DOCTOR
CRIPPEN

NICHOLAS CONNELL

AMBERLEY

For Barbara

First published 2013

This edition first published 2014

Amberley Publishing
The Hill, Stroud
Gloucestershire, GL5 4EP

www.amberley-books.com

British Library Cataloguing in Publication Data.
A catalogue record for this book is available from the British Library.

ISBN 978 1 4456 3465 4 (paperback)
ISBN 978 1 4456 2020 6 (ebook)

Typeset in 9.5pt on 12pt Sabon.
Typeset by Fakenham Prepress Solutions, Fakenham, Norfolk NR21 8NN
Printed in the UK.

CONTENTS

LIST OF ILLUSTRATIONS

ACKNOWLEDGEMENTS

This book was written in a period when many archives and libraries were experiencing cuts in staff and budgets. Despite this, the following repositories still managed to provide a great service; the British Library, the British Library Newspaper Library, Cambridge University Library, Camden Local Studies and Archives, Hertfordshire Central Resources Library, Islington Local History Centre, Metropolitan Police Records Management Branch and the National Archives.

It is due in no small part to their assistance that so much long-forgotten information about the 1910 North London cellar murder has come to light.

In his book *Jack the Ripper The Bloody Truth*, Melvin Harris acknowledged Richard Whittington-Egan 'who insisted that I write this book – and wouldn't take no for an answer!' I owe Richard a similar acknowledgement for persuading me to take another stroll down Hilldrop Crescent, for his continuous encouragement and for writing the foreword.

I would also like to thank the following for their invaluable help in finding material and supplying information: Kathleen Arthur, Stewart Evans, the late Stuart Goffee, the late Jonathan Goodman, Michael James Moore, Robin Odell, the late Heather Odgers, Jon Ogan, Mark Ripper, Neil Storey and Molly Whittington-Egan.

FOREWORD BY RICHARD WHITTINGTON-EGAN

So many times since its ur-enactment has the cautionary tale of little Doctor Crippen and the basement burial of the filleted, headless and limbless cadaver of his whilom spouse, in the obscurant gloom of the coal cellar of their villa on the Camden Town–Holloway outskirts of Edwardian London, been rehearsed that there might seem to be little left in the way of remains to pick over in the disturbed and disturbing earth and accumulated coal dust of their North London home, No. 39 leafy Hilldrop Crescent. But this is not the case.

Time and ill repute may have swept the old house away. So that No. 39 exists now, like some Holmesian locus – Pondicherry Lodge or the Copper Beeches – only in the imagination, cosseting its secrets.

Were its rooms and passages loud with the echoing dissonances of angry tirades of accusation and bitter counter-accusation, as limned by Filson Young in his introduction to the account of the case which he edited in Hodge's Notable British Trials series? Or heavy with the sullen silences of angry outbursts recollected in protracted disharmonies?

In the eye of the mind, one sees again, anew, the dark, below-stairs breakfast-room, unappetisingly cheek-by-jowl with the basement burial ground; the view through its grubby, net-curtained window of lingeringly Victorian fern-drenched garden. One sees, too, the grandish flight of stone steps to the front door, up which the visiting Martinettis ascended to dine and play whist with the Crippens on the last night of Belle Elmore's life.

Gone now; all gone. No. 39 annihilated by the breakers' hammers of the katabolic fifties to smithereens of uncharted eternity, its old bones of Victorian stone giving way to the bland new clay bricks of a block of council flats. Out in the silent stretches of the night the ear of memory catches the crackle of the crystal wireless telegraph apparatus sparking, in weird bluish incandescence, dot-and-dash Marconigram signals across the Atlantic to snare a fleeing murderer in its electric web.

Hawley Harvey Crippen, anonymous in life, has, in ignominious death, been metamorphosed into worldwide post-mortem celebrity as *the* most memorable of murderers. In recent times his supremacy has been questioned, his reputation libelled, by the importation into this classic case of a disquieting element of dubiety.

Was Crippen, as has been contemporaneously mooted, an innocent? Mr Connell confronts the derogatory whisper, pursues careful research, and delivers up a pretty convincing answer to this mean-minded attempt to deprive Dr Crippen of his hard-earned homicidal status.

The recent DNA juggling does not impress him. He brings, with noteworthy effort, his big analytical guns to bear. Unsubstantiated speculation is put to flight.

So, what manner of man was Peter Crippen, as he was wont habitually to designate himself? The generally received portrait is that of a humble, unassuming little personage, good-natured, kind-hearted, ever willing to do anyone a good turn, described by more than one acquaintance as the last man in the world that you would think capable of murder.

But, *res ipsa loquitur*. He was also an adulterer, a liar, a poisoner and a steel-nerved dismemberer – as well as a loyal, unselfish, warm, caring, heroically protective lover. A curious duality.

And what of Cora Crippen? How measures up the reality against the detrimental legend? In fairness, we have only the, surely biased, first-hand testimony of errant husband. And he can hardly be regarded as an impartial witness. Filson Young listened sympathetically to, accepted, and propagated Hawley Harvey's account of uxorial unpleasantness. Future writers on the case, impressed by the standard of the Notable British Trials volume, simply accepted without question Filson Young's Hawley Harvey-oriented version of Belle, and, passing down the subsequent literary chain, Cora's card was duly marked, her character thus besmirched, her persona decided upon.

The adjective 'blowzy', routinely attached to her, is not justified. Rather she was plump, dumpy, loquacious and vivacious to the occasional verge of vulgarity, handsome, beautifully dressed, liberally bejewelled, a pocket battleship, or schooner in full sail.

Now for the third member of the ill-starred trio. Her given name was Ethel Neave. The name she gave herself was the novelettish Le Neve. A better, more appropriate cognomen would have been Le Naïve – for naïveté, much-vaunted innocence, was her customarily projected image. Before Mr Connell's close research scrutiny, her *status sancta innocenta* dissolves. The revelation of her mulcting of money from the dissolved Cora's Post Office savings account, and her quasi-professional forgery of Belle's handwriting and signature on the withdrawal forms, is persuasive. These crude embezzlements – eight withdrawals, approaching cumulatively within a whisker of £200 – would seem to put to question, set one wondering as to, her guilty knowledge of her paramour's guilt. Ethel's fiscal acuity is later borne ample witness to by her shrewd marketing of her 'exclusive' life-story on at least four rewarding occasions.

Incidentally, the novelist Ursula Bloom is also detected in possible deceptive dissimulation. After her story *The Girl Who Loved Crippen* was serialised in the *Sunday Dispatch* in 1954, she laid claim to being the first to discover the erstwhile Miss Le Neve's latter-day marital identity and whereabouts. Miss Bloom either wilfully ignored, or carelessly failed to ascertain, the fact that over the years several seekers had run to ground, but desisted from making public, the new name and address of the shrinking *ci-devant* Ethel Le Neve.

The Crippen story is very much a tale of its time. It somehow contrives to embrace to entire atmosphere of the vanished world in which it was played out. The sudden verdure of the respectable Holloway residential enclave. Crumpets for tea. The muffin man's bell echoing through the afternoon streets.

Beyond Camden Town, Holloway, Islington, Pentonville, Scotland Yard – Norman Shaw's distinctive building – still standing beside the river; the London thoroughfares more thinly seeded by a more scant populace. The shadow of Sherlock Holmes still – just – discernible in sundry sympathetic quarters. Pea-soupers no longer wrapping the city in yellow blinkers, but wispy fogs, deceptively purblinding, still curling and swirling less ostentatiously about.

Eschewing many of what have, on the dubious grounds of their serial repetition, hitherto been taken for facts, Mr Connell has industriously and conscientiously scanned the newspapers, periodicals, books and official files of ten decades and dredged up all manner of lost comment, observation, and significant contradiction. He has encompassed much of this newly resurrected information in this soundly researched, carefully considered, authoritative and clear book, which, while correcting error, encroaches not upon previous preserves.

Richard Whittington-Egan

When a doctor does go wrong, he is the first of criminals. He has nerve and he has knowledge.

Sherlock Holmes, *The Adventure of the Speckled Band*

Most people would imagine that it would be impossible to write anything about this personage that is not already known.

Detective Inspector David Goodwillie on
Dr Crippen in 1925, *Thomson's Weekly News*

There never was a story like it, and never will be again.

Arthur Newton, Dr Crippen's solicitor,
Thomson's Weekly News

Male poisoners have, in all ages and countries, been largely found among medical practitioners.

Major Arthur Griffiths, *Mysteries of Police and Crime*

1

THE CASE OF THE MISSING ACTRESS[1]

Dr Crippen's famous disposal of his wife came to light less because of her absence than because her jewelry was observed adorning another woman – a circumstance even an English woman could not resist calling attention to.

Alfred Hitchcock, *New York Times*

Superintendent Frank Castle Froest was a man with a wide circle of friends and the door of his office at New Scotland Yard was always open to them. He was said to have possessed 'a faculty for making friends in all ranks of life ... He was naturally genial and good-natured.' Beneath the bonhomie 'he had most of the qualities of the perfect detective. He had resource, audacity, tenacity, a strength of purpose that carried him ruthlessly through obstacles if he could not go round them.'[2]

Froest did not look like a typical police officer. He was short and stocky and some likened him in appearance to a Prussian field-marshal when in uniform. When out of uniform Froest dressed immaculately, wearing a silk hat, patent leather boots, and carrying a carefully rolled umbrella. Known as 'the man with the iron hands', on account of his incredible prehensile strength, Froest was able to tear packs of cards in two and snap a sixpence 'like a biscuit'.[3]

On 30 June 1910 Froest received a visit from two of his friends, John Nash, a theatrical manager, and his wife Lillian, a music hall artist, professionally known as Lil Hawthorne. After hearing their tale, Froest summoned Detective Chief Inspector Walter Dew into his office. Dew and Froest went back a long way. They had hunted in vain for Jack the Ripper, enjoyed more success in capturing the notorious jewel thief Harry the Valet, and shared the disappointment two years previously when Florence Haskell was acquitted of the murder of her son Teddy at Salisbury, a crime of which they believed she was guilty.

At forty-seven years old and with twenty-eight years' service behind him, Dew was seriously thinking about retiring from the Metropolitan Police to become a private detective. Like Froest, Dew could easily be mistaken for something other than a policeman and, as a journalist observed,

> Mr Dew suggests the retired army officer rather than the detective. Imagine a man just above medium height, with a dark moustache, hair turning grey, a strong face tempered by a pair of kindly eyes, a clear-cut figure reminiscent of the barracks. A major in mufti is as good a description as any. You will find many like him in the famous military clubs in West End London.[4]

There was nothing to indicate that Nash's story was anything out of the ordinary. Dew later recalled, 'I certainly had no suspicion of the bigness of the case when the name of Crippen was first mentioned at Scotland Yard', but he would later describe the events which were to follow as 'the most intriguing murder mystery of the century'.[5]

The Nashes told Dew they had returned home to London from an American tour to hear that their American friend of Polish descent, Cora Crippen, was dead. Cora's stage name had been Belle Elmore, but her career as a music hall artist had never been as successful as she hoped. Many cruel things have since been written about Cora's singing talent, but she had been employed in various music halls, including appearing on the same bill as George Formby's father, George, at the Dudley New Empire in 1902.[6] London appearances at the Old Marylebone Music Hall, Clapham Grand and Holborn theatres did nothing to further her career and Walter Dew was probably right when he described her as 'a minor music-hall artist'.[7] Her act consisted of 'a tuneful song with a catchy chorus'.[8] Theatrical producer Clarkson Rose had seen her perform and remarked, 'She wasn't a top-rank artist, but, in her way, not bad – a blowsy, florid type of serio.'[9]

There must have been some truth in the stories of Cora's professional failings. Cora's friend Lottie Albert first met her at a small music hall in Oxford where 'her appearance was an utter failure. I found her overwhelmed with grief. Her most cherished ambition, that of becoming a personality in the music-hall world, had been shattered at one fell blow.' Belle Elmore looked like 'one who is utterly incompetent and suddenly realises it'.[10]

Cora was far more popular offstage and made friends easily. Realising her dreams of stardom would never materialise, but wishing to retain an association with the theatre, she joined the Music Hall Ladies' Guild, a charitable organisation founded in the autumn of 1906 to support women and children, members of their profession, who had fallen upon hard times. Cora became the Guild's honorary treasurer. Lottie Albert believed that this fulfilled Cora's ambitions to be connected with the theatre, and 'the music-hall failure, while a disappointment to her, was easily overcome. The good-nature and sound common sense with which she was endowed helped her to forget it and finally to put any thought of it aside.'[11] The Guild met every Wednesday at Albion House, a large block of flats in New Oxford Street.

John Nash believed Cora's American husband of seventeen years, Dr Hawley Harvey Crippen, was a dentist with some kind of American medical qualification. For reasons that are not known, Dr Crippen's friends called him Peter. The Crippens lived at 39 Hilldrop Crescent, a three-floored semi-detached house in Camden Town, North London.

Crippen was in partnership with Dr Gilbert Rylance, an American dentist with New Zealand qualifications. They worked together as the Yale Tooth Specialists and were also based in Albion House. Rylance and Crippen had gone into business together in 1908. In March 1910 they had entered a fresh arrangement whereby Crippen put £200 into the business and the pair would each take fifty percent of the profits.

Dr Crippen had also been engaged at £3 a week as manager of Munyon's Remedies, a mail-order patent medicine company which he had previously worked for in America and Canada. He ceased working for Munyon's on 31 January but carried on working in the same building. Crippen was also involved with other businesses – the Imperial Press Agency and Frankdel treatment for deafness. He had told the Nashes that Cora had left England for America on family business on 2 February and died there on 23 March, although several cheques had been presented during that period bearing her signature.

Inspector Dew was initially nonplussed. The cheques could have easily been signed by Cora before she left for America or been forged. The story he had heard was 'a somewhat singular one, although,' he mused, 'having regard to the Bohemian character of the persons concerned, is capable of explanation.' Nevertheless, Dew knew that the matter needed clearing up as 'the whole circumstances, one must admit, are mysterious, and this being so the persons referred to, the others, have made various enquiries with a view to clear the matter up but without any good result, nor can they discover any trace of Mrs Crippen going by any ship'. Before approaching the police, the Guild had hired a private detective to investigate Cora's whereabouts but he found nothing.[12]

Dew set about making his enquiries. He first spoke to the members of the Music Hall Ladies' Guild, taking a number of statements from Cora's friends. The Guild members all told a similar story.

Paul Martinetti, a retired music hall artist, and his wife Clara had known the Crippens for some eighteen months. On 31 January Dr Crippen had called at their home in Shaftesbury Avenue to invite them to dinner that night. Despite Paul being unwell earlier that day they accepted the invitation, arriving at Hilldrop Crescent around eight o'clock. They dined on soup followed by beef salad and spent the remainder of the evening playing cards. At some time during the evening Paul went to the toilet. The toilet window was open and he consequently caught a chill from the draught.

Clara Martinetti saw nothing unusual in Cora's behaviour that night. She described her friend as 'very jolly'. It had been 'the happiest party imaginable'. The Martinettis left Hilldrop Crescent around 1.30 in the morning. It was the last time they, or anyone else (besides Dr Crippen), would ever see Cora Crippen alive.

On the morning of 1 February Dr Crippen called at the Martinetti's flat around midday to see how Paul was. Clara told him that her husband was still in bed. She then asked after Cora and was told, 'Oh, she is all right.' Crippen visited again about a week later. By now Clara Martinetti had heard from the Guild's secretary, Melinda May, that Cora had apparently gone to America. Clara expected Cora to send her a card but nothing arrived either from the ship or from New York. When Clara told Crippen this he told her that his wife was not stopping at New York but heading straight to California.

At the Music Hall Ladies' Benevolent Fund's ball on 20 February, Clara saw Dr Crippen with his typist, twenty-seven-year-old Ethel Le Neve, who was wearing a brooch that looked very similar to one she knew Cora possessed. Clara and Lil Hawthorne thought Crippen was 'livelier than they had ever known him to be'[13] and Paul Martinetti noticed that Crippen 'looked very jolly' as he drank 'very freely of wine'. The theatrical newspaper *The Era* reported on the event, mistakenly describing Le Neve as Mrs Crippen.[14] Crippen visited the Martinettis once again after the ball. Clara repeated her concern that she had not heard from Cora, who was renowned as a good correspondent. He professed to be as surprised as she was. Crippen, however, had some worrying news. He said that he had heard from his American relatives that Cora was very ill and there was something the matter with one of her lungs, but he had also heard from Cora that she was 'not as bad as they say'.

The Martinettis received a letter dated 20 March that read,

Dear Clara and Paul,

    Please forgive me not running in during the week, but I have been so upset by very bad news from Belle that I did not feel equal to talking about anything, and now I have just a cable saying she is so dangerously ill with double pleuro-pneumonia that I am considering if I had not better go over at once. I do not want to worry you with my troubles, but I felt I must explain why I had not been to see you. I will try and run in during the week and have a chat. Hope both of you are well. With love and best wishes.

    Yours sincerely

    Peter

After a Guild meeting on 23 March, Clara Martinetti and fellow Guild member Annie Stratton went downstairs to find Dr Crippen at the entrance door. He said that he had received a cable saying Cora was dangerously ill, and he expected another at any minute to say that she had died. If he were to be widowed then he would go to France for a week for a change of air.

There was worse news to follow. On 24 March, Clara Martinetti received a telegram sent from Victoria station that read, 'Belle died yesterday at six o'clock. Please 'phone to Annie [Stratton]. Shall be away a week. Peter.' When Clara later went to offer her condolences to Crippen at Albion House, he informed her that Cora had died at Los Angeles with his relations. He subsequently told her that Cora was going to be cremated and her ashes would be sent to London.

Crippen had previously been married to an Irish-born nurse of English parentage called Charlotte Bell, who he had met when they both worked at the same hospital. The wedding took place in San Diego in 1887 and ended with the death of Charlotte on 24 January 1892. They had a son named Otto Hawley Crippen who was raised by Crippen's parents after Charlotte's death. When Otto was contacted in Los Angeles, his answers to the Guild's questions must only have heightened their confusion and suspicion:

The death of my step mother was as great a surprise to me as anyone. She died at San Francisco and the first I heard of it was through my father who wrote to me immediately afterwards. He asked me to forward all letters to him and he would make all the necessary explanation. He said he had, through a mistake given out my name as my step mother's death place. I would be very glad if you find out any particulars of her death if you would let me know of them, as I know as a fact that she died in San Francisco.

Even more perplexing news came from America. Following an enquiry from the Guild to the Los Angeles Chamber of Commerce, they were told that no one named Crippen had died there in March, although a man named Crippen had died in April.

Louise Smythson, a member of the Guild's committee, had known the Crippens for around fifteen months. She had last seen Cora Crippen at the Guild meeting on 26 January when she seemed to be in perfect health and high spirits. Louise had also seen Dr Crippen at the ball on 20 February where she asked him about Cora. Crippen vaguely replied that he had heard from his wife somewhere 'up in the wilds of the mountains of California'.[15] When pressed for an address, he gave Smythson his son's address in Los Angeles. When she asked where Cora died, Crippen brusquely told her that it was irrelevant as she was dead, and anyway, the Guild meant nothing to Cora's American friends.

Guild secretary Melinda May had known Cora Crippen for about two years. Like Louise Smythson, she had seen Cora at the meeting on 26 January when she appeared 'quite healthy and well, beautiful and bonny', but noticed that she was surprisingly absent from the 2 February meeting. May went round to 39 Hilldrop Crescent, where she was greeted by Ethel Le Neve, who handed her a pass-book, a paying-in book, a cheque book, a letter to Melinda and a letter to the committee. The letter to Melinda May was not in Cora's handwriting. It read,

39 Hilldrop Crescent, February 2nd

Dear Miss May,

Illness of a near relative has called me to America on only a few hours' notice, so I must ask you to bring my resignation as treasurer before the meeting to-day, so that a new treasurer can be elected at once. You will appreciate my haste when I tell you that I have not been to bed all night packing, and getting ready to go. I shall hope to see you again a few months later, but cannot spare a moment to call on you before I go. I wish you everything nice till I return to London again. Now, good-bye, with love hastily,

Yours, Belle Elmore, p.p. H.H.C.

Nor was the letter to the committee in Cora Crippen's hand:

39 Hilldrop Crescent, London, N.

To the Committee of the Music Hall Ladies' Guild.

Dear Friends,

Please forgive me a hasty letter and any inconvenience I may cause you, but I have just had bad news of the illness of a near relative and at only a few hours' notice I am obliged to go to America. Under the circumstances I cannot return for several months, and therefore beg you to accept this as a formal letter resigning from this date my hon. treasurership of the M.H.L.G. I am enclosing the cheque book and deposit book for the immediate use of my successor, and to save any delay I beg to suggest that you vote to suspend the usual rules of election and elect to-day a new honorary treasurer. I hope some months later to be with you again, and in meantime wish the Guild every success and ask my good friends and pals to accept my sincere and loving wishes for their own personal welfare.

Believe me, your [sic] faithfully,

Belle Elmore.

Lottie Albert was elected new treasurer that afternoon. When Melinda May saw Dr Crippen on 23 March, he told her that Cora was very ill, and that he was waiting for worse news.

Dr John Burroughs was the honorary physician to the Guild. His acquaintance with the Crippens stretched back to 1902. He described Cora as being 'a vivacious woman, I should say about thirty years of age, bright and cheerful, a very pleasant woman generally. She was very fond of dress, and dressed very well indeed. At times she wore a quantity of jewellery. As far as I know she was in the very best of health. She was a stoutish woman.' Cora was in fact thirty-six years old, which made her Dr Crippen's junior by twelve years. Like the other members of the Guild (eight or nine usually attended the meetings), Burroughs last saw Cora Crippen alive in January. He heard of her death via the Martinettis and sent Dr Crippen a letter of condolence:

Dear Peter,

Both Maud and myself were inexpressibly shocked and astounded to learn of poor Belle's death. We hasten to send our very heartfelt condolences on your great loss. As two of her oldest friends, why ever did not you send us a line? Do please give us some details of how and where she died. Maud is very much upset, and so anxious to hear. Only quite casually we heard she had suddenly left for America, and were daily expecting a letter or a card from her. Maud could not understand it, as Belle always wrote her on such important occasions, so could only think Belle wanted to cut all her old friends. And now to learn she is no more. It is all so sudden that one hardly realises the fact. We should so like to send a letter of condolence to her sister, of whom she was so fond, if you would kindly supply her address.

Yours sincerely,

J. H. B.

Crippen replied on black-edged mourning paper:

My dear Doctor,

I feel sure you will forgive me for my apparent neglect, but really I have been nearly out of my mind with poor Belle's death so far away. She was not with her sister, but out in California on business for me, and, quite like her disposition, would keep up when she should have been in bed, with the consequence that pleuro-pneumonia terminated fatally. Almost to the last she refused to let me know there was any danger, so that the cable that she had gone came as a most awful shock to me. I fear I have sadly neglected my friends, but pray forgive, and believe me to be most truly appreciative of your sympathy. Even now I am not fit to talk to my friends, but as soon as I feel I can control myself I will run in on you and Maud one evening. I am, of course, giving up the house, and every night packing things away. With love to both, and again thanking you for your kindness, I am, as ever, yours,

Peter.[16]

Besides the members of the Guild, Crippen had also communicated with Cora's family in America. Cora's younger sister Theresa Hunn had first met Dr Crippen around 1892 or 1893. Theresa's half-sister Louise Mills showed her a black-edged letter she had received from 39 Hilldrop Crescent:

My Dear Louise and Robert,

   I hardly know how to write to you of my dreadful loss. The shock to me has been so dreadful that I am hardly able to control myself. My poor Cora is gone, and, to make the shock to me more dreadful, I did not even see her at the last. A few weeks ago we had news that an old relative of mine in California was dying, and, to secure important property for ourselves, it was necessary for one of us to go and put the matter into a lawyer's hands at once. As I was very busy, Cora proposed she should go, and as it was necessary for some one to be there at once, she would go straight through from here to California without stopping at all and then return by way of Brooklyn, and she would be able to pay all of you a long visit. Unfortunately, on the way my poor Cora caught a severe cold, and not having while travelling taken proper care of herself, it has settled on her lungs, later to develop into pleuro-pneumonia. She wished not to frighten me, so kept writing not to worry about her and it was only a slight matter, and the next I heard by cable was that she was dangerously ill, and two days later after I cabled to know should I go to her I had the dreadful news that she had passed away. Imagine if you can the dreadful shock to me – never more to see my Cora alive nor hear her voice again. She is being sent back to me, and I shall soon have what is left of her here. Of course, I am giving up the house; in fact, it drives me mad to be in it alone, and I will sell out everything in a few days. I do not know what I shall do, but probably find some business to take me travelling for a few months until I can recover from the shock a little, but as soon as I have a settled address again I will write again to you. As it is so terrible to me to have to write this dreadful news, will you please tell all the others of our loss. Love to all. Write soon again, and give you my address probably next in France.

   From Doctor.

There was nothing in Crippen's behaviour since Cora's disappearance and supposed death to cause any undue suspicion. Between February and June Crippen had been attending work as normal and had been 'working very hard indeed'. He had taken to wearing a black hat and black armband.[17] When John Nash and Lil Hawthorne visited Crippen to offer their condolences, they found him in a distressed mood, nervous and sobbing. In what would later prove to be an appalling choice of words, Nash described Crippen as being 'much cut up'.

On 2 February Crippen had visited Attenborough's pawnbroker's

shop in Oxford Street and asked the manager, Ernest Stuart, for a
loan against a diamond ring and diamond earrings. Stuart considered
the items to be worth £100 and agreed to a £80 loan. One week later
Crippen returned to Attenborough's with a diamond brooch and six
diamond rings, for which he was given a loan of £115.

Crippen had given notice to his landlord that he was going to
leave 39 Hilldrop Crescent. The house was to play a pivotal role in
the story. It was owned by a builder called Frederick Lown, who
had let it to Dr Crippen for a three-year period in September 1905.
After three years the arrangement continued on a yearly basis at the
rental price of £52 10s per year. On 16 March 1910 Crippen told
Lown that he wanted to leave Hilldrop Crescent, as he had been left
some property in America, and that his wife had already gone there.
Crippen agreed to vacate the property on 24 June, but shortly before
that date he asked Lown if he could stay until 29 September. Lown
later asked after Cora Crippen and was shocked to hear Crippen tell
him that his wife had died in America.

Inspector Dew learned that Dr Crippen had journeyed to Dieppe
after telling Cora's friends that she was dead, staying for several
days with Ethel Le Neve under the name of Mr and Mrs Crippen.
Dew needed to know more and admitted to himself that, 'taken
as a whole, my inquiries had yielded little. I was no nearer solving
the problem I had set myself'.[18] It was time to have a talk with Dr
Crippen.

2

THE AMERICAN DENTIST

No story in the world of crime has ever created such widespread interest as that of Dr Hawley Harvey Crippen.

J. P. Eddy, *Scarlet and Ermine*

At this early stage of the investigation Dew did not harbour the grave doubts of Cora's friends about her apparent death, but he did have some suspicions:

> Mrs Crippen appears to have been a great favourite with all whom she came into contact with, always cheerful, and apparently in excellent health, and does not seem to have expressed any intention of leaving England, to her most intimate friends.
>
> … there are most extraordinary contradictions in the story told by Crippen, who is an American citizen, as is Mrs Crippen, otherwise Belle Elmore.
>
> From the action taken by the various friends of hers there can be but little doubt that Crippen has heard, or will soon hear, of the enquiries that have been made and, without adopting the suggestion made by her friends as to foul play, I do think that the time has now arrived when 'Doctor' Crippen should be seen by us, and asked to give an explanation as to when, and how, Mrs Crippen left this country, and the circumstances under which she died, which resulted in him causing the advertisement mentioned to be published.
>
> This course, I venture to think, may result in him giving such explanation as would clear up the whole matter and avoid elaborate enquiries being made in the United States.

The 'advertisement mentioned' was a death notice that Crippen had placed in the *The Era* on 26 March. It was brief and read 'Elmore

– March 23, in California, U.S.A., Miss Belle Elmore (Mrs H. H. Crippen).' A fuller obituary appeared in *The Music Hall and Theatre Review* written by Adelene Harrison, a journalist friend of Cora's:

> With deep regret I record the death of Miss Belle Elmore, the wife of Dr Crippen, the late hon. treasurer of the Music Hall Ladies' Guild. She passed away in California U.S.A., March 23. She was an old and valued friend of mine of many years, and the good work she did for the guild and her kindness to all will leave a tender remembrance in the hearts of those who knew her, mingled with sin of those who knew her, mingled with sin devoted to his bright little wife.[1]

And another was in *The Stage*: 'The Music Hall Ladies' Guild have lost a friend by the death of Miss Belle Elmore (Mrs H. H. Crippen), in California. She was honorary treasurer to the Guild for some time, but resigned from that position about two months ago in order to visit California.'[2]

Over five months had passed since Cora Crippen's disappearance when, on 8 July at around ten o'clock in the morning, Chief Inspector Walter Dew, accompanied by Detective Sergeant Arthur Mitchell, made an unannounced visit to 39 Hilldrop Crescent for what was to be the first of many trips to the quiet, leafy street off the Camden Road, containing sixty-eight houses built in the mid-nineteenth century.

They were admitted into the house by Crippen's seventeen-year-old French servant girl, Valentine Lecocq, who had been working there since 11 June. Ethel Le Neve came downstairs a few minutes later, wearing a brooch that would later be identified as one that had belonged to Cora Crippen. Dew thought that Le Neve 'was not pretty, but there was something quite attractive about her'.[3] He also considered her to be 'a nervous sort of girl'. In fact her real surname was Neave but she used the name Le Neve, taking her new surname from her father's stage name from when he used to sing at concerts in Norwich.[4] The detectives found Le Neve unhelpful, and got the feeling that she wanted to get them out of the house. She explained that Crippen was not in, and that she was Crippen's housekeeper. When Dew asked her if she was Miss Le Neve she admitted to it, but 'became a little agitated', asking if they could return later.

Dew insisted that she took him and Mitchell to Crippen, but she was reticent and offered to telephone him. This was unacceptable, and finally Le Neve went with Dew and Mitchell by tram car and cab to Crippen's office at Albion House. Dew had been reluctant to leave Le Neve alone, fearing she might telephone Crippen and warn him of their arrival as they made their way to his office. Le Neve went upstairs in a lift to fetch Crippen while Dew waited downstairs at a point where no one could leave the building without his knowing about it.

Crippen greeted the deputation, and the detectives were shown into his room, leaving Le Neve outside. Dew's first impression of Crippen was that he was 'an insignificant little man'.[5] The Scotland Yard man introduced himself and Mitchell, and explained that his wife's friends were not satisfied with his story concerning her death and that his own enquiries resulted in his feeling the same way. Crippen replied, 'I suppose I had better tell the truth,' and immediately confessed, 'the stories I have told them about her death are untrue. As far as I know she is still alive.' Dew suggested he make a full statement including a history of his life, which Crippen willingly did. Sergeant Mitchell, who was an expert shorthand writer, took down the following:

I am forty-eight years of age. After being questioned by Chief Inspector Dew as to the statements made by me that my wife, known as Belle Elmore, is dead, I desire to make a voluntary statement to clear the whole matter up.

I was born at Cold Water, Michigan, U.S.A., in the year 1862, my father's name being Myron Augustus Crippen, a dry goods merchant. My mother's name was Andresse Crippen, née Skinner.

My mother is now dead, but my father lives at Los Angeles, Cal.

I was educated first at Cold Water, Indiana, and California, and then attended the University at Michigan until I was about twenty, and finished my education at the Hospital College at Cleveland, where I took the degree of M.D.

I came over to England in 1883, and attended various hospitals to see the operations, and returned to the States, and was assistant for three or four months to Dr Porter, of Detroit. After that I went to New York and took a degree in specialist eye and ear work at the Ophthalmic Hospital. This would be in 1885.

After then I returned to Detroit, where I remained about two years as assistant to the same doctor. I then went to San Diego, where I practised as an eye and ear specialist for about two years. Before going to this place I was married to a lady named Charlotte Bell, of New York, and she accompanied me to San Diego.

We then came to New York. I have had only one child by my first wife. He was born at San Diego about 1887 or 1888, and his name is Otto Hawley Crippen. He is now married and lives at Los Angeles.

My first wife died, so far as I can remember, in 1890 or 1891. We were living at Salt Lake City, where I was practising as an eye and ear specialist. She was buried at Salt Lake City in my name.

After this my son went to live with his grandmother, my mother, until she died. I then went to New York, and went as an assistant to Dr Jeffrey, of Brooklyn, and I lived with him.

About 1893, while with Dr Jeffrey, I met Belle Elmore, who was being attended by him. Her name at that time was Cora Turner. I forget where she was living, but she was living alone. She was only about seventeen years of age, and I, of course, was about thirty.

She, at this time, was living under the protection of a man named C. C. Lincoln, a stove manufacturer, of Water Street, New York. She had been living with him, but he had given up his house and had taken a room for her and was paying all her expenses.

I took her to several places for some weeks, as I was very fond of her, and one day she told me Lincoln wanted her to go away with him. I told her I could not stand that, and would marry her right away, and a few days after this I married her at a minister's house at Jersey City. I forget his name and the name of the street.

I had been married to her some little time when she told me her name was not Turner, but Kunigunde Mackamotzki. She said her mother had been married twice, and her name then was Marsinger, and she was living in Brooklyn. Her mother had been dead some years. My wife told me her father was a Russian Pole and her mother was a German.

Her stepfather, so far as I know, is still living, and resides at Forrest Avenue, Brooklyn.

Her parents were in rather ordinary circumstances, but she had a good education, and spoke German well.

After getting married to her we went to St Louis, where I practised as consulting physician to an optician in, I think, Olive Street. His name was Hirsch, I think.

We stayed there about a year, and we returned to New York, where I took a position as consulting physician to the Munyon Company. We lived in the office at East Fourteenth Street.

I was in New York for only a few months when the company transferred me to Philadelphia. I was there with my wife for about a year, and was then transferred to the firm's place at Toronto, where I managed their business. I forget where I lived, but we were there only six months, and then returned to Philadelphia.

I was there some time, and while there, about 1899, my wife, who had a good voice, went to New York to have her voice trained, as she thought of going in for grand opera.

I paid all her expenses, and occasionally visited her at New York, and then in about 1900 I came to England alone, where I was manager for Munyon's at their offices in Shaftesbury Avenue, and I lived at Queen's Road, St John's Wood.

It was in April I came over, and she joined me in August, as she wrote and told me she was giving up her lessons in grand opera, and was going in for music hall sketches. To this I objected, and told her to come over here. She came, and we went to live at South Crescent.

When she came to England she decided to give sketches on the music hall stage, and adopted the name of 'Macamotzki', but she did not make anything at it. She gave a sketch at the Old Marylebone Music Hall, but it was a failure, and she gave it up.

After this she did not do anything in it for two or three years, until I had to go to America about two years after coming here. My firm sent for me, and I became manager in Philadelphia.

When I left England my wife and I were living at, I think, 62 Guildford Street, and she remained there while I was away. I remained in Philadelphia from November till the following June, and sent my wife money regularly.

When I returned I found she had been singing at smoking concerts for payment, and that an American music hall artiste, named Bruce Miller, had been a frequent visitor to her house.

She told me that this man visited her, had taken her about, and was very fond of her, also she was fond of him.

I may say that when she came to England from America her manner towards me was entirely changed, and she had cultivated a most ungovernable temper, and seemed to think I was not good enough for her, and boasted of the men of good position travelling on the boat who had made a fuss of her, and, indeed, some of these visited her at South Crescent, but I do not know their names.

I never saw the man Bruce Miller, but he used to call when I was out, and used to take her out in the evenings.

When I returned to this country, I did not take up my position at Munyon's but went as manager to the 'Sovereign Remedy Company', 13 Newman Street.

They failed about eight months afterwards, and I then went as physician to the Drouet Institute, Regent's Park, and afterwards at 10 Marble Arch, and they also failed.

From there I took a position with the Aural Clinic Company, 102 New Oxford Street, where I remained until they failed in about six months.

I then went back to Munyon's, 272 Oxford Circus, as manager and advertising manager.

I removed to Albion House as manager about eighteen months ago, after which I took it on as an agency, but as it did not pay, I, in February last, handed it over to the company again, but for the last two years I had been running the Yale Tooth Specialist Company, with Dr Rylance as partner, and am still doing so.

I ran what I termed the Imperial Press Agency, in connection with Munyon's, because by so doing I got their advertisements inserted at a reduction.

At the present time I am interested in an ear-cure business, called the 'Aural Remedy', at Craven House, Kingsway, and I work at an address in Vine Street.

I did not think anything of Bruce Miller's visiting my wife at the time.

After returning from America we went to live at 34 Store Street for about a year. During this time she adopted the stage name of 'Belle Elmore', although she had had it in her mind when she came over, but I persuaded her to use the other name.

She got an engagement at the Town Hall, Teddington, to sing, and then from time to time she got engagements at music halls. She went to the Oxford as a comedienne, and was there about a week.

She also went to the Camberwell, and also at a hall at Balham. She also sang at the Empire, Northampton, and various towns.

She would probably go away for about two weeks and return for about six weeks, but used to earn very little.

We remained at 34 Store Street for some time, and went to 37 same street for about two years, and about five years ago, in, I think, 1905, removed to 39 Hilldrop Crescent, for which I pay £50 a year.

It is quite four years since she ever went out at all to sing, and, although we apparently lived very happily together, as a matter of fact there were very frequent occasions when she got into most violent tempers, and often threatened she would leave me, saying she had a man she could go to, and she would end it all.

I have seen letters from Bruce to her, which ended 'with love and kisses to Brown Eyes'.

About four years ago, in consequence of these frequent outbursts, I discontinued sleeping with her, and have never cohabited with her since.

She did all the housework herself, with the exception of having a charwoman in occasionally.

About two years ago she became honorary treasurer of the Music Hall Ladies' Guild, and was here every Wednesday.

I never interfered with her movements in any way; she went in and out just as she liked, and did what she liked; it was of no interest to me.

As I say, she frequently threatened to leave me, and said that if she did she would go right out of my life, and I should never see or hear from her again.

On the Monday night, the day before I wrote the letter to the Guild resigning her position as treasurer, Mr and Mrs Paul Martinetti came to our place to dinner, and during the evening Mr Martinetti wanted to go to the lavatory. As he had been to our house several times, I did not take the trouble to go and show him where it was. After they had left my wife blamed me for not taking him to the lavatory, and abused me, and said, 'This is the finish of it. I won't stand it any longer. I shall leave you to-morrow, and you will never hear of me again.'

She had said this so often that I did not take much notice of it, but she did say one thing which she had never said before, viz., that I was to arrange to cover up any scandal with our mutual friends and the Guild the best way I could.

Before this she had told me frequently that the man she would go to was better able to support her than I was.

I came to business the next morning, and when I went home between five and six p.m. I found she had gone.

I realised that she had gone, and I sat down to think it over as to how to cover up her absence without any scandal.

I think the same night, or the next morning (Wednesday) I wrote a letter to the Guild saying she had gone away, which I also told several people.

I afterwards realised that this would not be a sufficient explanation for her not coming back, and later on I told people that she was ill with bronchitis and pneumonia, and afterwards I told them she was dead from this ailment.

I told them she died in California, but I have no recollection of telling any one exactly where she died.

Some one afterwards asked me where my son lived, and I told them.

I then put an advertisement in the *Era* that she was dead, as I thought this would prevent people asking a lot of questions.

Whatever I have said to other people in regard to her death is absolutely wrong, and I am giving this as an explanation.

So far as I know, she did not die, but is still alive.

It is not true that she went away on legal business for me, or to see any relations in America.

I did not receive any cables to say that she was ill, and it is not true that she was cremated at San Francisco, and that the ashes were sent to me, or that she sailed from Havre.

So far as I know, she has no claim to any title.

I have no recollection of telling any one my son was with her when she died.

We had a joint account at the Charing Cross Bank, subject to the signature of either, but it pleased her to think she was signing cheques, and she also did so, and several blank cheques were always already signed by her, and some of them have been changed by me since her departure, and there is one here now (produced).

When my wife went away I cannot say if she took anything with her or not, but I believe there is a theatrical travelling basket missing, and she might have taken this with some clothes.

She took some of her jewellery, I know, with her, but she left four rings behind – three single stone (or solitaire) diamonds, and one of four diamonds and a ruby, also a diamond brooch.

She had other jewellery, and must have taken that with her.

I have never pawned or sold anything belonging to her before or after she left.

Everything I have told you is true.

I do not know what clothes, if any, she took away; she had plenty.

Whenever we quarrelled, and she threatened to leave me, she told me she wanted nothing from me.

I have bought all her jewellery, and, so far as I know, she never had any jewellery presents, and I do not know that she ever had any money sent her, except that Bruce Miller used to send her small amounts on her birthday and at Easter and Christmas, to purchase a present.

She suffered from bilious attacks, and I have given her medicine for that – homeopathic remedies.

It is true that I was at the Benevolent Fund dinner at the Criterion with Miss Le Neve, and she wore the brooch my wife left behind. She has also worn my wife's furs.

Miss Le Neve has been in my employ, and known to me through being employed by the firms I have worked for, for the past eight years, and she is now living with me as my wife at Hilldrop Crescent. I have been intimate with her during the past three years, and have frequently stayed with her at hotels, but was never from home at nights.

After I told people my wife was dead Miss Le Neve and I went to Dieppe for about five days, and stayed at a hotel there (I forget the name, but the proprietor's name was Vacher) in the names of Mr and Mrs Crippen.

My belief is that my wife has gone to Chicago to join Bruce Miller, whose business on the music hall stage is a musical instrument turn, but I think he has now gone into another business, and has speculated and made money. Mr Didcot was his agent when he was over here.

I shall, of course, do all I can to get in touch with her, so as to clear this matter up.

She has a sister named Louise, whose name is Mills, living with her husband, who is a soapmaker living at Brooklyn. They live with my wife's stepfather, Mr Haaranger.

I do not know where any of her other relations live.

I cannot tell you how you can find or trace her, except as I have already said.

I will willingly go to my house with you to see if I can find any letters which may throw any light on the matter, and I invite you to look round the house, and do whatever you like in the house.

This is all I can tell you.

Any notes that I have changed through any one in this building were in connection with my business.

This statement has been read over to me. It is quite correct, and has been made by me quite voluntarily, and without any promise or threat having been held out to me.

This lengthy statement took around six hours to compile, partly due to the fact that it was taken between Crippen's consultations and tooth-pulling appointments. By lunchtime barely the introductory part of the statement had been taken, so Dew and Mitchell asked Crippen to join them for lunch at a small Italian restaurant close to Albion House. Crippen polished off a beefsteak 'with the relish of a man who hadn't a care in the world'.[6] After lunch they returned to the office, where Crippen finished his statement. It was read back to him and he signed each page.

Crippen's statement contains a number of assertions that only appear in the statement and are not corroborated by any other source. Nevertheless, they have been accepted as fact and repeated time and again in books and articles on the case. There is only Crippen's word that Cora threatened to leave him, that they were no longer sleeping together, that she had aspirations to be an opera singer for which he paid for her training, that she may have been intimate with Bruce Miller and the biggest lie of all, that his statement was all true.

Dew made it clear that at this time the question of arresting Dr Crippen had not entered his mind. He had only interviewed Crippen in order to get his explanation about what had happened to his wife, but he was not entirely satisfied with the story, saying, 'I cannot say that for a moment I considered his statement a reasonable one. I did not absolutely think that any crime had been committed. I was not satisfied with his statement.'

Despite his doubts, Dew was struck by Crippen's conduct and would often comment on his cool and collected manner:

> His replies came freely. There was no hesitation. From his manner one could only have assumed that he was a much maligned man eager only to clear the matter up by telling the whole truth.
>
> I was impressed by the man's demeanour. It was impossible to be otherwise. Much can sometimes be learned by an experienced police officer during the making of such a statement.
>
> From Dr Hawley Harvey Crippen's manner on this, our first meeting, I learned nothing at all.[7]

With hindsight, Dew thought that Crippen must have been expecting a call from the police at some time and that he had thought out his story in advance of that eventuality. Dew considered Crippen's statement had been 'an ingenious story. Half of it was true and half of it was false.'[8] Contradicting himself, Dew admitted that he had learnt one thing about Crippen: he was an 'accomplished liar',[9] as his statement had been so different from the story he told Cora's friends. But, as Dew pointed out, 'you can't charge a man with being a liar. My job was to find out if he was telling the truth now. Somehow I did not think he was.'[10]

Dew and Mitchell also took a statement from Ethel Le Neve. Like Crippen, there was nothing suspicious about her manner, although she was slightly embarrassed about admitting the nature of her relationship with her employer:

> I am a single woman, 27 years of age, and a Shorthand Typist.
>
> Since the latter end of February I have been living at 39 Hilldrop Crescent with Mr Crippen as his wife.
>
> I have been on intimate terms with Mr Crippen for between 2 and 3 years, but I have known him for 10 years. I made his acquaintance by being in the same employ as he.

I knew Mrs Crippen, and have visited at Hilldrop Crescent. She treated me as a friend.

In the early part of February I received a note from Mr Crippen saying Mrs Crippen had gone to America, and asking me to hand over a packet he enclosed, to Miss May.

About 4 p.m. same day he came to our business place, Albion House, and told me his wife had gone to America. He said she had packed up and gone.

I had been in the habit, for the past 2 or 3 years, of going about with him, and continued doing so.

About a week after he had told me she had gone to America I went to Hilldrop Crescent to put the place straight, as there were no servants kept, but at night I went to my lodgings; and I did this daily for about a fortnight. The place appeared to be all right, and quite as usual.

He took me to the Benevolent Fund Dinner, and lent me a diamond brooch to wear, and later on he told me I could keep it.

After this he told me she had caught a chill on board the ship and had got pneumonia, and afterwards he told me she was dead.

He told me he could not go to the funeral as it was too far and she would have been buried before he could get there.

Before he ever told me this I had been away with him for 5 or 6 days at Dieppe, and stayed at a hotel with him in the name of Mr and Mrs Crippen, but I cannot tell you the name of the place.

When we came back he took me to Hilldrop Crescent, and I remained there with him, occupying the same bedroom.

The same night, or the night after, he told me that Belle was dead. I was very much astonished, but I don't think I said anything to him about it. I have not had any conversation with him about it since.

He gave me some furs of his wife's to wear, and I have been living with him ever since as his wife, and have given up my lodgings at Constantine Road, and taken up my abode at Hilldrop Crescent.

My father and mother do not know what I am doing, and think I am housekeeper at Hilldrop Crescent.

When Dr Crippen told me his wife had gone to America I don't remember if he told me she was coming back or not.

I cannot remember if he went into mourning.

Dew might have been more suspicious after taking Le Neve's statement, for he observed that, 'Miss Le Neve has not told me she thoroughly believed what Dr Crippen has told her.' Nevertheless, Dew did not think she knew anything herself, as 'there was nothing in Miss Le Neve's manner which gave rise to anything in the nature of suspicions'.[11]

Ethel may have said that Cora Crippen had treated her like a friend, but years before Cora had told Maud Burroughs, 'I don't like the girl typist Peter has in his office.' She had asked Crippen to get rid of Ethel but he refused, saying she was indispensable to the business.

The manageress of Munyon's Remedies, Marion Curnow, later stated that on the day Crippen was interviewed by the police he called in on her with regard to two envelopes he had asked her to store in her safe at the beginning of March. They were marked 'Dr Crippen' and 'Dr Crippen, personal'. Crippen said to Curnow, 'If any one should ask you, know nothing', or 'say nothing', adding 'and if anything happens to me please give what you have there to Miss Le Neve.' Curnow replied, 'All right.' The envelopes contained deposit notes with the Charing Cross Bank for £600 and insurance receipts worth £300. In the other envelope was a watch and brooch.

Dew wanted to make a search of 39 Hilldrop Crescent, 'to see if we could find any papers which would throw any light on her movements'. Crippen consented to the request, saying that Dew was welcome to search the house any time he liked. There was no time like the present, so all four of them went to Hilldrop Crescent. On the way there Dew had much to contemplate:

> I was trying to get the hang of a case which was becoming more difficult at every turn.
>
> I certainly had no suspicion of murder. You don't jump to the conclusion that murder has been committed merely because a wife has disappeared and a husband has told lies about it.
>
> But he had lied. I couldn't get this fact out of my mind, and I was determined, if humanly possible, to find out why he had gone to such lengths to throw dust into the eyes of Belle Elmore's friends.[12]

Crippen was being perfectly courteous as his house was searched. Dew and Mitchell went through all the rooms, many of which were still adorned by pictures of Cora. Dew observed that, 'The rooms were in good order as a dwelling house would be ... there was nothing in the house to attract attention.' They then went out to the garden, and finally the coal cellar, whose evenly laid brick floor was covered with dust that did not appear to have been disturbed for years. Dew had no particular reason for looking in the cellar at that time other than wanting to make an examination of the whole house.

It was reached from a passage which led from the kitchen to the back door. There was no access from the outside to the cellar except for a coal-hole. Crippen and Le Neve stood watching in the doorway while Dew and Mitchell poked around. Mitchell then searched through the rafters of the house but found nothing. Everything appeared to be in order except for some rolled up carpets and packed boxes, but this could be explained as Crippen had given notice that he was going to move soon.

After searching the house, Crippen and Dew went to the breakfast room. Dew asked about the jewellery Cora had left behind and Crippen produced three rings and a rising sun brooch. Crippen was apparently being very helpful and asked what he could do to help find Cora. Would advertising be a good idea? Dew thought it would, and Crippen said he would place adverts in several American newspapers. He took a piece of paper and, with Dew's help, composed the following message:

'Mackamotzki'
Will Belle Elmore communicate with H.H.C. or
Authorities at once.
Serious trouble through your absence. $25 reward
Anyone communicating whereabouts to...

Dew and Mitchell finally left Hilldrop Crescent at eight o'clock after the inspector told Crippen, 'Of course I shall have to find Mrs Crippen to clear this matter up.' It was the last time Dew was to see Dr Crippen and Ethel Le Neve for some months.

3

THE CELLAR

Dr Crippen himself worried very little about the secret of the cellar.

Ethel Le Neve, *Thomson's Weekly News*

...there is sometimes nothing more horrifying than a revelation of what may be going on behind the discreet curtains of an outwardly respectable suburban house.

John Rowland, *Poisoner in the Dock*

When the young Walter Dew had joylessly hunted for Jack the Ripper he suffered with insomnia, and now it returned, possibly hinting that he was again working on something out of the ordinary:

I was dog tired, yet sleep I could not. My mind refused to rest. The events of the day kept cropping up.

What was behind it all? There was something, I now felt sure. Crippen had a secret which he was cunningly trying to hide. There would be no rest for me until I had found out.[1]

The day after interviewing Crippen, Dew circulated a description of Cora Crippen as a missing person throughout the Metropolitan Police district. On Monday 11 July Dew and Mitchell returned to Albion House to see Crippen, but neither he nor Le Neve was there. Dr Rylance had received a hand-written letter from Crippen that read 'I now find that in order to escape trouble I shall be obliged to absent myself for a time.'

Dew and Mitchell then went to 39 Hilldrop Crescent and were admitted by the French maid and Flora Long, the wife of one of Crippen's employees, William Long. The detectives searched the property again, and this time they made some startling discoveries.

In the wardrobe of the first floor bedroom Dew found a fully loaded revolver, while Mitchell discovered a box containing forty-five cartridges that fitted the gun. Dew did not know how long Crippen had possessed the gun, but it did not look new. According to Dew it was not there during his initial search when Crippen was present. He came to the dramatic conclusion that Crippen had the gun in his pocket at the time, and would have used it had anything been found.[2] Dew, who was a keen gardener when off duty, then dug up the garden and re-examined every room in the house and the coal cellar but found nothing suspicious.

Inspector Dew ascertained that on 9 July, some twelve hours after his initial visit, Crippen had left Hilldrop Crescent followed by Le Neve around an hour afterwards. They had both gone to Albion House as usual. Neither of them had any luggage besides Le Neve's reticule bag. Later in the morning Crippen gave William Long two pounds and asked him to buy a boy's suit, tie and braces, a brown bowler hat and size five boots. Long had asked Crippen if he was in any trouble. 'Only a little scandal,' replied Crippen, who was looking pale and ill that morning. Crippen visited a neighbouring office and exchanged a cheque for gold to the value of £37. At around 1 p.m. Crippen and Le Neve left the office unseen, leaving behind them Crippen's suit of clothes and Le Neve's hat.

Crippen's disappearance suggested only one thing to Dew:

My quarry had gone, but the manner of his going pointed to guilt.

My view was that a completely innocent man with nothing to fear would have seen the thing through. A man of Crippen's calibre would certainly have done so. I had already seen enough of him to know that he was not the type to do anything foolishly rash.

Here was the real clue.

His decision was a sudden one. Of that I felt convinced. A fair deduction seemed to be that he had been scared by the events of Friday.[3]

Valentine Lecocq had received a letter from Crippen saying,

Valentine,

Do not be alarmed (*N'ayent pas de peur*) if we do not return until late as we shall go to the Theatre this evening (*nous vaison au Theatre ce soir*)

H. H. Crippen

She had no friends in London and was sent back to France. When interviewed by the French newspaper *Le Matin* she said that she believed that Crippen and Le Neve were man and wife because Le Neve always wore a wedding ring. Her employers 'were always laughing and happy'. Le Neve did all the cooking, Lecocq did the housework while Dr Crippen would often go to the cellar to chop wood.[4]

Valentine Lecocq was not the only person who thought Crippen and Le Neve were married. Ethel had told her old school friend Lydia Rose in the second week of March 'you will be surprised to hear I was married last Saturday'. Her letter was signed 'Eth Crippen'. She had been sporting an engagement ring since the previous December. Rose was introduced to Crippen, whom she found 'a very fascinating man, with such a characteristic face that when one had once seen it they would never forget it'.[5] Crippen had told Dr Rylance that he had married Le Neve after Cora's death and invited the dentist to tea 'with him and his wife'.

Ethel once told her parents, 'I think if I ever marry, it will be with an old man – a man much older than myself.'[6] One day their daughter told them the shocking news that she had married Crippen at a registry office in West London and the ceremony had been witnessed by two of Crippen's friends. When Walter Neave asked to see the marriage certificate, Ethel 'turned pale, and trembled, and in a faltering voice she told me that she had handed it to Dr Crippen'.[7] She told her father that Crippen 'did not want any fuss made about the wedding; that he wanted it kept secret',[8] but there had never been any wedding.

Dew circulated descriptions of Crippen and Le Neve to domestic and foreign ports, requesting that they keep a look-out for the pair but not to arrest them. He then sent out enquiries throughout London to find out if any cabmen or carmen had removed boxes or packages from 39 Hilldrop Crescent since 31 January. On 12 July Dew and Mitchell carried out a further search of 39 Hilldrop Crescent, but again without result.

On 13 July, a breakthrough was made which turned Dew's investigation from one of trying to establish the whereabouts of Cora Crippen to what would turn out to be one of the most sensational murder cases of the twentieth century. With Crippen absent, Dew and Mitchell now had the house to themselves and the opportunity to search 39 Hilldrop Crescent without 'Crippen at my elbow to hamper me and perhaps throw me off the scent'.[9] Dew was beginning to consider the possibility that Cora had been murdered, but the house had yet to yield any clues other than the discovery of the advertisement Crippen had written on 8 July but had not sent to any newspaper.

Dew and Mitchell were 'completely fagged out' and Dew wanted to go home and sleep for twenty-four hours, but could not give up the search for Cora Crippen until the mystery was solved.[10] Dew decided to make a more thorough search of the cellar, which held a 'peculiar fascination' for him. Dew fancifully recalled, 'That house in Holloway had a strange attraction for me: always I had a reluctance to leave it: that sinister cellar seemed to draw me to it. A loose board near the door each time it was stepped upon seemed to creak out "Stop, stop".'[11] 'Maybe it was my sixth sense' was the only explanation he could offer.[12] Dew takes up the tale:

> 'Let us go along to the house and have another go at the cellar,' I said to my companion, and a short time later we were on our hands and knees probing once more at the bricks which formed the cellar floor. I was armed with a poker, and with this worked away too tired to say a word.
>
> Presently a little thrill of excitement went through me. The sharp point of the poker had found its way between two of the bricks, and one of them showed signs of lifting.
>
> I toiled away more hopefully now, all sense of fatigue vanishing in the excitement of hope. The brick came out. Then another and another. After this my work became easy.
>
> Mitchell ran to get a spade from the garden. With this I worked steadily for a few minutes. Then came evidence nauseatingly unmistakeable. The stench was unbearable, driving us both into the garden for fresh air.[13]

Dew and Mitchell fortified themselves with brandy and returned to their grim task. They had uncovered what appeared to be human remains. These were covered in a large quantity of lime, some of which was coarsely granular while some had set in hard lumps like concrete. Whoever had placed the remains there had made an elementary blunder. The lime had been mixed with water, making it a preservative rather than a destroyer of the flesh.

It is not entirely clear who made the breakthrough in the cellar. The passage above is taken from Dew's autobiography. He made several other statements about the incident at various times. When giving evidence at the Old Bailey, Dew took full credit for the find:

I went down with Mitchell on to my knees and probed about with a small poker which I had got out of the kitchen. I found that the poker went in somewhat easily between the crevices of the bricks, and I managed to get one or two up, and then several others came up pretty easily. I then produced a spade from the garden and dug the clay that was immediately underneath the bricks.

In another statement, Dew gives joint credit:

We went down on our hands and knees and carefully examined the brick flooring again, but everything appeared to be in order.

We then got a small poker and tested various parts of the flooring of the basement and probed about the brickwork of the cellar, and in doing so the poker, which has a thin point, went in between two of the bricks, which became loosened and Sergeant Mitchell and I then removed several bricks and found underneath a flat surface of clay.

In his report, Sergeant Mitchell said, 'I dug the poker between two of the bricks in the centre of the floor. I loosened and removed them, and Chief Inspector Dew then dug the floor up.' In a further statement, dated one day later, Mitchell said, 'I was present when the Chief Inspector found the human remains.'

Dr Crippen's disappearance was now explained. Among the remains were a Hinde's hair-curling pin with light and dark dyed hair attached, portions of ladies' undergarments, a portion of a man's pyjama shirt, a rotted man-size handkerchief knotted at two ends and a piece of coarse string. It was that which was not found that made the discovery all the more shocking. The head, limbs, bones and sexual organs were missing; everything that might help to identify the remains. Dew had 'that strange hunch ... that what we had found represented all that remained of the once charming and vivacious Belle Elmore'.[14]

Dew immediately sent for the local divisional police surgeon, Dr Thomas Marshall, and informed Sir Melville Macnaghten, the Assistant Commissioner of the CID at Scotland Yard, of the find. Macnaghten filled his pockets with cigars, grabbed Superintendent Froest, jumped into a car and sped to Hilldrop Crescent, where he handed the cigars out. 'I thought they might be needed by the officers – and they were!'[15] Dew occasionally smoked cigars and Froest continuously smoked strong cigars when working on murder cases as they helped him to think.[16] Dr Marshall arrived at around 5.40 p.m.

when the remains were partly exposed. He thought they were human but did not make a full examination that day. He returned at 9 p.m. when the remains were uncovered and just touched the surface of them, observing that 'they were emptied in like refuse of dustmen'. Dew ordered the photographing of the remains before covering them up.

Macnaghten and Froest explored the premises. Macnaghten was surprised to see bottles of whisky, claret, sherry and yellow chartreuse on the dining room sideboard. He observed Crippen's chair at the head of the table was only some fifteen or twenty yards away from where the remains lay and commented, 'How, for five long months, good digestion could have waited upon appetite in such circumstances has always been a marvel to me!'[17] The house was locked up for the night and guarded by the police, but the outside world was beginning to hear about what had transpired. The following morning, *The Times* reported,

Some persons who were passing the house last night were attracted by several slight explosions, and it then became known that the police were taking flashlight photographs of a body which is said to have been in the cellar for some months.[18]

As the crowds began to gather, the local newspaper sent its reporter to investigate 'The Green Crescent of the Crime', which was thus described:

Hilldrop-crescent is a quiet suburban place although in the inner ring of the Metropolis; and, reasoning superficially, it would be the last spot one would have dreamt of for the stage of a sordid murder. The exterior aspect of the quiet residential streets speaks of respectability: and in the placid atmosphere of well-to-do Suburbia the tokens of the grim deed seized the heart with a greater shock than they would have done in the denser and darker neighbourhood that lies not far away.

For this secluded crescent is situated just off the bustle and roar of several busy thoroughfares, and a stone thrown in any direction would fall in the thick of clustering human hives. It is no more than five minutes from Holloway-road with its ceaseless traffic; it is close to Caledonian-road with its constant goings-to-and-fro; on the other side the huge glass palaces rattle on their way to Tottenham Court-road. In a word, it nestles serenely in a back-wash of the whirling waters of the modern Babylon.

It is this strange contrast of peacefulness and quietude with the hurrying stretch of main thoroughfares that bound it and the network of mean and squalid streets that surround it, that seems to intensify the horror of the crime committed in its smug and snug precincts.

The crescent, then, is hidden away in the district which abounds in leafiness, and although not far off is a very different world of bricks and mortar, so cosily shut in is the essentially middle-class part that one can almost forget the grime and the encircling gloom.

Here it was – in this unlikely quarter – that the corpse of a beautiful woman was dug up.

Here it was that last night, as indeed all through the day, a knot of people stood shuddering, and conversing almost in whispers.

Here it was, in this green and salubrious road, that a garden gate was guarded by two stalwart men in blue – the guardians of a terrible interior that no prying eyes were permitted to look upon.

Here it was that detectives silently came and went; here came eminent professors and official photographers; and here came a coffin to bear away a woman's mangled remains.

It stands up, does that ill-fated house, behind large, spreading trees that almost conceal its frontage. In the sunshine of a summer day the green foliage gave almost a gay appearance to the scene.[19]

The remains were removed the next day under the supervision of Dr Marshall and Dr Augustus Pepper, a consulting surgeon from St Mary's Hospital and Home Office pathologist. They were placed in a coffin and taken to the mortuary. Two local police constables, Frederick Martin and Daniel Gooch, had helped Dew unearth the remains and place them in the coffin.[20] In recognition of their conduct during this unpleasant task, Dew spoke to Macnaghten, who promised them a 10s bonus.

Dew made a further discovery that would later prove to be vital. In a box under the bed in the first-floor bedroom there were two suits of pyjamas and one odd pair of pyjama trousers. The jackets bore the label of 'Shirt-makers, Jones Brothers (Holloway), Limited, Holloway, N.'

The news of the discovery of the remains was met with disbelief by the Crippens' friends and neighbours, who had perceived Hawley and Cora to be a devoted couple. Crippen had told Dr Rylance the story that Cora had gone to America on family business, and later that she had died. The press interviewed Rylance, who told them,

A more humble, unassuming little man I have never met, and to me it seems unthinkable that he would have committed so dastardly a crime.

In my judgement he was a smart man and a wonderful organizer, very exact, with fine business methods; in fact, one could not have desired a straighter representative.

Of late, I had observed that he looked worried. He had, of course, his bright moments, but generally he appeared to be distressed and perturbed by something or other, and I came to the conclusion that it was due to financial troubles.

His wife was a woman of charming manners. I frequently saw her here. What passes my understanding is how Crippen could have thrown her over in favour of his typist. It was a strange infatuation. She had little to recommend her so far as I noticed. The typist was a delicate woman. She was always ailing, and was jocularly known in this building as the woman who always answered inquiries with the same remark, 'Not very well, thank you.'[21]

A neighbour, Millicent Gillatt, who lived at 40 Hilldrop Crescent, revealed,

We first missed Mrs Crippen some time last February. My sister met Mr Crippen about that time, and he told her she had gone to America and that he intended to give up the house.

Both Mr and Mrs Crippen used to spend a great part of their time in the garden. He always seemed exceedingly fond of her, and used to follow her round in quite an adoring way.[22]

Another acquaintance stated that Crippen's devotion to Cora 'was remarkable'.[23] But Dew had already learned that after seventeen years of marriage, 'quarrels between them, I gathered, were not infrequent'.[24] These rows had been going on for some time. A German lodger had stayed at 39 Hilldrop Crescent from December 1906 to April 1907. He said that Cora 'frequently gave way to ill-temper, which led to painful discussions. Her husband, however, rarely lost his temper, even when he was the object of unjust remarks. He minimised the troubles, spoke gently, and allowed the storm to pass. He appeared to be exerting great self-control – his lips would go white and his hands involuntarily clench.'[25]

The Crippens' nationality ensured that the American press were following developments with interest and making their own enquiries. Crippen's former employer, Dr J. M. Munyon, told a journalist that he did not believe Crippen was capable of such a crime. Crippen 'was one of the most intelligent men I ever knew and was so proficient that I gave him a position readily, nor have I ever regretted it'. Munyon's son Duke gave his opinion on the Crippens, saying that Crippen 'was extremely jealous of her, and they often quarrelled. She was pretty and attractive and had many male friends. When Dr Crippen took her out, if she looked at other men he seemed to go insane.'[26]

In a somewhat surprising interview with the *Los Angeles Herald*, Crippen's son Otto calmly 'declared that his father no doubt committed the crime because of his infatuation for another woman. It is too bad to think that a man of his age would do such a thing. I am not a bit surprised, because I understood he passed most of his time in the company of various women who accepted his advances.'[27]

There was immediate concern that Crippen and Le Neve might have fled the country. Cablegrams were quickly sent out to various countries. The one sent to Ottawa, Canada, gave full physical descriptions of the pair:

Wanted for murder and mutilation of a woman Hawley Harvey Crippen alias Peter Crippen alias Francke, an American age fifty, 5 feet three or four, complexion fresh, hair light brown inclined sandy, thin bald on top, scanty straggling moustache, eyes grey, bridge of nose flat, false teeth, wears gold rim spectacles, may be wearing brown jacket suit marked Baker and Grey, round flat hat, Horne Bros. inside, wears hat back of head, rather slovenly appearance, throws his feet out when walking, slight American accent, very plausible and quiet spoken, speaks French and shows his teeth when speaking; and Ethel Clara Leneve[sic] travelling as his wife, age 27, height five feet five, complexion pale, hair light brown, large grey eyes, good teeth, good looking, medium build, pleasing appearance, quiet subdued manner, looks interested when in conversation, is reticent, walks slowly, probably dressed blue serge skirt, ditto three quarter jacket suit, large hat or may be dressed in boys dark brown jacket suit, grey hard felt hat, native of London, shorthand writer and typist.

The description of Le Neve was later amended when it was discovered that far from having good teeth, Le Neve had about twenty false teeth.[28] Further descriptions of the wanted couple appeared in newspapers in Spain, Sweden and Grand Canary, where large numbers of British steamers called. The descriptions also appeared in the British press, leading to numerous false sightings from all over England and Scotland.

Having alerted foreign police forces about the missing couple, Dew 'took on the almost equally big task of searching for evidence that would satisfy a jury that the woman who had met her fate in that gloomy looking house in Hilldrop Crescent was indeed Crippen's wife'.[29] He felt certain the remains were Cora Crippen's because she was missing, and her husband had lied about her disappearance and had subsequently fled. On 16 July Dew appeared at Bow Street police court to apply for a warrant against

HAWLEY HARVEY CRIPPEN, and ETHEL CLARA LE NEVE, alias, NEAVE, for having on or about the 2nd day of February 1910, at 39 Hilldrop Crescent, Camden Road, in the said County and district, wilfully murdered one CORA CRIPPEN otherwise BELLE ELMORE, supposed to be the wife of HAWLEY HARVEY CRIPPEN, and that they did mutilate and bury some of the remains in the coal cellar at the above address.

4

THE FUGITIVES

We sought him here, we sought him there,
Detectives sought him everywhere.
Is he in heaven, or hell, maybe,
The dem'd elusive Dr C.

Sir Melville Macnaghten, *Days of My Years*

I verily believe that they have both fled the Country together.

Chief Inspector Walter Dew

A coroner's inquest on the remains from 39 Hilldrop Crescent was held on 18 July at the chapel of ease, Holloway Road, Islington, but this location proved to be too small for the occasion and subsequent resumed inquests were held at the Central Library in Holloway Road. Frequent heavy showers failed to deter large numbers of curious onlookers who lined the approach to the coroner's court and mortuary. Among those attending the hearing were Ethel Le Neve's mother and a number of actresses who were connected to the Music Hall Ladies' Guild.

Coroner Dr George Danford Thomas swore in a jury to consider the cause of death of 'some human remains now lying dead', which they had viewed through a glass screen. Dr Thomas explained that the remains were believed to be those of Cora Crippen, adding that an adjournment would be necessary as there was not a great deal of evidence to be put before them at this time; but the police had the matter of finding Dr Crippen in hand, and the analysis of the remains was in progress.

Walter Dew gave his evidence. He outlined the extent of his investigations, including the discovery of the remains, and ended by saying that the police 'had not lost one minute, and search was being made everywhere for Crippen'. Dr Thomas heaped praise on Dew for making the find, saying, 'Many a man might have gone into that cellar and made no discovery. It had to remain for a detective with a genius for his work to go a step further, and it is due to the keenness of the inspector that this ghastly affair is brought to light.' Describing Dew as a genius was an overstatement. He had been tenacious, but there had been an element of luck in his discovery. If Crippen had not aroused suspicion by fleeing, or if he had filled the cellar with coal, Dew might not have been so diligent in his search. Dew admitted, 'If Crippen had taken the trouble to order a ton of coal, he'd be a free man to-day.'[1] Things might also have been different if Crippen had left Hilldrop Crescent on 24 June as he originally agreed with his landlord.

Dr Marshall detailed the preliminary findings of the post-mortem. He thought that the remains were female, but could not prove it because 'the perpetrator of the outrage had tried to obliterate not only all evidences of identity but all traces of sex'. Marshall thought that the cadaver was dissected in the cellar where it was found, 'and whoever did it must have taken his time about it, for it was a most deliberate and long process'.

As promised, Dr Thomas adjourned the inquest until Monday 15 August. The main difficulty faced at this stage was establishing that the pile of flesh had once been Cora Crippen. Here Dew had a lucky break. Outside the coroner's court he overheard Clara Martinetti say that Cora had undergone a serious operation and had quite a large scar on the lower part of her body which she had seen.[2] Among the remains there was a piece of skin bearing the mark of what could have been an operational scar.

Inevitably rumours began circulating about the crime and Dr Crippen. W. R. Bell, the brother of Crippen's first wife, Charlotte, said he had never been satisfied with what Crippen had told him about her death, which had been attributed to apoplexy and paralysis. His story of their life together suggests that Crippen's charm and respectability was all a façade:

Crippen set himself up as a dentist, but he got in some kind of trouble and they moved to 30th St., near Lexington-av. Again the authorities got after him and this time he moved – this was about 1890 – to some town out in California. I didn't hear from my sister much previous to this time; but I know that they moved once more from California to Salt Lake City, Ut.

Here the mystery began. Charlotte wrote to me that her husband was taking advantage of his medical and surgical knowledge and was compelling her – because of certain ordinary and to-be-expected circumstances, to undergo operations by the knife. She had undergone, she said, two dangerous operations. Her husband, she wrote, was then playing the part of an optician as well as a dentist, although he was really neither. Meanwhile, I should say, they had one little son, born in the first year of their marriage.

I was furious when I got these letters, and it was in my mind to go west and kill this man who was maltreating my sister. But I restrained myself. Then came the worst letter of all. Charlotte wrote something to this effect: 'My husband is about to force me to the knife again, and I feel that this will be the last time. I want my relatives to know that if I die it will be his fault.'[3]

Bell forwarded this letter to his brother, D. H. Bell, who lived in Dublin. He still had the letter and it was reported that the Irish police were enquiring into Charlotte's death, as were the police in Salt Lake City. Another story emerged in the American press that Scotland Yard were looking into the death of Charlotte.[4] None of these investigations were mentioned again, so it is difficult to know whether any police activity did take place or if the reports were groundless press speculation.

Melinda May remembered attending a New Year's Eve party at 39 Hilldrop Crescent on 31 December 1909, when Cora had told the guests, 'I'm so glad that we're together now, and I do hope that we shall all be together again this time next year.'[5] About a fortnight later Cora visited Albion House and complained of feeling so ill that she had told her husband the night before, 'Get up and fetch the priest. I'm going to die!' May was convinced that 'it was the result of an attempt which Crippen had then made to murder her by administering poison'.[6] Whether these suspicions were held before Crippen became a murder suspect, or if they only began after the remains were discovered, is a matter of conjecture.

Dew considered it was 'more than probable' that sooner or later Le Neve would try to communicate with her parents, who also lived in Camden Town, or her sister in Tottenham. He thought that Crippen might try to write to his employee William Long, who Dew discovered had withheld the information from him that he had bought a suit of boy's clothes at Crippen's request.[7] With this in mind he asked the Home Office to direct the postal authorities to look out for letters going to their addresses and forwarding them on to him under a Home Office warrant, later adding telegrams to his request. Scotland Yard had by now offered a reward of £250 for information leading to the arrest of Crippen and Le Neve.

It was at this time Dew's conduct in the case was brought into question. A question was put to the Home Secretary, Winston Churchill, by another Member of Parliament, William Thorne, who wanted to know, 'If he can state who is responsible for allowing Dr Crippen to get out of the hands of the police ... and it was in consequence of the pressing inquiries that caused Dr Crippen to vanish.' It was not until a fortnight later that Churchill responded to the question, which he dismissed as being an unfair one as Dew was engaged on special duty at the time and was therefore unable to defend himself.

Scotland Yard gave their answer, saying that until the discovery of the remains it had simply been a missing person case, the sort of which numbered around a hundred a week in London alone. It was not until there was evidence of foul play that the house could be searched more thoroughly.[8]

Dew later responded angrily to the criticism:

I came in for criticism. Certain people with no knowledge of police procedure and less of the law blamed me for allowing Crippen to go. I ought to have arrested him, they said. Ridiculous!

There was up to this time no shred of evidence against Crippen upon which he could have been arrested or even detained. Futile to talk of arresting a man until you know there has been a crime.[9]

On the face of things it had been Dew and Mitchell's surprise visit that had resulted in Crippen losing his nerve and fleeing, but his nerves may have been stretched to breaking point before the police called. During the week ending 24 June Crippen's landlord had arranged for some work to be done at the house. Three lengths of stack pipe were replaced and on the week ending 8 July a new door knocker was put on the front door. While Crippen could rest assured that neither Le Neve or Lecocq would disturb the fabric of the house, he must have been terrified that the builders might notice something about the cellar, or suggest work that needed doing near where the remains were buried. In addition, he had been visited by John Nash and Lil Hawthorne on 28 June. They had been out of the country since 23 March. Once back in England they went to see Crippen to offer their condolences and found him in an anxious state. After living in domestic bliss with Ethel for several months, having cut himself off from Cora's friends, it must have come as a very unwelcome shock to have builders traipsing through the house and old friends of Cora's turning up asking questions about her.

The Crippen case was now dominating the newspapers. Dew observed,

> There has never been a hue and cry like that which went up throughout the country for Crippen and Miss Le Neve. The newspapers were full of the case. It was the one big topic of conversation. On the trains and buses one heard members of the public speculating and theorizing as to where they were likely to be.
>
> All the elements to fire the public imagination were present. They were intrigued by the relationship between the doctor and his former secretary; repelled by the gruesome find in the coal cellar, and mystified as to how the victim had met her death. Every day that passed increased the fevered interest in the hunt.[10]

Now the events at Hilldrop Crescent were publicly known, rumours spread like wildfire and false sightings of the fugitives poured in from all over Europe. When a German named John Evert committed suicide at a Finsbury boarding house, word spread that he had in fact been Dr Crippen.[11] When a young woman committed suicide at Bourges on 13 July, a theory emerged from Paris that she had been Ethel Le Neve.[12] One joker signed the visitors' book at Salle Church in Norfolk on 14 July as 'H. H. Crippen of Hilldrop Crescent, London'.[13]

Remembering that, to his annoyance, his superiors had not asked for press help during the Whitechapel murders, Dew determined to follow his instincts and do the opposite, making an appeal to the French newspaper *Le Matin* for 'the Press to give us its assistance'[14] but this only led to more false sightings.

Mr Newton, a costumier with premises at Great Portland Street, reported that a man answering Dr Crippen's description had entered his shop 'and said he wanted to purchase a lady's costume and under clothes which he said was for himself'. A man fitting Crippen's description had been spotted in the south of France before crossing the frontier to Spain (provisional arrest and extradition orders had already been issued in France, Spain and Portugal). He was also 'seen' in Cardiganshire and Willesden.[15] Perhaps the strangest sighting was of Crippen and Le Neve in a small town on the South Coast getting into a hot air balloon.[16]

Journalist Philip Gibbs offered an explanation for the mass sightings. Crippen 'looked a respectable little man, with weak, watery eyes and a drooping moustache, so ordinary a type of middle-class business man in London that quite a number of people, including one of my own friends, were arrested by mistake for him when the hue and cry went forth'.[17]

The Times referred to Crippen as 'Dr' Crippen rather than Dr Crippen in their coverage. There was some doubt as to the validity of Crippen's medical qualifications. Dew found a diploma at 39 Hilldrop Crescent,

> Presented and Registered in the Office of the Clerk of the County of King's by Hawley H. Crippen, as his authority to practice physic and surgery, this 8th day of July 1900. This will certify that the within diploma is from a reputable Medical College, legally chartered under the laws of the State of Ohio.

This was good enough for Dew, who pointed out that the diploma proved Crippen 'was not drawing on his imagination in describing himself as a doctor, at any rate, so far as the U.S.A. was concerned'.[18] Crippen's American qualification would not, however, allow him to practice as a doctor in England.[19]

The Crippen case led *The British Medical Journal* to speak out against foreign medical practitioners and their qualifications:

> The crime could hardly have been accomplished had it not been for the fact that Crippen, thanks to his American degree, was enabled to procure poisons in any quantity he desired. But for this circumstance the chemists can hardly be held to blame, since, it has become the custom in this country to accept foreigners who dub themselves medical men at their own valuation. It is quite time that this free trade in medical practice came to an end, and for both the public and the authorities to adopt and maintain the legal interpretation of the term 'medical practitioner'. This is a person who in virtue of an approved curriculum at an approved institution had obtained admission to the Register kept by the General Medical Council. A large proportion of the degrees obtainable in America are not only absolutely worthless from the point of view of this country, but are frankly admitted to be so by Americans themselves.[20]

In 1898, Crippen had appeared as a witness at a trial heard at the County of London Sessions for a colleague who was accused of stealing money from Munyon's. Crippen referred to his colleague as 'Doctor' Deane, which the judge queried:

> Judge: You call him 'doctor'. What are his qualifications?
> Crippen: I don't know.
> Barrister: You are called 'doctor'. You are not qualified?
> Crippen: I don't pretend to be.[21]

Crippen's medical career had been rather a chequered one. From early respectability he was drawn to homoeopathy, but he soon slipped into the murky world of quackery. This might suggest an unscrupulous streak in Crippen's character as he engaged in a trade that offered diagnosis by post and dispensed cures for everything from kidney disease and asthma to the common cold.

Again at the 1898 trial, this practice was questioned:

> Barrister: You advertise 24 remedies, aren't they all the same?
> Crippen: No.
> Barrister: Can you tell me any other ingredients than sugar and water in these 'cures'?
> Crippen: I don't think I need answer that question.[22]

In his youth, Crippen had been quite a well-known figure in homoeopathic circles and in 1885 was employed as a special correspondent by *The American Homeopathic Journal of Obstetrics and Gynaecology*. He wrote articles, book reviews and travelled to Europe, reporting on the state of the homoeopathy business in Paris and Berlin. His writings prophetically hinted at what he had done after leaving Hilldrop Crescent. Berlin offered 'a very desirable contrast to the cloudy, damp, and smoky atmosphere of London',[23] while the lure of Paris 'tempted your correspondent to brave the dangers of seasickness and cross the English channel'.[24] Crippen and Le Neve had sailed to Europe.

5

THE INQUISITIVE SEA CAPTAIN

... one of those episodes that no novelist would dare to make up, such as Crippen's flight across the Atlantic with his mistress dressed as a boy.

George Orwell, *Decline of the English Murder*

Captain Kendall seemed to be very much impressed by our interest in anything connected with murder.

Ethel Le Neve, *Thomson's Weekly News*

In 1910 it was not necessary to have a passport to travel much of the world, and Crippen and Le Neve had reached Belgium by 10 July. On that day they had booked into the Hotel des Ardennes in the Rue de Brabant in Brussels. Later enquiries established they stayed there until 18 July. Crippen signed the visitor's register 'John Robinson, age 55 Merchant born in Quebec Canada last place of residence, Vienna'. The hotel's proprietress signed the book on behalf of Le Neve under the name of 'John Robinson Junior', for the typist was now masquerading as a boy. The only luggage they brought with them was a small basketwork trunk. To the staff at the hotel they appeared to be two people travelling for pleasure. They spent most of their time in their room, only leaving it for about two hours a day.

The story Crippen told the hotel staff was that he was a merchant travelling with his sick son and that his wife had died two months previously. Le Neve only spoke in whispers, which Crippen explained by saying that 'he' was deaf and suffering from an affliction of the throat. He added that they had come from Quebec and planned to go to The Hague, Rotterdam and Amsterdam, and spend a few days in the Cambre Forest before returning to Quebec. Other enquiries elicited that Crippen had said he was going to go to Vilvorde near Brussels, for the benefit of his 'son's' health.

On 13 July, the day Dew discovered the remains at Hilldrop Crescent, Crippen called in at the office of M. Baur, an agent of the Red Star shipping line. He asked for a second-class cabin on a ship bound for Canada. The only one available was the steamer *Montrose*, which was due to leave Antwerp on 3 August. Crippen (still using the name Robinson) did not book it but returned the next day. Then he was told that he could get an earlier berth by booking a ship which went via England to Canada. Crippen declined and booked a cabin on the *Montrose*, a 5,000-ton steamship that travelled at a speed of 13 knots.

Crippen made another visit to Baur on 15 July. He was then informed that the *Montrose* was now sailing early, on 20 July. Crippen collected his two tickets for cabin number five, which cost 275 francs each (around £22), paying with English gold. He then asked Baur if he could recommend someone in Brussels who might lend him some money, but Baur declined to give him that information.

The *Montrose* arrived at Antwerp on 15 July. The vessel had first been launched in 1897 and initially used to transport Boer War troops. By 1910 the *Montrose* had a reputation of being a modest and reliable ship. Its captain, Henry Kendall, had sailed from London the day before. He had been given a full description of Dr Crippen by the Thames Police, which also included the detail that Le Neve might be dressed as a boy and Crippen as a clergyman.

The passengers for the *Montrose* (all second and third class) boarded the ship on 20 July between 8.30 and 10.00 a.m. There were in total 20 second-class passengers, 246 third-class and a crew of 107, making a total of 373 souls on board. Kendall did not notice anything untoward about any of the passengers. That was until he went ashore and bought a Continental edition of the *Daily Mail*, containing photographs and descriptions of Dr Crippen and Ethel Le Neve.

Kendall's suspicions were aroused within three hours of the start of the voyage when he saw mister and master Robinson. Crippen had signed the manifest 'John Philo Robinson, age 55, Merchant, American, of Detroit, Michigan U.S.A.' Le Neve was described as 'John George Robinson, age 16, single, Student'. Mr Robinson was clean-shaven, but had several days of growth on his chin. When the captain 'saw the boy squeeze the man's hand I thought it strange and unnatural, and it occurred to me at once that they might be Crippen and Le Neve'. Kendall wished them the time of day and observed them keenly. Already he felt 'quite confident' that they were the fugitives, but he did not do anything else at that point as he wished to make sure he hadn't made a mistake.

The following day, Captain Kendall confided his suspicions to his chief officer, Alfred Sergent, and instructed him to help collect any English newspapers on the ship which mentioned the North London cellar murder. Locking himself in his cabin, Kendall took a newspaper photograph of Dr Crippen and pinned it up on a drawing board before chalking out his moustache and spectacles. He then cut out a cardboard frame and placed it over the photograph of Le Neve, obscuring her hat and hair. Looking out of his cabin port-hole, Kendall saw the Robinsons stretched out on deck chairs about 20 feet away. He was now convinced they were the London fugitives.[1] On 22 July, Kendall engaged Crippen in conversation on the subject of sea-sickness among passengers and the remedies used for curing it. Crippen's answers included some medical terms for certain remedies. This convinced Kendall that Robinson was a medical man.

In addition, Robinson fitted two of the points of description of Crippen. The bridge of his nose was flat, and there was a deep mark on his nose as if caused by the wearing of spectacles. Kendall also heard Robinson speak in French to the French passengers. This 'positively convinced' Kendall that his suspicions were justified. Kendall told Crippen stories he hoped would make him laugh out loud, to see if Crippen would open his mouth wide enough for him to ascertain if he had false teeth.[2] The captain tested Crippen two or three times by calling after him 'Mr Robinson', to which Crippen did not respond. It was only when Kendall repeated his call and Le Neve prompted him that Crippen replied, explaining that the cold weather had made him deaf.

Kendall now made an historic decision. He instructed his Marconi wireless operator to send the following message to the managing director of the shipping company who would pass it on to Scotland Yard:

> Montrose. 130 miles West of Lizard.
> Have strong suspicion that Crippen London Cellar
> Murderer and accomplice are amongst saloon passengers.
> Moustache shaved off, growing beard. Accomplice dressed
> as boy, voice, manner and build undoubtedly a girl.
> Kendall.

The wireless telegraph had come into existence in the late nineteenth century, and by the early twentieth century it was possible to send messages over ever-increasing distances. Before this it was necessary to send transatlantic messages via underwater cables that linked Britain and America. The *Montrose* was one of only about sixty ships in the world to be fitted with wireless.[3] Ironically, Crippen would often sit on deck and look up at the wireless aerial, listening to the cracking electric spark messages being sent by the operator. He once commented, 'What a wonderful invention it is!'

Kendall continued to keep the pair under observation. He noted that Le Neve

has the manner and appearance of a very refined, modest girl. She does not speak much, but always wears a pleasant smile. She seems thoroughly under his thumb, and he will not leave her for a moment. Her suit is anything but a good fit. Her trousers are very tight about the hips, and are split a bit down the back and secured with large safety pins.

He continually shaves his upper lip, and his beard is growing nicely. I often see him stroking it and he seems pleased, looking more like a farmer every day. The mark on his nose has not worn off since coming on board.

He sits about on the deck reading, or pretending to read, and both seem to be thoroughly enjoying all their meals. They have not been seasick, and I have discussed various parts of the world with him. He knows Toronto, Detroit, and California well, and says he is going to take his boy to California for his health (meaning Miss Le Neve). Has in conversation used several medical terms. Crippen says that when the ship arrives he will go to Detroit by boat, if possible, as he prefers it. The books he has been most interested in have been

Pickwick Papers
Nebo the Nailer (S .B. Gould)
Metropolis
A Name to Conjure With

And he is now busy reading *The Four Just Men*, which is all about a murder in London and £1,000 reward.

The Robinsons dined at the captain's table, where Le Neve's table manners were

most lady like, handling knife and fork, and taking fruit off the dishes with two fingers. Crippen kept cracking nuts for her, and giving her

half his salad, and was always paying her the most marked attention
… and the more I saw of them the more I was convinced and I sent a
further Marconi to Liverpool when in Mid Atlantic, saying that I was
fully convinced as to the identity, passengers not suspicious am keeping
everything quiet.

Dew, exhausted by the relentless and unsuccessful hunt for Crippen,
received the 'electrifying' news of Captain Kendall's suspicions one
evening via a telegram from the Liverpool police. As Dew read the
contents 'a wave of optimism swept over me. My fatigue instantly
vanished.'[4] Dew rushed from his Scotland Yard office and jumped
into a cab that took him to the residence of Assistant Commissioner
Melville Macnaghten, who had become 'obsessed with Crippen and
the hope of his capture'.[5] Dew handed Macnaghten the telegram,
which he read with raised eyebrows. The following conversation
ensued:

'What do you think?'
'I feel confident it's them.'
'So do I. What do you suggest?'
'I want to go after them in a fast steamer. The White Star liner
Laurentic sails from Liverpool to-morrow. I believe it is possible for
her to overtake the *Montrose* and reach Canada first.'
'Here's your authority, Dew, and I wish you all the luck in the world.'[6]

Despite endorsing Dew's voyage, Macnaghten was only too aware of
the risks it entailed. Dew knew every detail of the case and had spoken
to Crippen. His absence could create problems. 'But a decision had
to be arrived at … the die was cast, the Rubicon was crossed. If the
coup happened to come off, well and good, but, if otherwise, why,
then, the case would have been hopelessly messed up, and I didn't
care to dwell on the eventualities of its future.' Macnaghten's spirits
were somewhat deflated when he arrived at Scotland Yard the next
morning and asked Superintendent Froest, 'Well, what do you think
of last night's decision?' Froest was unimpressed by Macnaghten's
'sanguine view' of the chances of the Marconi message being correct,
although Commisioner Sir Edward Henry shared Macnaghten's
optimism.[7]

The Chief Constable of Liverpool had booked Walter Dew on
to the steamer *Laurentic* under the name of John Dewhurst. The
ship was going to sail from Liverpool at 6.30 p.m. on 23 July,

a whole three and a half days after Crippen and Le Neve had departed for Canada. The *Laurentic* could travel at about 3.5 miles per hour faster than the *Montrose*, and sailed directly to Quebec. She was due to arrive there on 31 July, a couple of days before the *Montrose*. Dew did not even tell his wife about his mission, named 'Operation Handcuffs'. He just said that he had to go abroad 'on a matter of great urgency'. This was not unusual, for Dew never discussed any of his cases with his family. His daughter Kate would later recall that her father 'was usually very reluctant to give any information or express any opinion on the work on which he was engaged'.[8]

Dew journeyed from Euston station to Liverpool, where he was met by a Liverpudlian police officer wearing a red rose in his buttonhole for identification. News of Dew's imminent departure had leaked and a number of reporters and photographers had assembled, but he managed to slip quietly on board and evade the gathered pressmen.[9]

While Dew was steadily gaining ground on the *Montrose* he made numerous attempts to contact Captain Kendall via the Marconi wireless, but his messages failed to get through. The range of the wireless was limited and messages had to be sent via other vessels within 150 miles of the two ships. Somehow the passengers on the *Laurentic* suspected that the man with the large dark-grey moustache was a Scotland Yard officer. Dew had 'made every possible effort to hide his identity. It was soon discovered, however, but by tacit consent of everyone his incognito has been respected.' This was disputed by Dew who said nothing, kept himself to himself, giving every appearance of being 'an Englishman out for a little pleasure jaunt'.[10] Despite what was at stake, Dew admitted, 'I had a most pleasant voyage.'[11]

Captain Kendall, meanwhile, continued his surveillance on Crippen and Le Neve. Crippen was very relaxed and he and Le Neve spent one night in the saloon

> enjoying songs and music, he was quite interested, and spoke to me next morning, saying how one song, 'We All Walked Into the Shop', had been drumming in his head all night, and how his boy had enjoyed it, and laughed heartily when they retired to their room. In the course of one conversation he spoke about American drinks, and said that Selfridge's was the only decent place in London to get them at.

Kendall thought he saw the outline of a revolver in Crippen's hip pocket when a gust of wind blew the tail of his jacket to one side.

From then on, he carried his own gun, and 'if he turned and fired on me I would shoot him dead'. The captain could have placed the couple under arrest, but he didn't have enough staff to put a permanent watch on them night and day. Furthermore, they hadn't caused the slightest trouble so far on the voyage, so he thought it best to observe them and play 'the complete simpleton'.[12]

Kendall sensed an almost sinister hold Crippen had over Le Neve:

> At times both would sit and appear to be in deep thought. Though Le Neve does not show any signs of distress, and is, perhaps, ignorant of the crime committed, she appears to be a girl with a very weak will. She has to follow him everywhere. If he looks at her she gives him an endearing smile, as though she were under his hypnotic influence.

As the voyage progressed Crippen became more and more restless. He asked Kendall where the ship stopped to be met by the pilot boat, how he came off, how far it was from the pilot station to Quebec, and said he was anxious to get to Detroit. Crippen told Kendall that he thought about settling down in California on a fruit farm.

Newspapers had been full of the story of the Atlantic chase because Captain Kendall had been sending back regular wireless messages to the British newspapers, which told of his progress and investigations. John Nash, who had originally reported Cora Crippen's disappearance, was elated and declared that the 'fact that Inspector Dew has gone is splendid. This means almost certainly that Crippen will be caught.'[13] Some telegrams were sent to the *Montrose* from New York asking for statements from Crippen, but these were intercepted by Kendall.[14]

Back in London Superintendent Froest was keeping his feet firmly on the ground, at least publicly. In a statement, Froest pointed out the realities of the situation, which were in stark contrast to the press excitement over the chase, which was seen as a foregone prelude to the capture of the fugitives. Froest said,

> He [Dew] will leave the details of the arrest to the Canadian police, who will of course, make their own arrangements. His position during the proceedings in Canada, which are identical with the proceedings which are taken for extradition orders in other countries, will be first to identify the people and then to wait until they are handed over into his custody by the Canadian police. He will act exactly as a foreign officer does who is in this country waiting for the extradition of a criminal for

whom he has been seeking. These proceedings will naturally take some considerable time, and it is not possible for Inspector Dew to arrive back in this country in time for the adjourned inquest, which is fixed for August 15. That is, of course, if he can identify the people. Speaking for myself, I am keeping a perfectly clear mind on the subject. We have so many houses built with cards which fall down when the last of the pack is placed on top, and for this reason we are pursuing every clue which comes to us, just as if the *Montrose* incident had never occurred. Investigations are being made in London and elsewhere by detectives with a view to building up the story of the crime which is, owing to several aspects of the mystery, somewhat incomplete.[15]

It was not just the newspaper-reading public who were eagerly following Inspector Dew's transatlantic chase. Late on 30 July Home Secretary Winston Churchill requested an update on the case, which was delivered to him at St James' Palace.

Dew's fears that the *Montrose* had beaten him to Canada were unfounded. As well as the assurances of the *Laurentic*'s captain, there was the sight of a pilot cutter coming out to meet the steamer at Father Point filled with press reporters and photographers. Dew surmised it never would have been there had the *Montrose* already arrived. To his annoyance they cheered, 'Three cheers for Inspector Dew!'[16]

Walter Dew's relationship with the American and Canadian press was always uneasy, principally because he steadfastly refused to tell them anything. Dew saw this as 'upholding the prestige of British justice and British police methods'.[17] Questions were met by blunt responses such as, 'Let me alone', 'I don't know anything about it', and 'I do not want any pictures taken at all'.[18] The newsmen could not understand Dew's reticence. 'They do things very differently in America,' Dew sighed. 'I prefer the British way.'[19]

6

THE ARREST

Has anybody here seen Crippen,
C R I double-P E N?
Has anybody here seen Crippen?
Seek him up and down.
He's done a bunk to Canada
And left his wife in a coal cellar.
Has anybody here seen Crippen,
Crippen from Camden Town?

Contemporary verse, *Versicles of Crime*

Father Point was a desolate outpost on the St Lawrence River, consisting of some wooden shacks, a wireless station and a lighthouse. Inspector Dew was put up in one of the shacks, where he sleeplessly awaited the arrival of the *Montrose* amid the din of the lighthouse foghorn and rowdy singing of the congregated journalists in the other huts. As Dew had no power of arrest in Canadian waters he was met by Chief Officer McCarthy and Detective Denis of the Quebec City police, who would arrest Crippen and Le Neve.

On 31 July 1910, Inspector Dew borrowed the uniform of a pilot boat officer before being rowed up to the *Montrose*, accompanied by a genuine pilot and McCarthy and Denis. Crippen was still blissfully ignorant of having been discovered, commenting to the ship's doctor, 'There seem to be a good many pilots in the boat, doctor.'[1] Captain Kendall had been forewarned by wireless about what was going to happen and was waiting for the disguised Dew on the bridge, where the pair shook hands.

While making his way towards the captain's cabin, Dew caught sight of and instantly recognised Dr Crippen, despite his now being clean-shaven and not wearing glasses:[2]

Presently only a few feet separated us. A pair of bulgy eyes were raised to mine. I would have recognized them anywhere.

The little man was Crippen. I thrilled with the realization that this was no wild goose chase after all. My search was ended. Miss Le Neve, I felt certain, would not be far away.

During my long career as a detective, I have experienced many big moments, but at no other time have I felt such a sense of triumph and achievement.[3]

Crippen was brought by McCarthy and Denis into Kendall's cabin, where Dew confronted him with the words, 'Good morning, Dr Crippen; I am Chief Inspector Dew.' Crippen simply replied, 'Good morning, Mr Dew.' Dew continued, 'You will be arrested for the murder and mutilation of your wife, Cora Crippen, in London, on or about the 2nd of February last.'

Dew recalled, 'Even though I believed him to be a murderer, and a brutal murderer at that, it was impossible at that moment not to feel for him a pang of pity. He had been caught on the threshold of freedom. Only twelve hours more and he would have been safely at Quebec.'[4]

Macnaghten compared the confrontation between Dew and Crippen with that of Henry Morton Stanley and Dr David Livingstone, almost forty years previously in Africa.[5] Livingstone had embarked on an African expedition in 1866 and was not heard of for years. The editor of the *New York Herald* dispatched journalist Stanley to find out what had happened to Livingstone. Stanley set out in 1871 and eventually tracked down Livingstone eight months later, greeting him with the immortal question, 'Dr Livingstone I presume?'

Chief Officer McCarthy and Detective Denis cautioned the now speechless Crippen. Detective Denis then searched Crippen and found several items from Cora Crippen's jewellery collection. There were also two printed cards bearing the name 'E. Robinson & Co., Detroit, Mich. Presented by Mr John Robinson'. On the back of one was written, 'I cannot stand the horror I go through every night any longer and as I see nothing bright ahead and money has come to an end I have made up my mind to jump overboard tonight – I know I have spoil [*sic*] your life – but I – I hope some day you can learn to forgive me. With last words of love, your H.' On the back of the other card was written, 'Shall we wait until tonight about 10 or 11 o'clock? If not, what time?'

Dew thought the writing was Crippen's, and believed they showed he would have committed suicide before the *Montrose* reached Quebec. He found Crippen's explanation of the cards unsatisfactory:

> He stated that two days before his arrival at Quebec, the Quartermaster of the *Montrose*, approached and showed him an unsigned letter, in which it said that the Police were going to arrest him on his arrival at Quebec, and he (the Quartermaster) offered to hide him amongst the cargo till all was quiet, and then at Montreal would facilitate his escape.
>
> Crippen alleged that it was arranged that Miss Le Neve should remain on board, as it was not supposed that Police wanted her, and that the cards found on him when arrested, in which he had written, that the horror was too much and that he intended jumping overboard etc., were written by him as part of the plot, and would have been produced by Miss Le Neve, when Police came on board.
>
> He further said that the Quartermaster was going to make a splash in the water at night, and then tell the Captain that he (Crippen) had jumped overboard.

Captain Kendall didn't believe the story either. It appeared in the *Montreal Daily Star* and led to the *Montrose*'s four quartermasters indignantly issuing a sworn statement refuting the story and of having had any dealings with Dr Crippen on the voyage.[6]

Leaving Crippen with McCarthy, Dew entered cabin five, where he saw Ethel Le Neve reclining on a settee. Her appearance had also altered since Dew last saw her. Not only was she dressed as a boy, wearing the same brown suit that William Long had purchased in London, but her hair had been cropped short. Dew thought Le Neve's disguise was unconvincing and found it 'difficult to believe that any person with an average amount of intelligence could ever have believed her to be a boy'. Dew said to her with his 'characteristic lisp',[7] 'Miss Le Neve', to which she replied, 'Yes.' Dew then identified himself and told her the charge she was facing. Le Neve did not reply, but became agitated and faint. Dew left Le Neve with a stewardess and returned to the captain's cabin to remove Crippen to another cabin. Crippen suddenly said, 'I am not sorry; the anxiety has been too much.' At no point did Crippen display any shock at hearing his wife had been murdered, nor did he ask Dew how she died. McCarthy handcuffed Crippen, explaining that, 'We must put these on, because on a card found on you you have written that you intend jumping overboard.' Crippen replied, 'I won't. I am more than satisfied, because the anxiety has been too awful.'

Dew made a further search of Crippen, finding more jewellery concealed about his person. Crippen asked Dew how Le Neve was. 'Agitated,' Dew replied, 'but I am doing all I can for her.' Crippen replied, 'It is only fair to say that she knows nothing about it; I never told her anything.' She had not seen any newspapers on the voyage thanks to the efforts of Captain Kendall and Chief Officer Sergent. 'I assure you Mr Dew,' Le Neve said, 'I know nothing about it, I intended writing to my sister when I got to Quebec.'

As soon as he could, Dew sent a telegram to Scotland Yard. 'Crippen and Leneve [*sic*] arrested wire later Dew.' The following day he sent another, 'Confirming former cable arrest made, arrive Quebec midnight Sunday. Suggest matron and Mitchell, Crippen threatened suicide, writing soon. Dew.'

The arrest of Crippen was the first instance of a murderer being captured thanks largely to wireless telegraphy technology. In 1845 John Tawell became the first murderer to be caught by a normal telegraph. He was observed getting onto a train at Slough after murdering his mistress. A telegraph was sent to Paddington station, and the police were waiting for him when he arrived.

The Times explained the importance of the wireless in the Crippen case:

> In the absence of wireless telegraphy the fugitives would have reached Canada in comparatively favourable circumstances. There would have been no apparatus of detention ready for their arrival. No doubt the captain's suspicions would have been made known in the proper quarters, and means might have been found to keep them under observation for a time. But there would have been no means of absolute identification, and the action of the authorities would plainly have been very much hampered. Wireless telegraphy enabled the captain, without altering his course, and without giving the alarm to the fugitives, to communicate his suspicions to his owners, who promptly handed them on to Scotland Yard.[8]

The *Montrose* arrived in Quebec early on the morning of 1 August. As with all the events surrounding the case, a crowd had gathered; this time it numbered around 500. Amid the flashes of camera lamps they saw a handcuffed Dr Crippen, holding his head down low, following Walter Dew down the gangplank. Ethel Le Neve followed, her boy's attire replaced by ill-fitting garments that belonged to the stewardess of the *Montrose*. Crippen and Le Neve were taken to the city gaol.

Isolated and enduring continuous pressure from the press for a story, Inspector Dew wrote a 'somewhat disjointed' twenty-three page hand-written report describing the arrest and his subsequent problems with journalists. 'I feel a little worn out after the somewhat strenuous and anxious life of the past month,' Dew told Chief Constable Bigham at Scotland Yard.

I was absolutely mobbed. Cameras were thrust in my face and I was practically at their mercy. I was importuned to say something, but I need hardly say that I refused.

In passing I cannot refrain from saying that the whole affair was disgraceful and should and could have been avoided and I was fearful lest this should in any way mar the success of my mission. Fabulous sums were offered me for information and permission to take the photograph of Crippen and especially Le Neve in boys' clothing.

My refusal to do this and declining to give information has of course gained me many enemies, as I have it on the best authority that owners of papers are complaining that no statements & information are forthcoming through them from Dew.

The result is that <u>daily</u> the most lying reports are published as to alleged statements made by me as to confessions etc. and indeed strange as it may seem, my life has been made a perfect burden.

I am followed and questioned in the most shameful manner, and my every movement is watched, they even intrude into my hotel and force their questions upon me at meals, and every possible ruse has been adopted to break through the reserve I have maintained from the first.

It has cost me a prodigious effort to continue to treat them with civility, but I think the fact of my having done so has annoyed them more.

Dew requested that he be allowed to have a free hand when it came to arranging the return voyage and said that Crippen would never be left alone, no doubt fearing he might try to attempt suicide. He emphasised that Crippen and Le Neve would be kept entirely apart and expressed concern that heavy bribes might be offered by the press to the matrons in order to get to Le Neve.

At the initial police court hearing, a crowd of 3,000 women blocked the entrance to the court in the fight for admission. All the available seats were occupied by women, with forty or fifty others standing. Crippen's physical appearance came as a disappointment to the expectant spectators. He was not 'the hypnotic marvel which cabled stories had held up. Instead, the cringing figure with stooped head gave the lie to expectations. Crippen whined where criminals with more backbone would have answered smartly and posed serenely. He rolled his swollen eyes and twitched his head.' Le Neve was no more inspiring. She 'leaned weakly upon the arms of her guards like one who had risen from a sick bed' before fainting and being carried out.[9]

The hearing itself was a formality. Crippen confirmed his name and acknowledged he knew Le Neve and the reason they were there. He also stated he was an American citizen, a Catholic and that he would not fight extradition. The 1881 Fugitive Offenders Act meant that fugitives from British justice wanted for offences carrying a sentence of twelve months or more could be arrested on a warrant in any part of the British dominions. When caught, the fugitive would appear before a magistrate and if the evidence presented 'raises a strong or probable presumption that the fugitive committed the offence', they would then be sent to prison for fifteen days to allow them to appeal before being extradited. This is what happened with Crippen and it meant that he and Dew would miss the resumed coroner's inquest in London.

Dew had anticipated a stay in Canada after Crippen's arrest. The intensity of the Canadian public's feelings of revulsion towards Crippen came as a surprise to him:

> I had plenty of opportunities for sensing public opinion in Quebec. The people there were incensed against Crippen. They looked upon him as a monster in human form. By some he had already been judged and found guilty. The ghastly murder and mutilation of Belle Elmore, followed by his flight from justice with Miss Ethel Le Neve as his companion, had roused public feeling against him to fever point.
>
> It was the same the world over. I have never known anything like it. Only those who can remember the case and the intense excitement and bitterness it engendered, can have any conception of the widespread antipathy towards the little man who was now in my charge.[10]

A rumour emerged on 4 August that Crippen had confessed to the murder of his wife. Dew stoutly denied this, saying, 'There is not an iota of truth in the rumour.' Froest described the suggestion as 'absolutely untrue', and the Canadian Provincial Premier, Sir Lomer Gouin, described the stories as 'tissues of lies'. They were lies, and they would later prove costly for the newspapers that had printed them.

Another bogus report said that Dew had been sent a telegram from Scotland Yard saying that the remains had been positively identified as being female. An 'absolute invention' was the exasperated Froest's verdict. Dew had not received such a communication from Scotland Yard and they had not had any more from Dew.[11]

Bizarre stories were published. Le Neve was offered £200 a week to star in a twenty-week tour, which included a music hall sketch called 'Caught by Wireless'. Crippen was offered £1,000 a week for a twenty-week engagement if he was acquitted.[12] At this time one of the strangest stories concerning Dew's investigations emerged. It was reported in *The Times* that Dew's wife Kate had expressed an opinion that Belle Elmore was still alive and that the whole Crippen case had been arranged as an advertising stunt.[13] Stranger still, Dew was reported as saying that the remains had not even been identified as human, let alone female and if Cora Crippen were to reappear alive she would be a great attraction on the stage and could name her price.[14]

Detective Sergeant Mitchell had left Liverpool and was making his way to Quebec aboard the *Lake Manitoba* to deliver extradition papers.[15] He was accompanied by Sarah Stone and Julia Foster, two stern-faced wardresses from Holloway Prison (there were no police matrons), to accompany Ethel Le Neve back home. When Mitchell was reunited with Dew on 14 August he handed him a letter from Chief Constable Bigham. Dew replied to Bigham, saying that he had received the two cables that the letter referred to. One of them appears to have contained instructions from Winston Churchill, for Dew wrote,

> The wishes of H.M. Secretary of State were anticipated by me, and I would remark that I have always made it a practice to treat prisoners with courtesy & consideration no matter what their position in life.
>
> If I have erred in this case it has been on the side of consideration and humanity, and at great cost to my own personal convenience & comfort.

Churchill had also expressed a desire that Crippen and Le Neve should be protected from the reporters and photographers. Dew was pleased to report that 'so far as I am personally concerned I succeeded in preventing all annoyance from these people, and I also think succeeded in preventing their photographs being taken, but no one except myself can ever realise at what a cost this was done'.

Dew went on to inform Bigham that he was 'devising a scheme' to get the prisoners back to England, as he was concerned about the strength of feeling the Canadians had against Crippen, which potentially jeopardised Dew's chances of bringing him back home safely:

> This of course will depend to some extent on the Police here, to whom sooner or later I must divulge my plans, but bluntly speaking, I don't trust them too much in respect to reporters, however I shall do my best to avoid publicity and annoyance to fugitives.

The Canadian and American journalists hoped that Sergeant Mitchell might be more forthcoming than Dew, but Dew told them in no uncertain terms that, 'Mr Mitchell is acting under my instruction, and I have instructed him not to discuss the case.'[16] Mitchell remained silent.

The adjourned coroner's inquest went ahead in London as scheduled on 15 August without Dew, Crippen or Le Neve. Also absent was the original coroner, Dr Danford Thomas. He had been suffering from ill health and decided to take a holiday between hearings. He died suddenly at the coastal town of Hastings. It was agreed that the assistant coroner, Walter Schröder, who was familiar with the facts, should replace him. Superintendent Froest appeared and said that he could not predict exactly when Dew and Mitchell would return with the prisoners but it would probably be in about three weeks time and suggested that the inquest be adjourned until then.

7

THE RETURN VOYAGE

The Crippen case was fraught with understatement, restraint, and characteristic British relish for drama.

Alfred Hitchcock, *New York Times*

Inspector Dew's plan to leave Canada unseen involved boarding a small steamer named *Queen*, which would meet the liner *Megantic* downstream. There was one small mishap as Crippen walked the gangway between the steamer and the *Megantic*. Handcuffed, and with his hat pulled down over his eyes, he walked into one of the ropes holding the gangway. It struck him on the chin and jerked him backwards, but Dew caught him before he fell into the sea.[1] On 20 August, so the story went, four people boarded the White Star liner *Megantic* under false names. Inspector Dew was Silas P. Doyle (in a parting shot a disgruntled journalist wrote 'Sillyass P. Doyle sails for England'),[2] Dr Crippen was Cyrus Field, Ethel Le Neve was Miss J. Byrne and Sergeant Mitchell was F. M. Johnson.[3] 'No one studying the liner's passenger list would have been any wiser,' boasted Dew.[4] This is contradicted by the surviving passenger list, which gives their correct names.[5]

On board, Dew read Crippen and Le Neve the warrant that charged them both with the wilful murder of Cora Crippen. Le Neve was also charged with being an accessory after the fact to that murder. After hearing the charge again Crippen simply said 'Right', while Le Neve said 'Yes.'

One American newspaper, perhaps frustrated by Dew's refusal to speak to the press, launched a scathing attack on the departing detective:

That ridiculous Inspector Dew has taken his two prisoners and departed. Atlas with the weight of the universe on his shoulders was never more impressed with the importance of his job than Mr Dew has been for the last twenty days. Pomposity and overweening conceit apparently pass at Scotland Yard for cleverness and efficiency.

Dew has been very funny while in America. And he has done a good service in destroying that traditional American awe and reverence felt for Scotland Yard and London police methods in general.[6]

Dew described the return voyage aboard the *Megantic*:

Crippen ate well and apparently slept well. I found him a good conversationalist, able to talk on almost any subject. For the most part we confined ourselves to general topics – books, the weather, the liner, the progress we were making, and so on – but several times every day he asked about Miss Le Neve.

One would never have guessed from Crippen's demeanour and manner, on that homeward voyage, that he was under arrest for murder, and that he had on his conscience a burden which few men could have borne without wilting.

The more I saw of this remarkable man the more he amazed me.

I was greatly impressed on the voyage home by the unswerving loyalty of Crippen to Miss Le Neve.

Every morning he asked first thing how Miss Le Neve was. He never seemed to care much what happened to himself, so long as her innocence was established.

One incident sticks out in my memory. When off the coast of Ireland we ran into a heavy storm. Most of the passengers became ill, including my girl prisoner.

Crippen was a good sailor. He remained unperturbed through it all, or would have remained unperturbed had he not learned of Miss Le Neve's condition. The news that she was seasick caused him great concern. He told me the best remedy was champagne, and that the patient should lie flat.

For a moment it didn't strike me that he had it in his mind that champagne should be given to Miss Le Neve.

He saw this, and looked pleadingly at me as he said: 'Oh, Mr Dew, please give her a little champagne and I will be eternally grateful to you.'[7]

Dew obtained a bottle of champagne that restored Le Neve immediately. Crippen 'was like a dog in his gratitude. He could scarcely have expressed greater pleasure had I told him that he could go free.'[8] Le Neve would later reveal that Dew also became seasick during some rough weather near Ireland. She found Dew's manner very paternal and she and Crippen referred to him as 'father'.[9]

Crippen never showed the slightest indication that he might lose his nerve as the ship neared England. Dew did not even notice any sign of depression, which might have been expected:

> His nerves must have been made of iron. Except that he was under constant supervision and was handcuffed when he was taken out for exercise, he lived the life of a normal passenger.
>
> He mystified me. He seemed quite happy. He gave no trouble, and never once tried the patience of Sergeant Mitchell or myself.
>
> The impression he gave me was that of a man with a mind completely at rest. Most of his time he spent reading. I used to fetch his books myself from the ship's library, being careful, of course, never to get him one with a crime or murder plot. He loved novels, especially those with a strong love interest.[10]

Sergeant Mitchell also found Crippen an easy prisoner to deal with. 'He chatted with me from time to time on various matters,' Mitchell recalled, adding that throughout the voyage Crippen 'seemed quite bright + jolly'.

Inspector Dew kept a close watch on Crippen during the return voyage, and several times saw his prisoner stripped. To his surprise the diminutive Crippen was strongly built, and Dew was relieved that his prisoner was so well behaved. He later told barrister Cecil Mercer, 'Well, I'm a much heavier man, but I should have been very sorry to have had to take Crippen on.'[11]

Crippen never mentioned his wife, and never showed any animosity towards his captor. Dew was often asked in later years why he treated Crippen with such kindness after his arrest. He did not consider that he had shown Crippen any more consideration than he had hundreds of other prisoners throughout his career. He thought that it was his duty to consider a prisoner innocent until they appeared before the proper tribunal and were found guilty. Despite this, Dew had 'never entertained a doubt as to his guilt'.[12]

Dew also spent a lot of time during the return voyage with Ethel Le Neve, who had fully recovered after the initial shock of her arrest. He made frequent daily visits to her cabin to see if there was anything she wanted. Dew found her almost as calm and collected as

Crippen. Le Neve showed great composure throughout the journey. Dew thought this was because she had a clear conscience and 'her fortitude was born of the knowledge of her own innocence and her faith in the integrity of the British Justice to which she was being surrendered'.[13]

Le Neve allegedly caused Dew a few problems on the return voyage. The detective told Cecil Mercer that, while Crippen was pining for her in his cabin on the opposite side of the ship, she was enjoying herself, joking and flirting with the ship's crew. In the end Dew had to move Le Neve to a less accessible cabin.[14]

Bernard Grant, a *Daily Mirror* photographer who had managed to obtain a berth on the *Megantic*, observed that the security around Crippen and Le Neve was very tight. Although both prisoners were allowed to choose their meals from the first-class saloon menu, the food arrived cut up. Steel knives were forbidden and the cords and tapes from the nearby lifeboats were removed, as was the wire on the electric ventilating fans, to prevent suicide attempts.

Each evening after dinner Crippen and Le Neve were taken separately to the top deck for exercise. This only took place once the deck had been cleared and all doors leading to it locked. A steward remained on duty outside the cabins at all times, while Sergeant Mitchell slept in Crippen's cabin and the junior wardress slept in Le Neve's. Dew would padlock the cabins at night.[15]

Grant, who had no luck when trying to interview Dew in Canada, hoped his resolve might weaken on the return voyage, but to no avail. Dew 'shut up like an oyster' whenever Grant mentioned the prisoners, and the journalist contented himself with convivial walks and deck games with the tight-lipped sleuth.[16]

On 24 August Dew took a handcuffed Crippen on to the deck to allow him some exercise. The prisoner asked Dew for 'a favour but I will leave it for Friday'. Dew told Crippen that he could give an answer then and there as well as he could on Friday so Crippen explained his request. 'When you took me off the ship I did not see Miss Le Neve. I don't know how things will go, they may go all right or they may go all wrong with me. I may never see her again and I want to ask you if you will let me see her – but I won't speak to her. She has been my only comfort for the last three years.' Dew considered the request to be a 'delicate matter', but did allow him to see, but not talk to her, on a train from Liverpool to London after the boat had docked.

Unknown to Le Neve at the time, she had now become the subject of a series of articles in the newspaper *Answers*, which began to appear as the *Megantic* neared Liverpool. The author was none other than her father Walter Neave. He believed his daughter was innocent, but wanted to give a more in-depth account of her life in order to finance any legal bills that were bound to start accumulating.[17]

As the *Megantic* approached the Liverpool landing stage, the waiting crowds spotted Dew on the deck, smoking a cigar and chatting with Inspector Duckworth of the Liverpool police, who had gone out in a boat to meet him. The sight of Dew indicated that Crippen and Le Neve were still aboard and they had not been surreptitiously landed already. The crowd thought that Dew would not emerge with his prisoners until late in the afternoon, but when a military and civic reception began to welcome the disembarking Canadian passengers and members of the Queen's Own Rifles, Dew rushed Crippen and Le Neve down the gangway, surrounded by police officers. One newspaper described it as, 'a very neatly contrived manoeuvre'.[18] The representative of the *Liverpool Courier* managed to get close enough to observe Crippen's pale, thin face and the stubbly growth of a sandy moustache.[19]

Dew was happy to be back in England. Not only had he dramatically captured Crippen and Le Neve, he had left behind the American journalists and was reunited with the English media, who reported,

> His [Dew's] comments on the methods of the American journalists with whom he came in contact were highly amusing, and there was no little feeling in his tone when he remarked, 'It is quite a pleasure to meet English Pressmen, for they are gentlemen.'[20]

The train carrying Crippen and Le Neve from Liverpool arrived at London's Euston station, where Crippen was greeted by boos and jeers from a waiting crowd who loathed him as much as the Canadian public. He and Le Neve were whisked off to Bow Street police court for two nights, until the Monday sitting of the court, when they were to appear before magistrate Robert Marsham, whom Dew described as 'a giant of a man with a ruddy face and an old-fashioned style of dress which gave him the appearance of a prosperous farmer. One of the finest gentlemen I have ever met.'[21]

Melville Macnaghten was hugely relieved. He later admitted to the journalist and crime writer Hargrave Adam how close Crippen had come to getting away with murder:

We had practically 'pigeonholed' the case. Officers had twice or three times been through Crippen's house without finding the slightest clue to go upon. There was nothing really in the attitude of Crippen himself to arouse suspicion. He placed no obstacles in the way of the police, in fact he actually helped them in their search of the house. Then when the thing was beginning to be regarded by us as 'disposed of' the man suddenly decamps! Well, of course that did it! It reopened the case, and at once gave us the impression that there really was something in that house. But if he'd had the pluck to have taken a long lease of his house instead of decamping, he would probably be alive to-day and the mystery of the disappearance of Belle Elmore an unsolved one![22]

Macnaghten added that fleeing with Le Neve had been his downfall because 'if he had gone away alone he might have baffled the police, for he was a man of the world and knew his way about it'.[23] Had Crippen done that, it would then have been the fate of another criminal to become the first murderer to be captured thanks to wireless telegraph and gain the lasting notoriety associated with it.

8

THE CROOKED SOLICITOR

...when she thought of the dreadful wickedness of that little American
doctor who dismembered his wife the tears actually came into her eyes.
George Orwell, *Coming Up For Air*

Arthur Newton was a well-known figure in legal circles. Barrister
Travers Humphreys described him as 'a public school boy, very
good-looking, with a charming manner and considerable gifts of
advocacy based upon an extensive knowledge of the world rather than
a knowledge of law'.[1] He added that Newton possessed a 'scheming
brain', and usually got what he wanted 'by fair means or otherwise'.[2]

Newton had been avidly following the story of the North London
cellar murder in the newspapers when he realised that the missing
suspect was a former client. Crippen had failed to make much of an
impression on Newton back in 1906. Newton remembered him as
a, 'short, insignificant figure, with weak, goggly eyes, protected by
gold-rimmed glasses, and a rather hesitating manner'.[3]

As a lawyer Newton was naturally familiar with the Bow Street
police court where he was reunited with his client. Being a somewhat
unscrupulous character, he had a more intimate knowledge of that
establishment than most. In 1890 he had been tried there on charges
of conspiracy to defeat the ends of justice. Newton had attempted
to prevent three telegraph boys from testifying that Lord Arthur
Somerset had committed acts of gross indecency with them at a male
brothel in Cleveland Street, London. He was ultimately sentenced to
six weeks' imprisonment.[4] 'God knows what he was paid to do it,'
said Cecil Mercer, who marvelled that Newton had avoided being
struck off as a solicitor. 'But he was a gentleman, and you couldn't
help liking him,' conceded Mercer, who hinted that Newton was not
above blackmailing police officers to get his way.[5]

One of Newton's clerks later explained how Newton had secured Crippen as a client, his less-than-pure motives for doing so and how he raised the money to pay for Crippen's defence:

> Quite simply he 'captured' Crippen as a professional speculation. It would have been worth taking on a case of this kind for its publicity value alone. Newton saw his way to get the publicity and the money, too.
>
> Newton arranged with a friend to cable Crippen to the effect that one who believed in his innocence was prepared if necessary to finance his defence.

Once Crippen had been snared, Newton set about raising money. He first obtained Crippen's permission to dispose of the contents of his house. Then he took a number of newspapers to court for statements they had made about the case that Newton could construe as contempt of court. Newton was paid costs in the successful prosecutions as he had bought the matter before the court. This still wasn't enough, so he took advantage of the great interest the case was attracting in America and accepted a payment of £1,000 from an American consortium. In return for their investment Crippen would undertake a two-month long lecture tour in America, if he was acquitted.[6]

Newton's client had aged markedly. The first words Crippen said to him were, 'I want you thoroughly to understand, Mr Newton, that my first anxiety is for Miss Le Neve. She is dearer to me than anything in the world, and, if it becomes necessary, I would sacrifice myself to save her. She knew nothing whatever about the matter.' Newton replied, 'I am assuming, Dr Crippen, that you are quite innocent.' Crippen responded, 'Certainly. But don't forget, whatever happens, your first thought is to be for Miss Le Neve.' Newton went to see Le Neve, whose appearance came as a disappointment, for 'she was not a beautiful woman, and I could see nothing in her to account for her strong hold on the affections of Crippen. She completely convinced me that she knew nothing, and that she believed that Belle Elmore had gone to America, as Crippen had told her.'[7]

A crowd numbering hundreds had gathered outside the court, many of them women and young girls. Only a handful managed to gain entrance, as the court was small and lacked a public gallery. The spectators had to stand behind a barrier at the back of the courtroom. Dew was amazed at the crowds the case attracted everywhere, commenting, 'No other murderer's personality has been quite so magnetic as that of Dr Crippen.'[8]

The prisoners entered. A journalist observed,

> There emerged a graceful, erect girl in dark-blue costume, with spreading dark-blue hat, her face half hidden in a motor veil of lighter hue. Behind her walked a plump-faced little man in a grey frock-coat rather too large for him. The man's big protuberant eyes were emphasised by an almost total lack of brows; and a very little nose and half-grown moustache, a fleshy little chin, a wide, upright forehead, and only sufficient hair to indicate a parting in the middle ... it was the vivacity of his face that made up his personality. The portraits of him which had been printed in the papers with his spectacles and severe aspect made him somewhat wooden. In real life, he carried the message of thoughtfulness, apprehension, sensitiveness. One would never have thought that he was a cold-blooded murderer. You could see the innate gentleness of the man as you looked at him.[9]

This initial hearing was a formality in order to have Crippen and Le Neve remanded until a later date. Travers Humphreys, representing the Director of Public Prosecutions, asked Mr Marsham if he would adjourn the hearing for eight days, to which he readily consented. Humphreys also pointed out that the likelihood was that Ethel Le Neve would only be charged as being an accessory after the fact.

The prisoners were hastily removed from the court by a side door and taken away by taxicab. Crippen's destination was Brixton Prison while Le Neve was driven to Holloway Prison.

An anonymous Bow Street gaoler later recalled Crippen's time there. Crippen

> looked tired and jaded, completely worn out, but conscious of the great ordeal which he knew he must face once he was in the grip of the police.
>
> I spoke to him about his journey, and he told me how glad he was in one way to have all the anxiety ended. But he never complained through all the monotony of the police-court proceedings, which lasted for many weeks. He was very keen to know what kind of treatment he might expect in Brixton Prison, and afterwards during his various visits to Bow Street he never once complained of the routine or the food or sleeping accommodation. In fact, he declared that the governor and warders did everything possible for his comfort and convenience. He had a great partiality for tea, and he always looked forward to this each afternoon of the Magisterial hearing.[10]

The case was attracting huge interest in the press all over the world. Melville Macnaghten observed, 'So far as my experience goes, no case has ever fascinated the British public, and, indeed, engaged the attention of the whole world, in quite the same way that the case of Dr Crippen did.' He dismissed it in one respect for 'from a detective point of view, it had no particular interest'. However, 'in its developments there were very many dramatic touches such as the man in the street loves to imbibe with his coffee at breakfast, and to inhale with his after-dinner cigar'.[11] A *Times* editorial attempted to explain this:

> It is due in part to the fact that Scotland Yard took the whole world into its confidence with unprecedented thoroughness. It enlisted not only the services of the official police of other countries, but also the formidable though unofficial detective service supplied by the extensive publicity afforded by the Press.
>
> The other reason for the keen interest with which this chase has been followed is the unprecedentedly large part played in the capture by wireless telegraphy. The ordinary telegraph has enormously increased the difficulties of fugitives from justice. It has frequently confronted an escaping criminal with a detective and a warrant just when he thought that he had baffled pursuit. But it could never have accomplished what has been done in this case by wireless telegraphy.[12]

Filson Young, who edited the *Trial of Hawley Harvey Crippen* for the Notable British Trials series, proffered another explanation of the appeal of the case. This was the paradox of Crippen's character. On the one hand he was utterly devoted to Ethel Le Neve, and regarded as a most kindly and mild-mannered man by those who knew him. On the other hand, he had just been arrested for a cold-blooded murder that was leaving the newspaper-reading public aghast with horror. Young observed that 'there are two sides to the story – the physical, which is sordid, dreadful, and revolting, and the spiritual, which is good and heroic', and Young observed it was rare in England to have a *crime passionel*. Furthermore, it was the newspaper 'silly season'. Summer was traditionally a quiet news time so the press had used the Crippen story to fill their pages, allowing their readers to know everything about the hunt for Crippen, while he and Le Neve were unaware of what was happening. Criminologist Nigel Morland suggested the timing of the story resulted in 'a vulgar intrigue' being blown out of proportion:

To start with, the story broke in July, a time when editors seek a freakish event – preferably slightly lunatic – to blow into epic proportions. Ready for it are millions in a holiday mood, which is certainly slightly lunatic; thus, a good beginning is soundly laid – and – let it be remembered – more than one murderer owes his permanent fame to the dog days of July.[13]

George Orwell would later suggest that the 'enormous ready-made fascination' with the case was due in part to 'the fact that the murder took place in the stable pre-1914 world, against a background of respectability'.[14]

Dew had his own theory to explain the unusual interest the case was attracting:

Think of the circumstances! The callous way in which the Doctor killed his actress wife, and the mutilation of her remains; the part played by Miss Ethel Le Neve, the 'other woman' in the case; the flight of the couple with the girl dressed as a boy, and their dramatic arrest on the other side of the Atlantic.[15]

The Americans were just as fascinated as the British:

Everywhere one goes in New York to-day – in the streets, tramway-cars, hotels – people congregate – men, women, and children – apparently interested in nothing else. Every feature of the case is eagerly discussed, often by persons entire strangers to each other.

The bulletin boards of the newspapers were again surrounded this afternoon by crowds clamouring for the latest details, just as they were last week when the pursuit by wireless across the ocean was in progress. As the edition of the evening papers follow each other in quick succession they are snatched from the hands of the swarming newsboys. Nothing like it has been seen since the days of the Spanish–American war. All classes seem to be equally affected.[16]

While Dew had been chasing Crippen and Le Neve across the Atlantic, investigations into the events at Hilldrop Crescent continued unabated. The drains and sewers of No. 39 were checked for human remains but none were found. The building, now under the constant supervision of a plain-clothes officer, had become something of a tourist attraction as scores of people filed past each day, while those with cameras took commemorative snapshots.

A statement was made at the end of July by metalworker Frederick Evans, who lived in Brecknock Road, Camden Town. Evans was 'fairly sure' that it was on the night of 4 February when he was returning home from the Orange Tree public house on Euston Road when, at around 1.20 a.m., he heard 'a terrible screech which terminated with a long dragging whine' that emanated from the direction of Hilldrop Crescent. Evans' first thought was of the Whitechapel murders, despite it being over two decades after the killings. Evans' back garden was some 3–4 yards away from the Crippens' and he frequently used to hear Cora singing. The Sunday after he had heard the screams Evans smelled burning from the garden of No. 39, which continued for several days.

Crippen had certainly been busy burning something. Islington dustman William Curtis recalled that, for three weeks from mid-February, he had to remove an unusually large amount of rubbish from 39 Hilldrop Crescent. The first week it consisted of burnt paper and women's clothing. In later weeks he removed quantities of a light, white ash that was not paper ash nor was it from a fire grate. Curtis was given a 3d tip for his efforts by a woman he thought might have been Ethel Le Neve.

Similar disturbances had been heard around the time of Cora's disappearance. Franziska Hachenberger of 36 Hilldrop Road was 'certain that when I heard the screams at the back of Hilldrop Crescent, was either on the early morning of the 1st or 2nd of February last … It was an awful scream, it was not easily forgotten.' Her father had also heard the scream which he thought happened at around 2 a.m. Miss Isaacs of 36 Brecknock Road had a garden that was adjacent to the Crippen's. She wrote a letter to a friend saying that she had heard 'a loud scream' coming from that direction. Lena Lyons and her lodger May Pole lived at 46 Brecknock Road which overlooked 39 Hilldrop Crescent. They both thought they heard two gunshots around seven o'clock one morning either at the end of January or the beginning of February.

The re-adjourned magistrates' court hearing took place on 6 September. Detailed medical evidence was put forward by Dr Pepper. His first impression had been that the remains *in situ* 'roughly corresponded in shape, breadth, and length with an adult human body'. After closer examination he came to the conclusion that they were from a human in the prime of life and stout of build. The remains bore signs of an old operation in the form of a scar.

Dr William 'Wilks' Willcox, senior Home Office scientific analyst, told the court that he had detected traces of an alkaloid poison in all of the organs he had been given to examine. He determined through his tests that the poison was hyoscine, amounting to just under one third of a grain. Hyoscine was usually given in doses of one one-hundredth or one two-hundredth of a grain as a last resort to quieten someone who was delirious, suffering from delirium tremens or acute forms of insanity. Willcox thought that whoever had given the victim the fatal dose of hyoscine must have administered a very large dose for so much to have remained in the body after such a long period. The large amount of poison in the intestines indicated that it had been taken by mouth and the person would have lived for an hour or more before succumbing to the effects of the drug. Once consumed in a large dose the poison would almost instantly put a person into a stupor, and possibly make them delirious. They would then become paralysed and comatose before death arrived.

Willcox thanked his good fortune that the remains had been covered with quicklime. 'That,' he said, 'was just what the expert wanted, because quicklime is an antiseptic, and it helped to preserve the viscera, without which I doubt if the hyoscine would have been discovered.' After carefully extracting the hyoscine, Willcox put some into a cat's eye and exposed the cat to bright light, resulting in its pupil dilating widely. For Willcox this was conclusive evidence. The cat, who became known as 'Crippen' to Willcox's students, made a full recovery.[17]

It was ascertained that on 19 January 1910 Dr Crippen had purchased five grains of hydrobromide of hyoscine at Messrs Lewis & Burrows chemist's in New Oxford Street, saying it was for 500 individual doses. This was a vast quantity and there was no good reason why Crippen would require it under normal circumstances.

The revelation of the discovery of hyoscine came as a great shock to Crippen. Barrister Cecil Mercer watched as 'the blood rose into his face, as I have never seen blood rise into a face before. It was like a crimson tide. It rose from his throat to his chin in a dead straight line ... from his chin to his cheeks ... from his cheeks to his forehead and hair ... till his face was all blood-red, a dreadful sight. And then, after two or three moments, I saw the tide recede. Down it fell, as it had risen, always preserving its line, until his face was quite pale.'[18]

The case was adjourned until the next day. A large crowd outside the court booed and shouted at the prisoners when they left.[19] The coroner's inquest was resumed at the Central Library in Holloway Road. However, this new, larger venue made it difficult for everyone present to hear the evidence being given. The evidence was of a more gruesome nature as Dr Pepper gave a detailed description of the remains:

> At the examination on July 15th he found one portion of skin 11in.
> by 9in., with some subcutaneous fat. The lower portion of the piece of
> skin was, in his opinion from the upper portion of the abdominal wall,
> and the upper portion from the chest. There was also a piece consisting
> of the covering of the lower part of the back and buttocks, a large piece
> from the upper part of the back, and a further piece measuring 7in. by
> 6in., which was from the lower part of the abdominal wall, and upon
> the skin of which there was a mark. There was also a piece of skin
> 15in. long, with fat and muscle attached, from the hip, and another
> piece of skin, with fat and muscle, from the thigh. There were several
> other smaller pieces. There was nothing except the hair which could
> be identified as coming from the scalp, or from the forearms, from the
> leg below the knee, from the hands, or from the feet. There was no
> trace either of the genital organs or of bone. There was one large mass,
> which comprised the liver, the stomach, the gullet, the lower 2½ in. of
> the windpipe, two lungs, the heart intact, the diaphragm, the kidneys,
> the pancreas, the spleen, all the small and the greater part of the large
> intestines. All this mass was removed in one piece.

Dr Pepper was asked whether he thought the mutilations could have been done by someone without anatomical knowledge or training. Pepper was sure that 'he must either have had real anatomical knowledge or have been accustomed to the process of evisceration of animals'.[20]

The penultimate hearing took place two days later. Arthur Newton questioned Dew about his intention to arrest Crippen. Dew explained that at their first meeting at Albion House he had no intention of arresting him. If he had he would not have put a number of questions to Crippen which he did:

> Newton: Did the question of whether you arrested him or not depend
> on the answer she gave to your questions?
> Dew: The question of arresting him did not enter my mind. I went there
> for information.
> Newton: 'Dr' Crippen's manner and from the details which he gave you
> at that time did you believe his statement?
> Dew: No, not altogether.
> Newton: Did you in substance believe it?

Dew: No, otherwise I should not have searched his house.

Newton: The search took place with his consent?

Dew: It did. I could not have gone to the house without his consent.

Newton: At any rate, after the statement he had given you and after the search did it then occur to you to arrest him?

Dew: I could not arrest him.

Newton: On the face of it, speaking generally, did you not at the time consider the statement a reasonable one?

Dew: No, I could not say I did not absolutely think that any crime had been committed. I thought it my duty to continue my inquiries, and I did so because I was not satisfied with his statement. I wanted to keep a perfectly open mind and to satisfy everybody – both 'Dr' Crippen and the public.[21]

The final hearing at Bow Street magistrates' court took place on 21 September. Crowds still milled around, waiting for the appearance of the prisoners. On this day Le Neve was taken to court by a four-wheeled cab, accompanied by a warder. She was spotted by a group of women who 'screamed out at the prisoner, and one of the knot pursued the cab to the gates of the station, shrieking opprobrious epithets. Miss Le Neve, leaning back in a corner of the closed vehicle, hid her face behind an open umbrella.'[22]

In summing up his decision, the magistrate, Sir Albert de Rutzen (who had replaced Robert Marsham), concluded that there was no doubt whatsoever that Crippen should stand trial for the charge against him. The case of Le Neve was more difficult, but de Rutzen considered there was enough evidence of Le Neve's complicity (which could have meant she just knew of the murder rather than having taken part in it) to allow a jury to decide her fate. They were, therefore, committed to trial at the Old Bailey. Arthur Newton said that both Crippen and Le Neve would plead not guilty when the time came.

While that was going on an auction was being held in Oxford Street of nearly 100 lots of furniture from 39 Hilldrop Crescent as Crippen was desperate for money to pay Newton's legal fees and, remarkably, considering the position he was in, anxious to pay the landlord of 39 Hilldrop Crescent the back rent he owed. The sale-room was crowded and all of the 1,000 catalogues had been snapped up an hour before the auction began. It was a good-natured sale, with much banter and flash photography taking place. Some lots met with higher prices than expected thanks to their infamous association. The highest bid was fourteen guineas for a cottage pianoforte.[23]

9

PRE-TRIAL PROCEEDINGS

> How dull the murders are getting nowadays. Not a patch on the old domestic poisoning dramas. Crippen, Seddon, Mrs Maybrick; the truth being, I suppose, that you can't do a good murder unless you believe you're going to roast in hell for it.
>
> George Orwell, *Coming Up For Air*

Crippen's decision to plead not guilty could have sealed his fate, for there may have been an alternative. As soon as Arthur Newton had been retained by Crippen, he wanted to offer the brief to Edward Marshall Hall, a charismatic parliamentarian whose forays into the criminal courts often attracted publicity. He had a commanding presence and 'a passion for showing off, tempered by an attractive simplicity and combined with a love of the marvellous, which made him on questions of fact somewhat of an impressionist. But there was about his personality something which even his most austere critics found hard to resist.'[1]

Unfortunately for Newton, Marshall Hall was on holiday abroad. When he called in at Marshall Hall's rooms in Temple Gardens he was met by the senior clerk, Archibald Bowker. Despite being very keen to accept the defence brief on behalf of Marshall Hall, who he knew would rise to the occasion, Bowker was wary because 'I knew Newton to be utterly unscrupulous ... he was not prepared to pay any of the fees until after the case was over, I became suspicious and insisted on a cheque with the brief'. Newton stormed out of the chambers when Bowker was forced to turn him down.[2]

Marshall Hall was convinced he could have proved Crippen's innocence of the charge of murder if the accused man would only admit to everything except intent to murder, thus resulting in a conviction for manslaughter. Marshall Hall's biographer set forth the potential defence:

Crippen, in order to spend the night with his paramour, whether at home or elsewhere, drugged his wife with a new and rare drug of which he knew little, and of which he had lately purchased five grains. To be on the safe side he gave her a large dose, which turned out to be an overdose; or perhaps his continual dosing of her necessitated a big dose to ensure unconsciousness. In the morning he found his wife dead, and in a panic he made away with the remainder of the hyoscine, and with all a surgeon's skill cut up her body, rising above his inexperience with the inspiration of despair. Then, hurriedly wrapping the flesh in an old pyjama jacket of his own, he buried it in quicklime, thinking it would thus be destroyed; as a matter of fact the quicklime had the reverse effect, and preserved the remains. Then he proceeded to write to a number of his friends a transparent tissue of lies. Crippen admitted that Miss Le Neve had slept at Hilldrop Crescent on February 2nd. Might she not have slept there on one or both of the previous nights, and frequently before that, while his wife was drugged with hyoscine and unconscious?[3]

Marshall Hall knew that Crippen's not guilty plea would be disastrous. He thought that Crippen would not have agreed to his line of defence anyway as it could have made Le Neve an accomplice if she had been in the house with him as Cora Crippen lay dying or dead. Crippen would never allow any suggestion of guilt towards Le Neve.[4] Newton would have to find a defence team who were willing to try to convince a jury that Crippen knew nothing of the human remains found in his house.

At Brixton Prison, Arthur Newton's young clerk let slip to the chief warder that Newton had brought an agreement for Crippen to sign which sold the rights for the story of his life to an American newspaper. This was yet another means by which Crippen was going to pay his legal fees. There was more chicanery involved. Newton had held several interviews with Crippen, supposedly to prepare his defence, but one of his clerks had also been present and taken down Crippen's life story in shorthand.[5] The interviews took place within sight, but out of hearing, of the prison staff.

The matter was put before Winston Churchill. The Home Secretary considered that there had already been such immense publicity and sensationalism surrounding the case that the publication of Crippen's memoirs could hardly add to it. Therefore he ordered that they should 'not fetter the accused on grounds of taste', and as the money would be used for his defence the story could be sold. Newton's misuse of his position was a different matter. Churchill advised that Newton must be censured for his improper conduct.

Another of Newton's clerks had interviewed Crippen and was struck by the man's character:

> And yet, feeling convinced that he was a liar and a murderer, I could not help feeling sorry for him. Looking at him and listening to his slow, hesitating, nervous speech I simply could not visualise him as a cold-blooded assassin.
>
> There he was, a little sandy man with drooping moustache and gold-rimmed glasses, blinking at us and stammering with thin fingers playing at his upper lip.
>
> You would have taken him for a timid, kindly little shop-walker, ready to serve you with the utmost politeness, but always, in the back of his mind, thinking of his neat little suburban home and the neat little wife waiting to greet him there.
>
> Always apologetic, always deferential, he contrived to remain aloof from the actual drama and terror of the case. To all outward appearance he might have been a client slightly perturbed at the prospect of a summons for riding a bicycle without a light.[6]

The coroner's inquest finally concluded on 26 September. In his summing up the coroner addressed several questions that the case had raised. Were the remains human? Yes. What was the sex of the remains? The medical evidence could give no decisive opinion. What was the identity of the remains? Unknown, but the fact that they were found at 39 Hilldrop Crescent, along with the disappearance of Cora Crippen and Dr Crippen's subsequent actions, heavily suggested that they were those of Cora Crippen. The jury left to consider their verdict at 4.37 p.m. They returned at 5.20 p.m. and returned a verdict of murder against Dr Crippen, being of the opinion that the remains were those of Cora Crippen and that she died as a result of poisoning by hyoscine.[7]

Bruce Miller's name had been raised at the very outset of the investigation when Crippen told Inspector Dew that he believed his wife had left him for Miller. Miller had been tracked down in Chicago by Pinkerton's detective agency after the American police failed to locate him. Now working in real estate and with a wife and two children, Miller, though friendly towards the Pinkerton agent, appeared reluctant to return to London to give evidence at Crippen's trial. Not only did he not want any scandalous publicity, he was currently involved in a large land deal that could result in a significant commission. He 'does not want to go unless absolutely necessary' but if he had to 'he will give full testimony and says he certainly can defend the character of Belle Elmore'. Miller was offered $15 per day, along with his passage and expenses, but this would represent too great a loss of earnings. He insisted on $25 per day plus all expenses both ways.

Miller gave a statement to Pinkerton's about Cora saying that 'her character was of the very best, far beyond reproach'. They had continued to correspond after he returned to America. He had last heard from her in a Christmas card in 1909. Miller's birthday was 14 April and he was surprised not to receive a card from Cora, as she had been in the habit of sending them. In a personal letter to Inspector Dew the former music hall performer explained his relationship with Cora:

Miss Elmore and I were the best of friends and I have watched the case with the most intense interest, never suspecting that I would be mentioned in it in any way, until the newspaper men came to see me and then I said as little as possible. However there has been little discression [sic] used in quoting my statements, though they have said nothing that will really do any harm.

If Dr Crippen has only made the charge that Miss Elmore eloped with me, I do not see that I would be of any service in the case, as I have not seen her for six years, and as I have been in this place during the past four years, proof of this could be had without my presence.

If on the other hand he makes any attempt to defame her character on my account, there is nothing he can say that I am not willing to face him in, but I do not think he will make any further charges because he well knew of our friendship, and, while he never took the pains to meet me even when he was in the house, and has delivered some of my letters to her in person, and that I have always written to her at their residence and have often recd a reply, from the provences, some one must have forwarded them to her, and they were undoubtedly in his possession first.

Besides I have photographs of Miss Elmore that he took of her with a kodak, and according to her statements, he knew that I have them. Again while I was playing in the provinces, I was taken ill, and wrote to her and mentioned what the trouble was and in her reply she told me that the Doctor told her to tell me to take certain remedies.

Now, while I will acknowledge that I thought a great deal of her, and we were the very best of friends, she was always a lady to me in every respect and I always treated her as a gentleman should.

As you no doubt was one of the first to go through the house, you no doubt found my little cards, candy boxes &c. with my name on, and when I left there were two of my photos enlarged and hanging on the wall in her parlor. Now that Dr Crippen knows all this I do not think that when his trial comes up that he will mention my name again, and I do not think that you will want me in the case either.

If I am wanted, I regret that on account of a big real estate deal that I have on, that my thirty days option will not be up till October 14th and it will perhaps take a few days to close up after that, it looks to me at the present time, impossible to get away before about the 20th of October, but if things progress favourably and I can leave before, I will do so.

Financially, I can hardly afford to leave, as I will have to drop my fall work in the way of building and wait until Spring, and as I am making about $10,000.00 a year, you can see what that means to me. However I am willing and ready to stand up and defend the character of a most honourable woman, and a good friend.

Now, if I should come I would like to come into the country incog. and have a consultation with yourself and the prosecuting Attorney before anyone is aware that I am there, then I will act strictly to your advice.

You have won my admiration in this case to such an extent that I trust as a friend, and know that you will protect me in this to the best of your ability.

Before the trials of Dr Crippen and Ethel Le Neve took place, the issue of the reward for his capture had to be resolved. Captain Kendall of the *Montrose* had made a claim for the £250 that was offered. Dew thought that Kendall's claim could not be disputed, as he was the first person to recognise Crippen and Le Neve as the fugitives and he had immediately reported his suspicions. Dew had carefully questioned others on board the *Montrose* and was satisfied that Kendall was entitled to the bounty.

There was an element of doubt, as the deputy coroner had received a letter, signed 'One of the Public', saying that a steward on the *Montrose* had been the first to realise that Mr Robinson was Dr Crippen. This steward had formerly been a barman at the Brecknock Tavern, Camden Road, where he had seen Crippen drinking. Dew had noticed this story in a couple of periodicals 'of no particular standing', and dismissed it. As far as he was concerned, the money rightfully belonged to Captain Kendall, who duly collected a cheque at Scotland Yard. The cheque, however, was never cashed. Kendall framed it and hung it on his stateroom bulkhead.[8]

At long last the remains found at Hilldrop Crescent could be laid to rest. It was now late September and the remains were causing concern to the Islington Public Health Department, who held them in their mortuary. They wrote to Melville Macnaghten explaining that the *disjecta membra* 'are likely to cause a serious nuisance'.

Inspector Dew checked with Dr Pepper, Dr Marshall and the Director of Public Prosecutions to make sure they had no further need of them. They did not, and Arthur Newton had no objection towards the burial, but unsurprisingly 'demurred somewhat to their being buried in the name of Belle Elmore or Cora Crippen'. No doubt it might have helped his cause if the remains had not been positively identified, but the coroner's burial order clearly stated, 'Do hereby authorise the burial of the remains of the body of Cora Crippen alias Belle Elmore late of 39 Hilldrop Crescent, Islington, age 34 years' (she had really been thirty-six).

Cora Crippen's old friends of the Music Hall Ladies' Guild took charge of the funeral arrangements. Dr Burroughs had written to Mrs Ginnett, saying, 'I feel that a fitting funeral should be given to her … the Police are anxious, if possible to trace other parts of her body … the awfulness of the crime does not bear thinking of. The man must indeed be a fiend.'[9] They desired a private ceremony and did not want the press to intrude. A cortège consisting of a hearse and two mourning coaches left the undertaker's in Camden Road at 2.45 p.m. on 11 October and took a direct route to St Pancras Roman Catholic Cemetery in Finchley.

One resourceful journalist managed to gatecrash the funeral. Joseph Meaney, dressed entirely in black, was shoved into the last carriage just as it was pulling away. Meaney found himself among six female music hall artistes who supposed he was some relative of Cora's. Despite the protests of the reporters, kept outside the cemetery gates by the police, Meaney gained admission to the chapel where he scribbled down notes in shorthand on a bound copy of the funeral service. He recorded 'a very earnest and dignified appeal by the priest to the people in the chapel to behave with the utmost decorum at the graveside, and add their own prayers to his for the peace of the murdered woman's soul'.[10]

10

REX V. CRIPPEN
PART ONE: PROSECUTORS AND DEFENDERS

We had so much evidence against Crippen, we didn't use it all.
                                        Cecil Mercer, counsel for the Crown

The trial of Hawley Harvey Crippen for the murder of his wife was held at the Central Criminal Court, popularly known as the Old Bailey. It lasted five days, from Tuesday 18 October to Saturday 22 October 1910. The presiding judge was Richard 'Dicky' Webster, the Right Honourable Lord Alverstone, Lord Chief Justice of England. It was said that it was unlikely that 'in thirty-two years at the bar any man ever had more work to do, or earned more money'.[1]

Alverstone was described as being of 'medium height, with an impressive cast of features, a kindly disposition, though stern and inflexible when the occasion demanded'. As well as being hard-working, he impressed the newspaper editor and politician T. P. O'Connor, who gushingly wrote, 'Never was a man endowed with such a memory for detail; and never was there a man who could master in so short a space of time such a collection of facts. It was almost uncanny.'[2] Alverstone's view of the Crippen case was that it was 'an extraordinary one'.[3] He had apparently taken a great interest in the North London cellar murder from the time of the discovery of the remains.[4]

Representing the Crown were Richard Muir, Travers Humphreys and Samuel Ingleby Oddie, assisted by Cecil Mercer and acting under instruction from the Director of Public Prosecutions, Sir Charles Mathews.

The question of how much Le Neve knew would have to wait for her trial. Crippen and Le Neve were to be tried separately and on different charges. Muir and Humphreys were concerned that if they were tried together for the same crime, one of the jurymen might be 'so influenced by the appeal on behalf of Le Neve that he might decline to convict Crippen'. Separate trials would also simplify the job of the prosecution.

When Crippen learned that he was to face the ferocious and daunting Richard Muir, he said despairingly, 'It is most unfortunate that he is against me. I wish it had been anyone else but him. I fear the worst.'[5] Thorough, grim and remorseless, Muir worked relentlessly in preparing his cases, leaving nothing to chance. Samuel Oddie worked in Muir's chambers. He described Muir as

> an indefatigable worker. His work was his life. He had no amusements and no relaxation. He always took work home every night, and after his evening meal and a short snooze over the paper, he drew up his chair to the table and set to work on his briefs at which he continued nightly up to one and two in the morning. Yet he was always the first to arrive in the chambers and the last to leave.[6]

Mercer had mixed feelings. He considered Muir the best at what he did, but too inflexible and limited. He was a hopeless defender, but

> give him a dead case, and he'd screw the coffin down as could nobody else. But everything had to go according to plan. He couldn't turn quickly, as counsel should be able to do. But, by God, he was a glutton for work. And he was safe as a house. A very admirable man. No sense of humour at all – he didn't know what it meant.[7]

Not everybody was so impressed by Muir. Former chief clerk at Bow Street magistrates' court Albert Lieck remembered Muir because he 'was the only man who ever sent me to sleep, actual heavy slumber, in court. He was ponderous beyond belief, though thorough and dangerous enough. He had an unpleasant way of pressing his case too hard against the accused.'[8]

Muir had built up an impression of Crippen:

> He is not the ordinary type of man one would expect to commit a murder and then to cut up the body of his victim and dispose of it. Rather is he the sort of man I would expect to find running a successful swindle. He has a certain amount of craftiness and cunning, as well as considerable self-assurance.
>
> There is no doubt that his life with his wife had been one of unending misery, and apparently he found a good deal of relief and a certain stolen happiness with Ethel Le Neve.

I suppose one cannot look upon the cutting up of his wife's body as being such an outrageous or aggravating feature as it might have been with anyone else. He had more than a passing knowledge of medicine and surgery and to such a person, no doubt, the dissecting of a body would not create such a revolting impression as it would in an ordinary individual.[9]

Travers Humphreys was on holiday in Filey with his wife and two sons when he was summoned back to London by the Director of Public Prosecutions. Humphreys was certain that Crippen had murdered his wife. He believed that Le Neve might have 'had an inkling that something serious had happened' when she was asked to disguise herself as a boy but thought that had she known the full facts she would have immediately left Crippen.[10] Despite the incredible public interest the case was creating, Humphreys thought that the evidence against Crippen was so overwhelming that from a legal point of view it would be 'of little interest for the lawyer'.[11]

Oddie was given the junior brief for the Crown. He was chosen over Humphreys' junior, Cecil Mercer, because of his medical experience. As it was a poisoning case Oddie did not rate Crippen's chances for his attitude was that the 'average Englishman is a decent sort of fellow who does not like homicide and looks upon secret poisoning as a low-down dirty game, and indeed it is'.[12]

Cecil Mercer was constructing the case against Crippen. He wasn't remotely impressed by Crippen. '"He had such charming manners," they used to say. Perhaps he had. To my mind, he was repulsive: but most women seemed to like him, and that's the truth.'[13] He was struck by Crippen's eyes, 'since he had protruding eyes, the effect, when he looked at you, was really most repulsive, for the glass being thick and the eyes very close to the glass, some trick of magnification lent them a horrible look. His gaze was most disconcerting.'[14]

The prosecution team were sure Crippen had killed his wife, but no one besides Crippen knew exactly how it had happened. Cora might have realised her terrible fate when it was too late to save herself. Mercer made the interesting point that 'until the poison was found, we had no reason to think Crippen had poisoned his wife'.[15] Dr Marshall had initially admitted, 'I came to the conclusion that it was a homicide and have no doubt a murder was committed, but there was nothing to tell me how she met her death.' When Dew discovered some pieces of string measuring fifteen and eleven inches and a handkerchief among the remains, he wondered if they might have been used for strangulation.

Mercer made the following reconstruction of Cora's murder from the evidence:

That certain things happened we know: exactly how they happened, we cannot be sure. Though much of what I tell you must be assumed, every conclusion was most carefully drawn, and myself I have no doubt that the very gruesome picture which I shall present differs hardly at all from the tale which would have been told, had someone been there to see.

Belle Elmore was partial to stout. Whilst she was in her bedroom, getting undressed, Crippen brought her a glass of stout. But into the stout, he had put some hyoscine. It is a deadly poison, inducing convulsions and coma, preceding death. It is very slightly bitter, but stout would conceal the taste.

Belle Elmore drank the stout, and Crippen undressed. By the time the coma had supervened, Crippen was in his pyjamas. He seized his wife's hair and dragged her out of the room and down the stairs. She was still in her underclothes.

All this was according to plan, for the crime was premeditated. The grave he had dug was waiting, under the coal-cellar's floor.

Well, he dragged the body downstairs and into the kitchen. He got it on to the table, above which was burning a lamp. This must have meant a great effort for the body was a dead weight and Belle Elmore was not a small woman by any means. That done, he stripped the body, in which, as like as not, there was still some life. His knives and scalpels were ready, and so he cut her throat. That blood he caught in a bucket and poured away. When the veins had been drained, he cut off her head.

How he disposed of her head, no one will ever know. And a human head is a difficult thing to destroy. And nobody had any theories. The head was gone.

He then dissected his wife from A to Z. Only a man who had some surgical training could have done this: and only a very strong man could have completed her dissection within a very few hours. But Crippen, though he was small, was immensely strong.

When the dissection was done, Crippen proceeded to remove the flesh from the bones. This, too, was a formidable task. But he undertook it because he proposed to bury the flesh, but burn the bones. He could not trust his lime to destroy the bones: and he could not trust the fire to destroy the flesh. By now the monster was working stripped to the waist, for the labour was very heavy, and he was up against time.

As he removed the flesh, he took the pieces and laid them in the grave. They were difficult to handle – they slipped: so he used the top of his pyjamas, to carry them in. But one piece of flesh, he laid aside. For he dared not trust that piece even to lime.

Years before, Belle Elmore had had an operation which women sometimes have. It was a major operation. And the scar which it left ran right up the middle of the abdomen. When the operation was performed, she may have been slim. But as she grew stout, the scar stretched, until it became a thin, isosceles triangle – I should say, eight inches in length. Such a scar may fairly be termed 'a distinguishing mark'. So Crippen had to make sure that the scar was destroyed. Accordingly, from the abdomen, he cut out a slab of flesh some ten inches square. And this, as I have said, he laid to one side.

For hours the work went on. At six o'clock in the morning, he'd very nearly done. And then something – no one will ever know what – something occurred, to make Crippen lose his nerve. I always think it likely that it was some sound – a milkman's cry, perhaps ... which showed that the world was stirring ... that people were waking up. Be that as it may, panic was Crippen's portion for half an hour. And his one idea was to get what was left away and out of sight. Almost all the flesh was gone, except the slab which was bearing the tell-tale scar. In his frenzy, he snatched this up and thrust it into the grave. It was, in fact, the very last piece of flesh which he put in. In went his pyjama-top, too, and Belle Elmore's underclothes, and tufts of hair, some false as well as real. But never a bone.

And each time he laid a portion of flesh in the grave, he sprinkled it lavishly with lime. He also had a bucket of water. And so often as he sprinkled his lime, he soused that lime with water – he slaked his lime.

Well, the last slab of flesh went in, with the other bits and pieces as I have said. Then he threw in lime by the handful, covering everything thick and thrusting lime down by the sides of the shocking heap. And then he slaked the lime, drenching it all with water, as fast as he could. He had some earth ready, some earth he had taken out, when he dug the grave. In this went, on top and down the sides: and when all was tight and level, back went the bricks with which the cellar was floored. He laid these roughly in lime, for the lime was there. Then he smeared the coal-dust over the top of the grave. Where he hid the bones for the moment, I've no idea. But during the days that followed he burned them into the back-garden, bit by bit.[16]

The reports of gunshots from Crippen's neighbours led Oddie to formulate his own theory about Cora's death, which would account for the use of a gun:

> It must be remembered that he was a doctor and that his wife was very fat. Fat people are more prone to fainting attacks caused by indigestion and flatulence than other people. I believe he intended to poison her with hyoscine, and to say that she had often had attacks of heart failure before, owing to her weak heart, and particularly after heavy meals, and that she had had such an attack on the night of the 31st January, 1910, which had unfortunately proved fatal. My theory is that after her death he intended to send for a doctor in the early hours of the morning and to tell him this story of her death, at the same time explaining that he was a medical man himself. My long experience of the facile way in which some general practitioners issue certificates of death leads me to think that in all probability Crippen could in this way have got a death certificate showing syncope and fatty disease of the heart as the cause of his wife's death.[17]

Oddie reasoned that as the body would show no visible sign of hyoscine poisoning a doctor would accept that her heart had failed because a post-mortem would inevitably reveal a fatty heart. The final dinner party was contrived to provide witnesses to say how much Cora ate and drank and on what friendly terms the Crippens were on that night. However, Crippen gave Cora too much hyoscine in a whisky nightcap. This led to Cora becoming hysterical, shouting and shrieking.

> This was not at all according to plan, and as it was extremely likely to result in his being hanged, I believe Crippen shot his wife in the head with the revolver to stifle her cries ... there now being a gunshot wound in his wife's head, it is easy to understand why he had to dispose of the remains and inform enquirers that his wife had gone to America.[18]

There was a great certainty about the Crown's case. Mercer later said 'we had no doubt' that Cora died on the night of the dinner party. When pressed, he refused to elaborate how they knew. 'We just did' was his blunt reply.[19] It nearly wasn't that night. When Paul Martinetti fell ill, Cora asked Clara, 'Will you stay here tonight dear?' How would Crippen have reacted if the Martinettis had stayed? Might he have changed his mind about killing Cora, or just done it on a later date?

Muir was unhappy that the police had allowed Crippen to flee England in the first place, and felt that since Dew had brought his prisoners back he had been less than energetic in helping to put together the case against them. He went so far as to suggest Dew 'must be suffering from sleepy sickness'.[20] This view was echoed by Travers Humphreys, who recalled, 'We made more than one attempt through Dew to obtain further information, but without success',[21] but few detectives could sustain Muir's twelve-hour shifts, which Humphreys described as his colleague's idea of 'a reasonable working day'.[22]

Humphreys explained his grievances with Dew's investigations. He began by complimenting Dew on his inquiries before Crippen's arrest. The initial statement he had taken from Crippen was admirably done, and was 'thorough and complete; in fact, it took the form of a very effective cross-examination. Moreover, it was probably the fear that further investigation by this highly inquisitive officer would lead to a thorough search of the premises that caused Crippen to lose his nerve and flee the country.' However, Dew's 'subsequent lack of energy must be animadverted upon'.[23] Humphreys visited 39 Hilldrop Crescent and was surprised to see that Cora Crippen's furs had remained at the house, rather than being removed as evidence and made exhibits for the trial. He was dissatisfied with Dew's explanation of why he had left the furs at the house and instructed him to take them away, as he was convinced that the jury would see them as evidence that Cora would not have left for America in the middle of winter without them.[24]

The accusations of Dew's tardiness were disputed by the Director of Public Prosecutions, whose office sent Macnaghten a letter on 26 October thanking Dew and Mitchell 'for the unfailing and valuable services which they rendered to my staff, and to my Counsel, both in the investigation of these cases before the Magistrate, and at the trial of them at the Central Criminal Court'.

Acting for Crippen's defence were Alfred Tobin, Huntly Jenkins and Henry Delacombe Roome, who were instructed by Arthur Newton. Tobin had allegedly been chosen by Newton after he had left Marshall Hall's chambers in a bad temper after failing to secure the services of 'The Great Defender'. Three doors up the lane he saw Tobin's name on a door and hired him.[25] Another account had it that Tobin was recommended to Newton by F. E. Smith, who would later defend Ethel Le Neve.[26] Tobin was not a bad choice. He was clever, industrious and experienced and possessed 'the most ecclesiastical voice of any member of the Bar'.[27] Tobin's 'cheerful and plausible manner made him an effective defender of prisoners',[28] but he was now facing an unenviable task in arguing that Crippen was not guilty of murdering his wife.

11

REX V. CRIPPEN PART TWO: THE TRIAL

The first and second days of the Crippen trial were gruesome beyond words.

The American Law School Review

The case is not a pleasant one: on the contrary, this case is painful from beginning to end.

Lord Chief Justice Alverstone

Dr Crippen stood trial first. An American lawyer was watching the proceedings and observed as

> the wiry little Dr Crippen was led to the front of the dock, and boldly faced the Lord Chief Justice. The accused gazed about the crowded court with evident satisfaction. He appreciated that he was the centre of attraction, and returned the curious stares of the brilliant assemblage with a faint smile. Monocles and opera glasses were directed at him, to his apparent gratification.[1]

Tabloid crime reporter Vincent Wray had also obtained a ticket to watch the trial. He had expected Crippen to have 'hard drawn lips, deep set eyes, furrowed brows – a man, in short, who had cruelty written in every line of a distorted face.' Instead he saw

> a miniature Pickwick. His brow was bulging and benevolent, his eyes twinkled behind his spectacles, and he looked just the sort of man who would have protested against everything that suggested cruelty to man, woman, or dumb animal.
> His voice, too, was low and mellifluous, and his manner was courteous and gentle. Instantly there leaped into my mind the mighty story Stevenson penned about Dr Jekyll and Mr Hyde.[2]

Day one of the trial began with the clerk of the court reading out the charge. 'Hawley Harvey Crippen, you are indicted and also charged on the coroner's inquisition with the wilful murder of Cora Crippen on the 1st February last. Are you guilty or not guilty?' Crippen replied, 'Not guilty, my lord.'

Richard Muir made the opening statement for the Crown. Muir's biographer described him as 'essentially a logician: he had no patience with high-flown rhetorics, and he made it an invariable practice to open his cases so that a man of the meanest intelligence could easily understand what they were about'.[3] In his opening speech the plain-speaking Muir suggested a financial motive for the murder in addition to a romantic one:

> The position, therefore, was this – his affection fixed upon Ethel Le Neve, and himself desirous of establishing closer relations with that young woman; the physical presence of his wife an obstacle to those relations; the fact that he had no money another obstacle. If Belle Elmore died both those obstacles would be removed, because Belle Elmore's money, and property which could be converted into money, would enable him to keep Ethel Le Neve, which at that time he was unable to do.

Muir continued,

> Her friends said she was a good correspondent; but from the moment that Mr and Mrs Martinetti left the house in the early morning of 1st February she passed out of the world which knew her as completely as if she were dead. She left behind her everything she would have left if she had died – money, jewels, furs, clothes, home, and husband. The prisoner made up his mind that she had left never to return. He at once began to convert her property, and on 12th March Ethel Le Neve, who had been seen wearing a brooch and furs belonging to Belle Elmore, went permanently to live with him at 39 Hilldrop Crescent. Crippen was therefore quite certain that his wife would never return.

Muir then raised the question of why Crippen felt the need to flee the country if his statement to Dew had been correct, and his wife was still alive. Crippen had not offered any explanation. Then there was the question of who, other than Crippen, had the opportunity to bury the remains in the cellar, and why would they have been buried there if the death had been a natural one?

Most of the first three days of the trial consisted of evidence for the prosecution. An uncomfortable Bruce Miller had been given a first-class passage from America to England aboard the *Deutschland*, on which he travelled under the pseudonym of 'C. C. Brown' ('Cora Crippen Brown' eyes perhaps?). His appearance on the first day of the trial would have been the first time he had ever been in the same room as Dr Crippen. Miller testified that he had not seen Cora Crippen since April 1904, but they corresponded occasionally. Tobin hoped to establish that Cora and Miller had been lovers, therefore making it seem more feasible that she would have left Crippen to join Miller in America:

> Tobin: Did you ever tell her that you loved her?
> Miller: Well, I do not know that I ever put it in that way.
> Tobin: Did you indicate to her that you did love her?
> Miller: She always understood it that way, I suppose.
> Tobin: Then you did love her, I presume?
> Miller: I do not mean to say that. I did not exactly love her; I thought a great deal of her as far as friendship was concerned. She was a married lady, and we will let it end at that. It was a platonic friendship.
> Tobin: Do you know the difference between friendship and love?
> Miller: Yes.
> Tobin: Were you more than a friend?
> Miller: I could not be more than a friend. She was a married lady and I was a married man.

Miller did admit to having kissed Cora, but said, 'I always treated her as a gentleman, and never went any further.' He further denied having 'improper relations' with Cora when asked directly by Muir and Alverstone. Vincent Wray recorded that the bald-headed Miller had drawn himself up and 'almost flung his reply' to Tobin, before leaving the witness box and glancing contemptuously at Crippen.[4] Was Miller's affectionate behaviour towards Cora, both in correspondence and in person, just an example of theatrical familiarity or was there more to it? There is no evidence that Cora and Bruce Miller had an affair, nor is there explicit proof of the true nature of their relationship. One early writer on the Crippen case neatly explained the relationship, 'which, if not proved guilty, at least never was proved to be innocent'.[5] But if the association had been so significant, it seems strange that not one of Cora's friends mentioned it. In Crippen's statement to Dew he had merely said that his wife and Miller were fond of each other. The defence and subsequent writers on the case interpreted this as proof of an affair. One person who did comment on the matter was Miller's wife. She told her local newspaper that her husband and Cora 'were merely friends. His letters were only those of a friend to a friend. They had no love affair. There was nothing in their relationship which was not perfectly proper.'[6] There was, of course, no question about Dr Crippen's relationship with Le Neve, which they both described as 'intimate' to Dew.

Walter Dew had been the first of the witnesses to arrive at the Old Bailey on the second day of the trial, when he was called to give evidence. Dew spent more than two hours in the witness box and began by detailing the visit to Scotland Yard of the Nashes and continued up to his interviews with Crippen and Le Neve on 8 July. At this point Travers Humphreys read out to the court the lengthy statements that Crippen and Le Neve had given to Dew and Mitchell.

As Dew's testimony continued, he explained how he had searched 39 Hilldrop Crescent in the presence of Crippen, and later, in his absence, how further searching had lead to the discovery of the *corpus delicti* in the cellar. A press observer described Dew's performance as 'very suave, perfectly cool, and self-possessed. Mr Dew is scrupulously fair to the prisoner. He not only assents to Mr Tobin's suggestion that he was not anxious to conceal anything, but he adds to it the perfectly voluntary statement that he did not attempt to.'[7] Dew concluded by briefly mentioning his chase and arrest of Crippen and Le Neve. Travers Humphreys had been gentle with him despite the fact that he thought Dew had been resting on his laurels too much on his return to London. He was not about to say anything in court that disparaged the police or Dew.

Much of the trial was taken up by the detailed discussion of medical evidence, primarily whether a piece of skin found upon the remains bore the mark of a scar or otherwise. This was a vital point because it could go towards identifying the corpse as being Cora Crippen, who had an operational scar on her abdomen.

The first doctor to give evidence was Dr Pepper. The Home Office pathologist had given evidence at many important trials over the years. A colleague said that as a witness, Pepper had 'an absolute certainty of his facts and a quiet competence in the witness-box, which, whilst it made a great impression upon the jury, was the despair of opposing counsel'.[8] He thought that the remains had been buried in the cellar shortly after death and that they had lain there for between four and eight months. When asked whether they could have been there prior to 21 September 1905, Pepper emphatically replied, 'Oh, no, absolutely impossible.' That was the date when the Crippens had moved into 39 Hilldrop Crescent and would prove to be crucial later on in the trial.

Pepper thought that the piece of skin in question was from the lower front part of the abdomen. He was convinced that the mark upon it was a scar, and a microscopic examination of it had reinforced his view. 'Even I could see it was a scar – a scar which had stretched,' Cecil Mercer asserted. He asked Pepper if there were any doubts. 'How can there be?' the pathologist replied. 'As she grew stouter, it stretched. I've seen them again and again.'[9]

Tobin cross-examined Dr Pepper and tried to establish that whoever dismembered the body possessed great anatomical and medical skill. By this he was suggesting that Crippen would not have had the requisite skill to have undertaken such a task. Pepper was too experienced to allow himself to be led:

Tobin: As to the great dexterity you have already told us that was required to remove these organs in the way they were removed, it would require a really practised hand and eye, would it not?
Pepper: Certainly.
Tobin: A man frequently accustomed to dissect bodies or to conduct post-mortem examinations, or matters of that kind?
Pepper: No, a person who had previously done it, but not necessarily continuously. If a person had once learned how to do it he could do it.
Tobin: Suppose a student in the hospitals learnt it, and then there was a long lapse of time afterwards – fifteen years or so – surely the hand and eye have to be pretty well accustomed?
Pepper: I think he could do it quite as well after ten years as he could at the time. It is not a minute dissection; it is a particular kind of work.

On the third day of the trial Dr Bernard Spilsbury, a pathologist from St Mary's Hospital, gave evidence. Like Travers Humphreys, Spilsbury had his holiday interrupted by the Crippen case. He remained in London while his wife and baby went to Minehead without him.

Even in this early court appearance Dew gained the impression that Spilsbury 'was a man who knew what he was talking about'.[10] He was 'a new, dominating voice in the courts of justice … Tall, handsome, well-dressed, a red carnation in his buttonhole, his bearing in his first capital case was as detached, imperturbable, and confident as it was when he was at the height of his fame.'[11] Spilsbury had made notes on the case and concluded that Crippen had 'skill in evisceration – acquisition of hyoscine – access to textbooks'. Cora Crippen was 'American. 35. Vivacious – good company – attractive – dressed well – jewellery – fast life. Private: very overbearing – bad temper.' As well as being the case that made his name, the Crippen case would be the one which made the most lasting impression on Spilsbury. Years after the trial he read, reread and annotated his copy of the Notable British Trials Crippen volume until the spine broke and the pages became loose.[12]

Spilsbury had been a student of Dr Pepper, and would succeed him as Home Office pathologist. Pepper's conclusion about the mark on the skin had been 'an old scar. Probably more than a year old. It might be many years old.' Spilsbury also thought the skin was from the lower abdomen and he clearly stated 'that mark is undoubtedly an old operation scar'. Spilsbury's opinions did differ from those of Pepper on the matter of the killer's anatomical skill. He answered Tobin's questions coldly and unemotionally:

> Tobin: Dealing with the question of the remains, must the person who removed the viscera have been a person of very considerable dexterity?
> Spilsbury: He must certainly have had considerable dexterity, yes.
> Tobin: And must that removal have been done by somebody with a very considerable anatomical knowledge, or somebody accustomed to evisceration?
> Spilsbury: Certainly some one having considerable anatomical knowledge.
> Tobin: And accustomed to evisceration?
> Spilsbury: Yes, one who has done a considerable amount of evisceration.

Next to testify was Dr Marshall, the police surgeon. He concurred that the skin was from the lower part of the abdominal wall and stated, 'I formed the opinion that it was a scar mark, and that is still my opinion.'

Crippen's defence produced their own medical experts, who contradicted those who had concluded the mark on the skin was a scar. Dr Gilbert Turnbull, the Director of the Pathological Institute at the London Hospital emphatically stated 'it cannot possibly be a scar', but he conceded that the skin was from the lower abdomen. Another expert for the defence, Dr Reginald Wall, said that 'in my opinion it is not a scar'.

The medical evidence turned to the issue of the cause of death. Dr William Willcox had tested the viscera of the corpse for poisons, eventually finding traces of the alkaloid poison hyoscine. Willcox had a slight speech impediment, so spoke in a slow and sometimes hesitant manner, which served to emphasise his testimony. Once described as 'the most deliberate and painstaking expert witness who ever stepped into the box',[13] Willcox had 'no doubt it was hyoscine' which was 'gummy syrupy stuff', but used medicinally in the salt form of hydrobromide of hyoscine. He had found two-fifths of a grain of the drug in the organs he had examined, which he estimated would mean that there would have been more than half a grain in the whole body, easily a fatal dose. Willcox had never known hyoscine to have been used in a murder case before, but thought that in this instance it would have been taken orally and the victim would have lived for at least one hour but no more than twelve. Dr Arthur Luff, the honorary scientific advisor to the Home Office, who boasted 'a peculiarly long experience of alkaloids produced by putrification', agreed entirely with Willcox's findings.

Connecting Crippen with large quantities of hyoscine proved simple. Charles Hetherington, a chemist who, like Crippen, worked in New Oxford Street, was acquainted with Crippen, who had been a regular customer at his shop. Around 17/18 January 1910, Crippen had called in at the chemist shop and ordered five grains of hyoscine hydrobromide, which he said he wanted for homoeopathic purposes. This was a huge quantity, and Hetherington had to place a special order, which Crippen collected on 19 January. He signed the reason for purchase column in the poisons register as 'homoeopathic preparation'. Crippen had often bought drugs from the chemists including cocaine (for preparing dental anaesthetic), morphia and mercury, but never before hyoscine.

The Crown had completed presenting their case. Now it was the turn of the defence. Tobin pointed out that every witness who knew Crippen described his character in glowing terms. He was, according to people who knew him, 'amiable', 'kind-hearted', 'good-hearted', 'good-tempered', and 'one of the nicest men I ever met'. How could such a man suddenly become 'a fiend incarnate'? Furthermore, Crippen's behaviour did not appear to have changed immediately before Cora's disappearance and he carried on working as normal immediately afterwards. He said that Cora's disappearance 'was a strange thing, but strange things happen at all times, and would happen again to the end of time'. If this was all he could offer it was apparent that Tobin was going to struggle.

Tobin continued, 'The position, therefore, was this. There was an illicit intimacy between Mrs Crippen and Bruce Miller, and an illicit intimacy between Crippen and Le Neve – the latter might be another reason for Mrs Crippen's departure. Where was she now? Why did she go? She went because she had long disliked Crippen, and her dislike had turned to hate. Who knew where Belle Elmore was? Who knew whether it was Belle Elmore's flesh that was buried in the cellar? Who knew for a certainty whether Belle Elmore was alive to-day or not? Who knew for certain whether she was abroad, whether she was ill or well, alive or dead? In a case of life and death, and in a charge of murder, they had to know, to know beyond all reasonable doubt, before they could find a verdict that would send a fellow-man to death.'

Crippen's flight could be explained. 'Feeling there was that high mountain of prejudice which he had erected by his lies against himself, he did what innocent men, threatened with a charge, have done before. He resolved in his folly to fly.' Finally, Tobin reminded the jury that they had to be sure that the remains had not lain in the cellar of 39 Hilldrop Crescent for years and that they were indeed those of Belle Elmore.

When Crippen went into the witness box he explained that the reason he made such a large purchase of hyoscine was for 'a nerve remedy in a homoeopathic preparation, that is, reduced to extremely minute doses'. He admitted purchasing the five grains of hyoscine on 19 January but claimed to have diluted them into 500 minute doses, two-thirds of which he had already dispensed. He had wanted 'to prepare some special nerve remedies for some very obstinate cases'. Crippen was unable to provide any record of his disposal of over 300 doses of hyoscine. The remaining doses were allegedly in a cabinet in Crippen's private room at Albion House. Arthur Newton went there to look for them but found nothing.

Crippen claimed to be very familiar with the use of hyoscine, having first used it at Bethlem mental hospital in England, and had since used it as a nerve remedy in homoeopathic preparations. Muir asked him if he knew of any medical textbook that advised the administration of hyoscine orally for any disease. Crippen cited Hempel and Arndt's *The Dictionary of Homoeopathic Materia Medica*. Alverstone said that the Court would have to obtain a copy of that book but by the fifth and final day of the trial a copy still had not been found. Tobin had found another book, *Retrospect of Medicine*, that contained references to the use of hyoscine.

Despite the failure to find a copy of *Materia Medica*, John De Villiers, a senior member of staff at the British Museum, wrote an account of the book search in his 1931 autobiography. De Villiers said that one Saturday morning Crippen's solicitor turned up at the museum pleading for a copy of the book as it was the only one that could be found in London. The British Museum at that time held the vast library that is now the British Library. It was not a lending library so De Villiers had to take the book to the Old Bailey without permission. As he would not be parted with the volume, Alverstone allowed him to take a seat on the Bench.[14]

While the debate over the book did take place on a Saturday, De Villiers' story is contradicted by the trial transcript in which Tobin states that efforts were made to obtain a copy until eight o'clock the previous night (Friday). But Tobin did say to Alverstone that he had a copy of Braithwaite's *Retrospect of Medicine* 'which has only this minute been handed to me'. Perhaps that was the book brought by De Villiers.

Crippen stuck rigidly to his story about returning home from work one day at his normal time of 7.30 p.m. to find his wife gone, and that the statements he had subsequently made concerning her death had all been false. When examined by Huntly Jenkins, Crippen explained his motives for saying Cora had died:

> Crippen: I said that my wife had left me, that she afterwards became ill, and that subsequently her death took place. I admit all that.
>
> Jenkins: Were those statements true or false?
>
> Crippen: The statements that I made were false.
>
> Jenkins: Why did you make those statements?
>
> Crippen: She told me I must do the best I could to cover up the scandal, and I made those statements for that reason; I wanted to hide anything regarding her departure from me the best I could, both for my sake and for hers.
>
> Jenkins: Was the statement that you made to Inspector Dew a false or a true statement?
>
> Crippen: It was quite true. Inspector Dew was very imperative in pressing upon me that I must produce my wife, or otherwise I would be in serious trouble. He also said that if I did not produce her very quickly the statements I had made would be in the newspapers the first thing I knew. I made up my mind next morning to go to Quebec, and, in fact, I did go.

Dew had not told Crippen that he would be in serious trouble if he did not produce his wife, nor did he say anything about publishing details in the newspapers. 'Obviously, this was a thing I should never have dreamed of doing', was Dew's indignant response. Crippen was lying under oath, just as he had lied to Cora's friends and lied to the police.

Crippen also gave an account of his arrest:

> Jenkins: Was Inspector Dew's coming on board at Father Point a surprise to you?
>
> Crippen: It was at Father Point – well, I did not expect him at all. I thought there had been a cable to the Quebec police; I did not expect Inspector Dew; that was a surprise to me.

Jenkins: Inspector Dew says that you said on arrest, 'I am sorry; the anxiety has been too much.' What were you referring to then?

Crippen: I was referring to this, that I expected to be arrested for all these lies I had told; I thought probably it would cast such a suspicion upon me, and perhaps they would keep me in prison – I do not know how long, perhaps for a year – until they found the missing woman.

Crippen was at pains to point out that all he had told Ethel Le Neve about the affair was that Cora had left him and that she had died.

The third day of the trial concluded with Jenkins once again questioning Crippen. Jenkins may have doubted that his client realised the urgency of his predicament, for when he visited him in prison to discuss the defence, Crippen made him wait, saying, 'I have a cup of cocoa here and it's just as well to drink it before it gets cold.'[15] In court Jenkins almost casually asked Crippen an obvious but necessary question:

Jenkins: Those remains that were found at your house in Hilldrop Crescent – have you any idea whose they were?

Crippen: I beg your pardon.

Jenkins: The remains that were found in the cellar at Hilldrop Crescent?

Crippen: I had no idea. I knew nothing about them till I came back to England.

The judge could barely contain his incredulity at Crippen's defence. At one point he asked the prisoner, 'Do you really ask the jury to understand that your answer is that, without your knowledge or your wife's, at some time during the five years, those remains could have been put there?' Crippen weakly replied, 'I say that it does not seem possible – I mean, it does not seem probable, but there is a possibility.'

One of Arthur Newton's clerks despairingly described Crippen's defence of ignorance as a 'preposterous story'.[16] If Crippen could not even persuade his own defence team of his innocence what chance was there that the jury would believe him?

On the fourth day of the trial Crippen was recalled and this time he was cross-examined by Richard Muir. Whispers passed around the court. 'What is Muir like as a cross-examiner?' someone asks. 'Very slow, but very direct,' is the reply, 'with a wonderful way of asking awkward questions.'[17] Muir's incisive questioning was a stark contrast to what Crippen had experienced the previous day with Jenkins:

Muir: On the early morning of the 1st February you were left alone in your house with your wife?

Crippen: Yes.

Muir: She was alive?

Crippen: She was.

Muir: And well.

Crippen: She was.

Muir: Do you know of any person in the world who has seen her alive since?

Crippen: I do not.

Muir: Do you know of any person in the world who has ever had a letter from her since?

Crippen: I do not.

Muir: Do you know of any person in the world who can prove any fact showing she ever left that house alive?

Crippen: Absolutely not; I have told Mr Dew exactly all the facts.

Muir: But you have made no inquiries?

Crippen: I have made no inquiries.

Muir: It would be most important for your defence in this case on the charge of murder if any person could be found who saw your wife alive after the Martinettis saw her alive; you realise that?

Crippen: I do.

Muir: And you have made no inquiries at all?

Crippen: I have made no inquiries at all.

Muir later elicited from Crippen that when Dew charged him with the murder of his wife, Crippen didn't even ask him about how she had died even though he claimed he still thought Cora was alive at the time.

The crucial evidence of the pyjama top found with the remains made Crippen's already fragile defence seem all but futile. Dew had told the prosecutors that the Messrs Jones Brothers, who sold the green-striped pyjamas to Crippen, could only say that the jacket was similar to those they occasionally sold to Crippen and that they could not give a precise date as to when Crippen had bought them. Muir and Humphreys felt sure there was more information to be gained from Jones Brothers and on the eve of Crippen's trial they sent Sergeant Mitchell back to the store with a series of questions explaining why they thought the information was obtainable. The answers showed that the pyjamas had been delivered to the shop on 7 December 1908 and sold on 5 January 1909. Crippen told the court that he had bought all of the pyjamas that Dew had found at Hilldrop Crescent since he and Cora had moved to that address. Crippen thought that the newer pyjama suit had been purchased by himself in September 1909.

Regardless of the date of purchase, Muir had established one fact. The material used in the pyjama trousers that Dew found and its accompanying top found with the remains were not manufactured and could not have existed until November 1908, therefore the jacket, produced in the court in a glass jar, could not have got among the remains prior to November 1908, well after the Crippens had moved into Hilldrop Crescent.

It was such a vital piece of evidence for the Crown's case that Muir had been worrying whether he could establish the facts about it in their favour and hoping that the defence would not find out what he was doing. As the information had arrived at such a late date the prosecution thought it would be unfair to produce it without giving the defence prior warning. The defence could have asked for the trial to be postponed while they found experts to examine the pyjama evidence.[18] When asked how the pyjamas could have ended up in his cellar, Crippen replied, 'I don't know.'

Richard Muir was relentlessly blunt in his questioning of Crippen, who was becoming less convincing in his answers, despite maintaining his composure. Dew was spellbound by Muir's cross-examination and said, 'Crippen was clever, but not clever enough. There were gaps in his armour which Mr Muir's skill was able to pierce.'[19]

Muir: When did you make up your mind to go away from London?

Crippen: The morning after Inspector Dew was there – the 8th or 9th.

Muir: Had you the day before been contemplating the possibility of your going away?

Crippen: I would not like to say that I had made up my mind. When Inspector Dew came to me and laid out all the facts that he told me, I might have thought, well, if there is all this suspicion, and I am likely to have to stay in jail for months and months and months, perhaps until this woman is found, I had better be out of it.

Judge: Mr Crippen; do you really mean that you thought that you would have to lie in gaol for months and months; do you say that?

Crippen: Quite so, yes.

Muir: Upon what charge?

Crippen: Suspicion.

Muir: Suspicion of what?

Crippen: Suspicion of – Inspector Dew said, 'This woman has disappeared, she must be found.'

Muir: Suspicion of what?

Crippen: Suspicion of being concerned in her disappearance.

Muir: What crime did you understand you might be kept in gaol upon suspicion of?

Crippen: I do not understand the law enough to say. From what I have read it seems to me I have heard of people being arrested on suspicion of being concerned in the disappearance of other people.

Muir: And that is why you contemplated on the afternoon of 8th July flying from the country?

Crippen: Quite so – that, and the idea that I had said that Miss Le Neve was living with me, and she had told her people she was married to me, and it would put her in a terrible position; the only thing I could think of was to take her away out of the country where she would not have this scandal thrown upon her.

In the light of Crippen's devotion to Le Neve, this was a considerably more plausible response than his previous answers.

Another point raised by Muir was that Crippen had written letters to Cora's friends and relatives telling them that she was dead. How did he know that she would not write to them herself, if indeed she had simply left him to live with Bruce Miller?

Crippen may have held his nerve during Muir's questioning, but his answers could not have been creating a favourable impression on the jury:

Muir: You thought you were in danger of arrest?

Crippen: Yes.

Muir: And so you fled the country?

Crippen: Yes.

Muir: Under a false name?

Crippen: Yes.

Muir: Shaved off your moustache?

Crippen: Yes.

Muir: Left off wearing your glasses in public?

Crippen: Yes.

Muir: Took Le Neve with you?

Crippen: Yes.

Muir: Under a false name?

Crippen: Yes.

Muir: Posing as your son?

Crippen: Yes.

Muir: Went to Antwerp?

Crippen: Yes.

Muir: Stayed in a hotel there?

Crippen: Yes.

Muir: Stayed indoors all day?

Crippen: Oh, no.

Muir: Practically all day?

Crippen: We did not; we went to the Zoological Gardens, and walked all over the place.

Muir: Enjoying yourselves?

Dew's final assessment of the cross-examination was that it had ended in the Crown's favour but he had gained a strange kind of admiration for Crippen, whose composure had not cracked throughout his questioning, which had lasted three hours and forty-eight minutes:

And so, hour after hour, the cross-examination went on. On the whole, Crippen came out of the ordeal well, but there were times when the penetrative questioning of Mr Muir laid bare the weaknesses of his case.

No person, with experience of criminal court procedure, could have escaped the impression that the little doctor was seeking cleverly, if unconvincingly, to give innocent interpretations to facts all pointing strongly to his guilt.

A lesser man – that is lesser in education and self-control – would have collapsed completely under the searching cross-examination for the Crown.[20]

Another observer, court official William Bixley, recalled

I never saw a trace of perspiration, not even during the four hours of his cross-examination, despite the strain shown in his immobile hands … the only emotion he ever showed was a quick sense of humour so that he never failed to smile when some witty remark or amusing comment was made by one of the witnesses.[21]

Cecil Mercer saw something else when Crippen was amused:

Crippen wasn't human. I once saw him laugh in court – throw back his head and laugh, at something his solicitor said. He opened his mouth wide and bared his teeth. He looked like a cat, or a tiger – you know how a cat, when it cries, will open wide its mouth and bare its teeth. I was quite close to him, and the startling similarity hit me between the eyes. Crippen was an animal.[22]

1. Hawley Harvey Crippen. (Author's collection)

2. Cora Crippen. (Author's collection)

3. Alias Belle Elmore. (Author's collection)

4. Lil Hawthorne, who informed Scotland Yard of Cora Crippen's disappearance. (Author's collection)

Above left: 5. Superintendent Frank Froest. (Author's collection)

Above right: 6. Chief Inspector Walter Dew. (Stewart P. Evans)

7. 39 Hilldrop Crescent. (Author's collection)

8. The remains of Cora Crippen. (The National Archives)

Left: 9. The basement of 39 Hilldrop Crescent. (The National Archives)

Below: 10. Inspector Dew (far right) and colleagues in Crippen's back garden. (The National Archives)

METROPOLITAN POLICE

MURDER

AND MUTILATION.

Portraits, Description and Specimen of Handwriting of HAWLEY HARVEY CRIPPEN, alias Peter Crippen, alias Franckel; and ETHEL CLARA LE NEVE, alias Mrs. Crippen, and Neave.

Wanted for the Murder of CORA CRIPPEN, otherwise Belle Elmore; Kunigunde Mackamotzki; Marsangar and Turner, on, or about, 2nd February last.

Description of Crippen. Age 50, height 5 ft. 3 or 4, complexion fresh, hair light brown, inclined sandy, scanty, bald on top, rather long scanty moustache, somewhat straggly, eyes grey, bridge of nose rather flat, false teeth, medium build, throws his feet outwards when walking. May be clean shaven or wearing a beard and gold rimmed spectacles, and may possibly assume a wig.

Sometimes wears a jacket suit, and at other times frock coat and silk hat. May be dressed in a brown jacket suit, brown hat and stand up collar (size 15).

Somewhat slovenly appearance, wears his hat rather at back of head. Very plausible and quiet spoken, remarkably cool and collected demeanour.

Speaks French and probably German. Carries Firearms.

An American citizen, and by profession a Doctor.

Has lived in New York, Philadelphia, St. Louis, Detroit, Michigan, Coldwater, and other parts of America.

May obtain a position as assistant to a doctor or eye specialist, or may practise as an eye specialist, Dentist, or open a business for the treatment of deafness, advertising freely.

Has represented Munyon's Remedies, in various cities in America.

Description of Le Neve alias Neave.—A shorthand writer and typist, age 27, height 5 ft. 5, complexion pale, hair light brown (may dye same), large grey or blue eyes, good teeth, nice looking, rather long straight nose (good shape), medium build, pleasant, lady-like appearance. Quiet, subdued manner, talks quietly, looks intently when in conversation. A native of London.

Dresses well, but quietly, and may wear a blue serge costume (coat reaching to hips) trimmed heavy braid, about ½ inch wide, round edge, over shoulders and pockets. Three large braid buttons down front, about size of a florin, three small ones on each pocket, two on each cuff, several rows of stitching round bottom of skirt; or a light grey shadow-stripe costume, same style as above, but trimmed grey moire silk instead of braid, and two rows of silk round bottom of skirt; or a white princess robe with gold sequins; or a mole coloured striped costume with black moire silk collar; or a dark vieuxrose cloth costume, trimmed black velvet collar; or a light heliotrope dress.

May have in her possession and endeavour to dispose of same:—a round gold brooch, with points radiating zig-zag from centre, each point about an inch long, diamond in centre, each point set brilliants, the brooch in all being slightly larger than a half-crown; and two single stone diamond rings, and a diamond and sapphire (or ruby) ring, stones rather large.

Absconded 9th inst., and may have left, or will endeavour to leave the country.

Please cause every enquiry at Shipping Offices, Hotels, and other likely places, and cause ships to be watched.

Information to be given to the Metropolitan Police Office, New Scotland Yard, London S.W., or at any Police Station.

E. R. HENRY,
The Commissioner of Police of the Metropolis.

Metropolitan Police Office,
New Scotland Yard. 16th July 1910.

11. Police wanted poster for Crippen and Le Neve. (Author's collection)

Above left: 12. Charlotte Bell, Crippen's first wife. (*The Umpire*)

Above right: 13. Dr Augustus Pepper. (*The Lancet*)

14. Inspector Dew at the coroner's inquest. (*Illustrated Police News*)

15. Ethel Le Neve disguised as a boy. (*The Bystander*)

Left: 16. Captain Kendall of the *Montrose*. (*The Graphic*)

Below: 17. The *Montrose*'s lounge. (Author's collection)

CANADIAN PACIFIC S/S MONTROSE THIRD CLASS LOUNGE

CANADIAN PACIFIC S/S MONTROSE THIRD CLASS BOOKSTALL.

Above: 18. The *Montrose*'s bookstall. (Author's collection)

Right: 19. Captain Kendall observing the Robinsons. (*Illustrated Police News*)

CAPTAIN KENDALL'S SUSPICIONS WERE AROUSED.

20. Sending a wireless message from the *Montrose*. (*Illustrated Police News*)

21. Assistant Commissioner Sir Melville Macnaghten. (Author's collection)

INSPECTOR DEW LEAVES
LIVERPOOL FOR CANADA.

22. Inspector Dew boarding the *Laurentic* at Liverpool. (*Illustrated Police News*)

TRUTH STRANGER THAN FICTION.

HOLIDAY
FICTION
ALL THE
LATEST
PUBLICATIONS

HOLLOWAY
MYSTERY
TODAY'S
SENSATIONAL
STORY

BATTERSEA
MYSTERY
LATEST
CLUES

CRIPPEN
DRAMA
LATEST
WIRES
FROM
QUEBEC

JOHN BULL (holiday making): Detective stories, sensational novels? No thank you, guess I can find all the sensation I want in the papers!

23. The Crippen story dominated the news. (*Daily Chronicle*)

24. A typically inaccurate depiction of the arrest of Crippen and Le Neve. (Author's collection)

Above left: 25. Home Secretary Winston Churchill. (*The Graphic*)

Above right: 26. Sergeant Mitchell, Crippen and Inspector Dew board the *Megantic* at Canada.(Author's collection)

27. Inspector Dew escorting Crippen off the *Megantic* at Liverpool. (Author's collection)

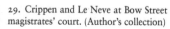
28. Arthur Newton, Crippen's solicitor. (Author's collection)

29. Crippen and Le Neve at Bow Street magistrates' court. (Author's collection)

30. Inspector Dew giving evidence at Bow Street. (*The Bystander*)

31. Cora Crippen's grave in St Pancras Cemetery. (Author's collection)

Above: 32. Brixton Prison.
(Author's collection)

Left: 33. Sir Charles Mathews,
Director of Public Prosecutions.
(Author's collection)

34. Lord Chief Justice Alverstone.
(Author's collection)

35. Richard Muir, prosecuting
counsel. (Author's collection)

36. Travers Humphreys, prosecuting counsel. (Richard Whittington-Egan)

37. Samuel Ingleby Oddie, prosecuting counsel. (Author's collection)

38. Cecil Mercer, prosecuting counsel. (Author's collection)

39. Edward Marshal Hall, who was unable to defend Crippen. (Author's collection)

Left: 40. Alfred Tobin, defence counsel. (Author's collection)

Below: 41. The Old Bailey. (Author's collection)

Central Criminal Court, London

Above: 42. Gilbert Rylance (in top hat) and Paul Martinetti arrive at the Old Bailey. (Stewart P. Evans)

Right: 43. Inspector Dew outside the Old Bailey. (Stewart P. Evans)

Above: 44. The jury for Crippen's trial. (*The Bystander*)

Left: 45. Crippen being led away after receiving his death sentence. (*Illustrated Police News*)

46. F. E. Smith, Ethel Le
Neve's defence counsel. (*The
Graphic*)

47. Judge Darling of the
Court of Criminal Appeal.
(Author's collection)

48. Pentonville Prison. (Stewart P. Evans)

49. The execution of Dr Crippen. (*Illustrated Police News*)

Right: 50. The rosary held by Crippen and the ring he wore when executed. (Richard Whittington-Egan)

Below left: 51. Scottish comedian Sandy McNab outside his new home, 39 Hilldrop Crescent. (Author's collection)

Below right: 52. An early edition of Ethel Le Neve's memoirs. (Stewart P. Evans)

CRIPPEN'S HOUSE, 39 Hilldrop Crescent, London, N. With Sandy McNab, the new owner, standing at gate.

PRICE THREEPENCE

ETHEL LE NEVE
HER LIFE STORY

With the True Account of Their Flight and Her Friendship for

DR. CRIPPEN

TOLD BY HERSELF

Ethel C. Le Neve

COPYRIGHT

Thomson's Weekly News

LATEST CERTIFIED CIRCULATION 623,984 COPIES WEEKLY

3409. [REGISTERED AT THE GENERAL POST OFFICE AS A NEWSPAPER.]   SATURDAY, SEPTEMBER 18, 1920.   (ESTABLISHED 1855)   PRICE TWOPENCE

Poignant Human Document Begins To-Day.

My Life Story by Ethel Le Neve

In this remarkable human document, the first instalment of which appears below, Ethel Le Neve tells the full story of her life. After a silence maintained for over ten years, she has decided to tell the world all she knows of Dr Crippen and the world-famous case.

In the course of her story she makes many startling admissions and clears up once and for all, as the only person who knows, many points which have been discussed and argued over again since those fateful days in 1910.

Ethel Le Neve.

Dr Crippen and Ethel Le Neve in the dock at Bow Street.

Crippen's House at Hilldrop Crescent.

SECURED A SITUATION

A QUIET AND CULTURED MAN

AN INVITATION TO DINNER

BECAME GREAT FRIENDS

53. One of Ethel Le Neve's newspaper memoirs. (*Thomson's Weekly News*)

Above left: 54. Ethel Le Neve in 1928. (*Thomson's Weekly News*)

Above right: 55. Donald Pleasence portrayed Crippen sympathetically in 1962, along with Samantha Eggar as Le Neve. (Author's collection)

DR. CRIPPEN SAVED FROM A WATERY GRAVE.

56. Crippen's effigy saved from the 1925 flood at Madame Tussaud's. (*Illustrated Police News*)

Chicago, Ill.
Oct. 22 - 1910.

Dr. Hawley Harvey Crippen.
Brixton Prison.
London,
England

Doctor:-

As I saw your coniction coupled with the death penalty, I come from seclusion long enough to try and save your worthless life at least; as I don't want to be responsible for your demise, if I can save you in this way, but I will never come forward personally, as I am happy now.

I informed the judge; now save yourself.

Belle Elmore Crippen.

57. A hoax letter, purportedly from Cora Crippen. (The National Archives)

58. A genuine letter from Cora Crippen. (The National Archives)

59. Margaret Bondfield House, built on the site of 39 Hilldrop Crescent. (Author's collection)

Above left: 60. Inspector Walter Dew in retirement. (Author's collection)

Above right: 61. Walter Dew's autobiography. (Author's collection)

12

REX V. CRIPPEN PART THREE: THE VERDICT

> Every episode in the revolting story pointed directly towards Crippen
> as the murderer, which the jury pronounced him to be.
>
> *The Lancet*

In Alfred Tobin's closing speech for the defence, he laid out the case
in favour of Crippen's innocence. He explained to the jury that 'the
burden of proof rested on the prosecution, and if on a single material
point there could be reasonable doubt it was not for him to appeal
for mercy; he had only to claim what was the right of the prisoner'.

According to Tobin, Crippen's failure to look for his missing wife
was simply explained by the fact that he was glad to be rid of her and
able to live with Le Neve. 'It was idle to suppose,' he pointed out,
'that he would be other than relieved at her departure from Hilldrop
Crescent. One would have supposed that he did not care, or that he
would prefer her to be away.'

Tobin claimed, as had Crippen, that Le Neve had spent the night
of 2 February at Hilldrop Crescent, although the prosecution refuted
this, as there was only Crippen's dubious word for it. Although Ethel
had spent nights at Hilldrop Crescent in February, she moved from
her landlady's, Mrs Jackson's, on 12 March. It was inconceivable,
Tobin said, that Crippen could have murdered Cora on 1 February
before spending the whole day at work and then dismembering her
corpse before tidying up and regaining his composure to such an
extent that Le Neve noticed nothing the next day.

The prosecution had made a great deal of the fact that Dr Crippen
was a liar, as shown by his letters to Cora's friends and relations
informing them of her death. Remarkably Tobin said that these
letters were almost an act of kindness on Crippen's part for, 'those
friends would have been glad indeed to find that Dr Crippen's story

of her illness and her death was quite untrue, and further, they would have thought none the worse of Dr Crippen for having told those lies in order to try and cover up his wife's disappearance and his wife's shame'.

The flight of Crippen and Le Neve, in disguise and under false names was thus explained by Tobin, who was stoically trying to make the best of a bad job:

> They had to consider what was the reason for his flight, or his folly, if they liked. They had to realise the time of his flight, and what had just been said by Inspector Dew. They had to remember the lies Dr Crippen had told, and that he had admitted that they were lies. They must not forget what Inspector Dew had said to him, 'I am not satisfied about your wife,' and, 'There will be serious trouble in store for you unless you find your wife' [which Dew had never said]. A man who had lost sight of his wife for all those months, who had no notion where she was, and who remembered that he had told lie after lie as to the reason for her disappearance, might be thoroughly alarmed when an officer of the law appeared and said there would be serious trouble in store for him about this disappearance. Dr Crippen realised the mass of prejudice he had raised against himself by the lies he had told, and was flight, although an act of folly, a clear proof of guilt?

Alfred Tobin told the jury that they must be entirely satisfied that the remains were female, before they could even address the question of whether they were those of Cora Crippen. 'Suspicion was not enough.' He also raised the question of Crippen's anatomical skill:

> There was another thing which was admittedly needed, and that was a dextrous hand, well versed in anatomical operations. So far from being dextrous in anatomy, he was, compared with the skill required by an anatomical surgeon, a very commonplace manager for Munyon's remedies. Something else was needed. There was needed the fiend incarnate to do a deed like that; but the prisoner's reputation was that of a kind-hearted, good-hearted, amiable man.

Tobin did not offer any explanation for how human remains ended up in Crippen's cellar. He asked the jury if they could believe that a man who had committed such a terrible crime could go about his day-to-day business with no one noticing any change in his demeanour. 'Were they to be told that during the doctor's close intimacy with his friends in London, and with his business people in London, they would never have detected any trait such as cruelty or something of that kind in his nature? The characteristics of the man who would do a deed like this were absolutely absent.' Edward Marshall Hall had visited the court during the trial. He later told a journalist, 'When I took the opportunity of snatching that hour at the Old Bailey, and hearing the line which the defence had taken to try to save Crippen, I walked out appalled.'[1]

The fifth and final day of the trial heard the closing speech for the Crown, presented by Richard Muir. Muir had been staggered by Tobin's assessment of Crippen as a kind man:

> Let them examine the foundation for that theory. The prisoner had admitted that over a long series of months he had led a life of studied hypocrisy, utterly regardless of the pain which the lies which he was telling and was acting would inflict upon friend or sister of his wife. Letters full of grief of a bereaved husband were written to Mrs Martinetti, to Dr Burroughs to be seen by Dr Burrough's wife, to Mrs Mills, the half sister of Cora Crippen. There was that letter of his carrying the sobs of the bereaved husband across the ocean to harrow the feelings of his wife's relations. He put on mourning, wrote on black-edged paper, mocked the grief of his wife's dearest friends, who thought they were sympathising with him, when they wished to lay a last tribute of love upon the far-off grave of their dead friend. He said, 'A wreath is no use; she is not being buried, she is being cremated; her ashes will soon be here' – and then with his tongue in his cheek – 'you may have your little ceremony then.' Ashes to be fetched across the sea! They were asked to say then that he was too kind-hearted to have done this deed.

In addition to Crippen's lies, there was his hypocrisy. He had hinted that Cora had been unfaithful with Bruce Miller despite the fact that they 'had never cast eyes on each other for six years'. Besides this, 'the man who brought those accusations against his wife was the man who was himself carrying on an intrigue with Ethel Le Neve, extending over three years, and who said in the witness-box that he believed his wife knew nothing about it'.

Muir pointed out that there was no evidence to show that the remains were not those of Cora Crippen. However, the evidence had overwhelmingly pointed to the fact that Cora Crippen was dead. The hair found among the remains was naturally dark brown which had been bleached to a lighter colour and 'Belle Elmore had dark brown hair bleached to a lighter shade. It was true that other women had dark brown hair bleached to lighter colour, but there was no suggestion that any woman with hair of that sort was missing in London within the limits of the time which were involved in that case.' Muir reiterated the prosecution's claim that the mark on the piece of skin was an abdominal scar and 'Belle Elmore had been operated upon in that region in the year 1892 or 1893'.

Most damagingly, the remains had been riddled with hyoscine, and Crippen had purchased large quantities of the drug. Summing up, Muir said, 'Ask yourselves in this most important case these questions. Where is Belle Elmore? Is your answer to be that she is dead? Then, whose remains were those in the cellar? Is your answer to be Belle Elmore's? If not Belle Elmore's, what conceivable explanation is there? None in the world. Who mutilated her body and put the remains there? Who but the prisoner had the opportunity, the skill, the access to the pieces of pyjama jacket which were found in the grave? How did she die? Is your answer to be of hyoscine poisoning? If not, how did that person die? No sign upon the internal organs which were left, no sign on post-mortem examination, of any cause of death at all except hyoscine poisoning. If your answer is to be that she died of hyoscine poisoning, where did she get it and who administered it? Crippen bought it – it was not much known – on 19th January, and Belle Elmore disappeared from this world on 1st February.'

Lord Alverstone lucidly summed up the case to the jury. Put simply, 'That is the crime of murder charged here against Dr Crippen, that he wilfully and intentionally killed his wife, poisoned his wife, and that he mutilated the body, and buried the remains in the cellar at 39 Hilldrop Crescent in order to conceal his crime.' The jury had to consider two questions. The first: 'Were the remains found at 39 Hilldrop Crescent the remains of Cora Crippen? If they were not, there is an end of this case. If you find that they were the remains of Cora Crippen, then you have got to ask yourselves, was her death occasioned by the wilful act of the defendant Crippen? If not, again the defendant is entitled to be acquitted. Those are the two issues that you have got to consider, and those are the issues upon which I shall ask you in a short time to concentrate your attention.'

Alverstone had been intrigued by the enigmatic Dr Crippen: 'Whatever the truth in this case, the defendant is an extraordinary man. He has committed a ghastly crime; he has covered up that ghastly crime, or endeavoured to, in a ghastly way, and he has behaved with the most brutal and callous indifference after the crime has been committed. If he is an innocent man, it is almost impossible, as you may probably think, to fathom his mind or his character, again absolutely indifferent to the charge made against him of murder; having, according to him, I will not say a ready means, but at any rate the means of doing his utmost to establish his innocence, no step taken of any sort or kind by him.'

It was the judge's opinion that 'the fact that Dr Crippen has lied on material points in this case is a very important matter for your consideration'. Another 'very serious matter' was why, if Cora had left Crippen on 1 February, did she not take her jewellery and furs with her?

As to the matter of whether Cora Crippen was still alive, Alverstone thought there were two problems with this. Firstly, how could Crippen have written the mourning letters 'except with the knowledge that the wife could not appear? Friends in America, gone to America, friends at home making inquiries; put off, hoodwinked – we need not care about the dates, but hoodwinked in a disgraceful way by mourning black-edged paper, and so forth. Do not consider it from the point of view of taste. Consider it from the point of view of upon which side the truth lies. If you come to the conclusion that the game was so enormously dangerous that Dr Crippen could not have possibly carried it out if he thought his wife might appear again, you will ask yourselves, can you believe the story that his wife left him on 1st February.'

Cora might even have come forward herself: 'The man was arrested, as you know, in consequence of the agency of this new invention, wireless telegraphy; there is no doubt about that; it is a matter that could not have been established but for that invention; that part is common knowledge; he is arrested in Canada, and then the story is known all over the world. It is a very serious suggestion to make to you, as it is made by the counsel for the defence, that Belle Elmore may still be alive. If Belle Elmore is alive, is it possible to think that this has not come to her knowledge? Does that man in the dock mean to suggest that so bad is this woman who was his wife for eighteen years, and whom, apart from her being angry and bad tempered, he does not make any serious complaint against – that she is so mean and so abominably wicked as to allow this man to stand his trial in the dock without making any communication or anything of the kind? That is what you have got to consider in this part of the case.'

After a brief adjournment Alverstone continued his summing up. He addressed the issues of how long the remains had been buried, saying that 'perhaps the most important thing is the pyjama jacket'. Were the remains those of Cora Crippen? Alverstone said 'that they are the remains of a woman now is really not seriously disputed', as they were partially clothed with a woman's vest and found with hair curlers. There were suggestions that it was Cora Crippen on account of the hair colouring and pyjama top but the evidence was 'not so certain' as was the evidence suggesting the remains were those of a woman.

Alverstone described the alleged scar on the piece of skin as 'the battleground in this case'. 'Now is that a scar or not?' he asked, before warning the jury that 'in order to satisfy you that it is not Cora Crippen, the defence must have satisfied you that there is no scar there. Coupled with the pyjama and the camisole and the combinations and the vests, you have to ask yourselves have you any doubt that that is the body of Cora Crippen?'

The penultimate point was 'what was the cause of death, who put that body there, was it the same person who killed her or not?' Alverstone thought that the jury would 'be of the opinion that the person who caused the death of Cora Crippen took steps to get rid of the body. That is the natural thing a man would do who had committed a great crime.' If she had not been poisoned, could the jury account for her death by any natural cause? The defence had not put forward an alternative suggestion to hyoscine poisoning, so the only explanation of her death was that 'some one gave Belle Elmore hyoscine, and she became unconscious, comatose, and died, and there was the dead woman in the house'.

Finally Alverstone addressed the jury on the subject of Crippen's behaviour, which he considered to be 'a most important part of the case'.

Now, you have had Inspector Dew's statement put before you, and you heard it read more than once. The only important thing in Dew's statement for the present consideration is, not the lies that the accused told, which he admits now were lies, namely, the letters and all the statements about his wife being dead – but the things he said were true were not consistent with the facts as proved. He was at trouble to show Inspector Dew the jewels, and those are the same that were found sewn in his undervest when he was arrested at Quebec; he was at trouble to show Dew that his wife must have taken the other jewels with her. Now, one has to make every allowance for a man in a difficult position; he says, 'She had other jewellery, and must have taken that with her,' but, when you are dealing with a man who is supposed to be speaking the truth, and who is asking you to believe that his wife had gone away, you cannot forget the fact that he had pawned a very considerable portion of that jewellery on 2nd February, the day after she disappeared, and on 9th February, seven days afterwards. He says, 'I have never pawned or sold any jewellery belonging to her before or after I left her.' He says afterwards, 'I thought it was my property.' It may be that that taken by itself may be so construed; it may be so understood; but the important thing is that he said that she had taken it with her and he follows that up by the statement about pawning. Then he says, and I suggest to you that it is one of the most important things, 'I shall, of course, do all I can to get in touch with her and clear this matter up.' Gentlemen, on that day he, with the assistance of Inspector Dew, drafts an advertisement offering a reward, to be published in the papers, to endeavour to find Belle Elmore. He never sent it. If he believed that his wife could be found, why should not he have sent it?

Alverstone then told the jury of 'a test applied in these Courts'. That test was, 'How did the man behave when the charge was brought against him?' 'You have it that, living there in the same name, carrying on his business, consorting with Ethel Le Neve for practically six months, the day after the inspector goes to his house he alters his name and flees – goes to Antwerp, appears under the name of Robinson, induces Le Neve to disguise herself as a boy, passes Le Neve off as his son, and endeavours to escape to Canada; and he would no doubt have got there but for Inspector Dew being able to catch him.'

When Dew arrested Crippen, the fugitive told his captor, 'It is only fair to say she knows nothing about it.' Alverstone wondered, 'What did that "it" mean?' The judge concluded by reiterating that 'there has been ample opportunity for getting hold of Cora Crippen if she is really alive'.

After Lord Alverstone's summing up the jury retired to consider their decision at 2.15 p.m. and returned just twenty-seven minutes later. They unanimously found Crippen guilty of murdering of his wife. Crippen maintained his composure and said, 'I still protest my innocence.'

John De Villiers from the British Museum gave an eye-witness account of Crippen's reaction when the sentence was passed:

On entering the dock to hear the verdict he took off a light overcoat, carefully folded it inside out and hung it over the dock rail; then pulled down his white linen cuffs and composed himself to listen. I should have regarded him as the least interested man in court. I have always wondered whether his demeanour was owing to absence of moral responsibility or to dope.[2]

Lord Alverstone passed the dread sentence:

Hawley Harvey Crippen, you have been convicted upon evidence, which could leave no doubt on the minds of any reasonable man, that you cruelly poisoned your wife, that you concealed your crime, you mutilated her body, and disposed piece-meal of her remains; you possessed yourself of her property, and used it for your own purposes. It was further established that as soon as suspicion was aroused you fled from justice, and took every measure to conceal your flight. On the ghastly and wicked nature of the crime I will not dwell. I only tell you that you must entertain no expectation or hope that you will escape the consequences of your crime, and I implore you to make your peace with Almighty God. I have now to pass upon you the sentence of the Court, which is that you be taken from hence to a lawful prison, and from thence to a place of execution, and that you be there hanged by the neck until you are dead, and that your body be buried in the precincts of the prison where you shall have last been confined after your conviction. And may the Lord have mercy on your soul!

The case had caused a sensation although, with perhaps the exception of the medical arguments, it had not been one of any great legal importance. Travers Humphreys admitted as much and his junior, Cecil Mercer, described it as a 'dead case', meaning that Crippen had never stood a chance. The evidence against Crippen was so overwhelming that the prosecution never bothered to call the man who delivered the lime to Crippen.[3]

One of the few things to impress Mercer about the trial was Tobin's vigorous defence of his client. He thought Tobin 'put up an excellent show. How he contrived to do it, I have no idea, but he appeared to have convinced himself of Crippen's innocence.'[4] Alverstone concurred, thinking that Crippen had been 'ably defended'[5] by Tobin while Marshall Hall's senior clerk, Archibald Bowker, recalled 'his conduct of the case was justly admired by the Temple'.[6]

The verdict had been pronounced and the world outside the walls of the Old Bailey was desperate to know it as soon as possible. Fleet Street reporter Joseph Meaney had secured a precious ticket to attend the trial on the last day. His editor issued him with three coloured handkerchiefs. Once the verdict was given, Meaney was instructed to wipe his nose with a red handkerchief for guilty, white for not guilty and blue for a disagreement among the jury. A colleague was waiting by a glass-panelled door to pass on the news. However, in all the excitement, Meaney pulled out all three handkerchiefs and waved them up and down, before remembering to blow his nose on the red one, thus alerting the world to the result.[7]

An important question remained unanswered. It was never established what had happened to Cora Crippen's head, bones and other missing parts. A newspaper report mentioned mysterious visits made by Crippen to the neighbourhood of Regent's Canal. On each occasion he had taken a heavy bag with him.[8] Doctor Pepper made a passing remark about a limb found in the River Thames at Greenwich, but nothing conclusive came of this. Oddie thought Crippen had dismembered Cora in the bath and disposed of her head and bones piecemeal at night in the canal or River Thames.[9]

One theory was that Crippen had disposed of Cora's head in a bag over the side of the cross-channel steamer when he and Le Neve had gone to Dieppe in March. Melville Macnaghten thought this was the likeliest explanation and admitted that it is what he would have done had he been in Crippen's position.[10] Le Neve refuted this theory, claiming they had only taken two small handbags with them which were barely big enough for their luggage and that they had sailed during the day when Crippen might have been spotted throwing a bulky package overboard.[11]

The Lord Chief Justice had matters of a less weighty nature to deal with after leaving the Old Bailey. A keen billiards player, he had agreed to present a trophy to the winner of a tournament final between Melbourne Inman and Tom Reece. Inman won, leaving Reece to ruefully quip, 'I think the Lord Chief should have presented the cup to Crippen and passed sentence on Inman!'[12]

13

REX V. LE NEVE

When Dr Crippen asked me to disguise myself and run away with him, instinct ought to have told me there was something terribly wrong.
                                        Ethel Le Neve, *Thomson's Weekly News*

My innocence I felt sure must be established. I told myself that I was guiltless of any crime, and that no jury could dare to convict me.
                                        Ethel Le Neve, *Thomson's Weekly News*

The curious thing about Ethel Le Neve's trial is that it was not meant to have happened. Richard Muir thought that the judge would ask him what evidence he had to establish Le Neve as an accessory after the fact in the murder of Cora Crippen. Muir 'would be bound to say that he had no sufficient evidence in support of that charge'. An official from the Director of Public Prosecutions' office noted, 'I was strongly disposed to agree with his view, on the ground that the great point was to secure a conviction of Crippen, and that the result of the proceedings against Le Neve was of very little importance, especially as it appeared to be improbable that two trials would in fact be held'.

Cecil Mercer agreed with Muir. 'Our case against her was, of course, very thin. We had next to nothing at all. I mean, we could not prove that, either before or after, she was aware of the crime. Naturally enough we didn't press the case. Crippen was what we wanted, and he was in the bag.'[1]

For whatever reason, Le Neve's trial did go ahead and Muir had to do the best he could. While Muir knew he had not got the evidence to prove that Le Neve was guilty, he may have suspected she was. When Dr Crippen had been sentenced to death, Muir made the enigmatic statement, 'Full justice has not yet been done.'[2]

With Dr Crippen awaiting his appointment with the hangman,

Ethel Le Neve stood trial at the Old Bailey on Tuesday 25 October 1910. She would have been found guilty if the jury could be satisfied that she had helped Crippen escape, knowing that he was a murderer.

Once again Richard Muir, Travers Humphreys and Samuel Oddie were the counsel for the Crown, but Le Neve had a different team defending her from that which Crippen had. Appearing for her defence was Winston Churchill's best friend, Frederick Edwin Smith. Popularly known as 'F. E.', he was

> strikingly handsome, six feet one inch in height, of a distinguished figure, slightly marred by sloping shoulders. His clothes, although not in any one particular out of the ordinary, gave the impression that he was over-dressed. The hat worn on the back of his head, the red flower in his button-hole, the very long cigar always carried in his mouth, made him a ready subject for the caricaturist.'[3]

Oddie had a high opinion of his opponent, describing him as 'a human phenomenon. His vitality was only equalled by his extraordinary brain-power.'[4]

Arthur Newton had wished to brief Smith for Crippen's defence, but F. E., who would later have the reputation of being 'the cleverest man in the kingdom', had enough foresight to see the inevitable outcome of that trial. He pointed out that as Crippen and Le Neve would be tried separately, it would be necessary to employ separate counsel and shrewdly opted to defend Le Neve, preferring the likelihood of a small victory to a great defeat.[5]

Smith viewed Le Neve as 'an easy victim. She came from the lower middle classes; Crippen was her superior, and in her eyes a man of great education and position. She was young, a gentle, affectionate girl, not unattractive, though anaemic and liable to neuralgia. Sent out into the world at a tender age, condemned to earn her living in a monotonous avocation and to spend her leisure in drab, uninteresting lodgings, it is not surprising that the opportunity offered by Crippen to this soft and ductile young woman proved a temptation which she could not resist.'[6]

Richard Muir opened the trial by explaining that Le Neve was charged 'in effect, with assisting Hawley Harvey Crippen to escape from justice at a time when she knew that he had been guilty of the murder of his wife'. There was no question on either side that Crippen had been rightly convicted of the murder. Muir elaborated what the prosecution aimed to prove:

What was the state of knowledge that prisoner had, and what was her intention with regard to the acts which she undoubtedly committed. Guilty knowledge and guilty intention are issues in this case, and upon such issues a jury can rarely have direct evidence at all. It hardly ever happens that the state of a person's mind can be judged by anything but that person's actions, and, therefore, you will look at the facts in this case with a view to discovering what was the knowledge of the prisoner at the time that the acts in question were done, and what was her intention with regard to the acts which she herself did.

According to Muir, a vital point in the case was Le Neve's behaviour around the time of Cora Crippen's death. Le Neve had been lodging with Emily Jackson in Camden Town since September 1908 and the pair enjoyed a close relationship. In correspondence Le Neve called Jackson 'My dearest Mum' and 'My dear Ma'.

In an earlier statement, Jackson had given some details about her life with Le Neve. About two weeks after Le Neve had moved in she had suffered a fourth-month miscarriage. Jackson 'never saw the baby' but heard Le Neve tell the doctor present she had been to the lavatory and 'felt something come from her'. She refused to say who the father had been.

Around the end of January or the beginning of February 1910, Le Neve was in a depressed state. She pulled and clawed at her hair, 'looked straight ahead into a recess in the corner of the room and shuddered violently'. Soon afterwards 'she came home one night more pleasant than I have ever seen her, and said "Somebody has gone to America".' Le Neve started to spend nights at Hilldrop Crescent and in late February she told Jackson that she had married Crippen. On 12 March Dr Crippen picked her up in a cab and they first went to a pub with Emily and her husband where they drank a quart bottle of champagne that Crippen bought. She then moved in permanently with Crippen.

Muir presented his case:

Mrs Jackson says that about January last prisoner began to look ill and troubled, and that one night towards the end of January, or in the beginning of February – she did not fix any date – prisoner came home very ill. She would take no supper, and went to bed. Her appearance, according to Mrs Jackson's description, was the appearance of somebody who had suffered a great shock, who was stricken with horror at something that had happened. Prisoner was asked for an explanation, but little or none was forthcoming that night. The next morning, again, this young woman was in the same condition. She was practically unable to eat her breakfast, and her condition was such that Mrs Jackson saw she was quite unfit to go to her work as a typist, and persuaded her to remain at home.

That was no ordinary illness. It was something which seemed to strike the prisoner with horror. Whatever it may have been, it was contemporaneous, or nearly contemporaneous, with the murder of Mrs Crippen. This is a fact which cannot be disputed.

Muir told the jury that they would have to decide what caused Le Neve's distressed state. He obviously wanted them to think that it was the knowledge of Cora's murder. Le Neve's troubled state was soon replaced with cheerfulness:

She says that 'the doctor' has promised to marry her. She comes home wearing Mrs Crippen's clothes and jewels, and makes presents to Mrs Jackson of enormous quantities of clothing that Mrs Crippen had left behind her. She says that Mrs Crippen has gone to America, and she and Crippen visit Mrs Jackson on more than one occasion. She also had the knowledge that Crippen for a large sum of money had been pawning some of Mrs Crippen's jewellery. You must ask yourselves, 'What is the explanation of this?' Is it likely that any woman would suppose that the wife was going away from the husband leaving behind her furs, jewels, and everything practically that she had in the world, to be worn by any woman to whom Crippen liked to give them?

According to the prisoner, Crippen never told her, so far as she could remember, whether Mrs Crippen was coming back or not. But immediately she began to wear Mrs Crippen's jewels and go out in public in them – wearing the brooch at a dinner and ball of the Music Hall Artistes' Benevolent Fund, a place where all Mrs Crippen's friends would be gathered together. You will have to ask yourselves whether there was not in her mind such knowledge that Mrs Crippen would never come back as this indictment imputes to her, otherwise she never would have gone about with Mrs Crippen's husband, wear Mrs Crippen's clothes and jewels, and give away some of Mrs Crippen's clothing to friends.

When it came to the Atlantic flight,

What was it the prisoner knew which induced her to cut off her hair and masquerade as a boy, and condemn herself practically to perpetual silence, because she dare not speak in public in the hearing of any person lest her voice should betray her? The explanation which lies on the surface of those facts is that the prisoner knew that Crippen was flying from justice for the murder of his wife. What other explanation is there? Absolutely none.

Emily Jackson was called to the witness box where she gave her account of Le Neve's strange behaviour around the end of January 1910:

During the latter part of January I observed that there was something strange about Miss Le Neve's manner. She became very miserable and depressed. Upon one occasion in the latter part of January Miss Le Neve came home looking very tired and strange. She was greatly agitated and went to bed without supper. I went into the bedroom after her. I could see that her whole body was trembling, and that she was in a terrible state. I asked her what was the matter, but she did not seem to have the strength to speak. I asked her again, and she said she would be all right in the morning.

I said to her that I was sure there was something dreadful on her mind, and that if she did not relieve her mind she would go absolutely mad. She said, 'I will tell you the whole story presently.' A little while afterwards she said, 'Would you be surprised if I told you it is the doctor?' I said, 'What do you mean; do you mean he was the cause of your trouble when I first saw you?' [i.e. the miscarriage]. She said, 'Yes.' I said, 'Why worry about that; it is past and gone?' She burst into tears again, and said, 'It is Miss Elmore.' Up to that time I had never heard the name of Miss Elmore in my life. I wondered what she meant, and asked her, and she said, 'She is his wife, you know. When I see them go away together it makes me realise what my position is.' I said, 'My dear girl, what is the use of worrying about another woman's husband?' and she said, 'She has been threatening to go away with another man, and that is all we are waiting for, and when she does that the doctor is going to divorce her and marry me.'

Crippen was telling Le Neve the same story he told Dew; that Cora was going to run off with Bruce Miller. Le Neve repeated it to her sister, Adine Brock, who recounted that Cora 'was always nagging him and some man in America wanted her (Mrs Crippen) and if she went away from him he would get a divorce and would marry my sister'. It is another contentious assertion for which Crippen is the only source. Had Crippen genuinely believed it, or was it a yarn he was spinning to appease Le Neve, who clearly wanted marriage, as she had been wearing a ring and telling people she was married? Could it be that Le Neve was tired of waiting for Cora to leave and had given Crippen an ultimatum that led him to kill Cora?

F. E. was so confident that the Crown's case against Le Neve was groundless he announced to the Court that he did not propose to call any evidence for the defence. He knew that it was up to Muir to prove that Le Neve was guilty and not for him to argue her innocence. Smith undermined the prosecution's case when he cross-examined Emily Jackson. He established that Le Neve was frequently ill, and that the illness Muir had referred to actually took place at the beginning of January 1910, well before Cora Crippen's disappearance.

Muir proceeded with the Crown's closing speech. He reminded the jury of Le Neve's behaviour at Emily Jackson's house and her flight under a false name. Then he said, 'Le Neve was arrested on 31st July. She was told of the charge made against her – the charge of murder, and the charge of being accessory after the fact. She made no reply. On 21st August on her way home she was told the charge, and made no reply. On 27th August, at Bow Street police station she was told of the charge, and made no reply; and when committed for trial, with every opportunity for making a statement she made none.'

Then Smith made the closing speech for Le Neve's defence. He put forward the suggestion that Le Neve was a naïve innocent who fell under Crippen's spell: 'What was the misfortune of this girl, little more than a child, when it became necessary for her to earn her living? She had the extreme misfortune to come across the path, at the age of seventeen, of one of the most dangerous and remarkable men who have lived in this century; a man to whom in the whole history of psychology of crime a high place must be given as a compelling and masterful personality.'

Smith attributed the Atlantic flight to the fact that 'Crippen had acquired this enormous power over her, and she was utterly ignorant of the laws of England. She was confronted with the problem as to whether she would stay in England or go with him.'

He criticised Muir's suggestion that Le Neve knew of the murder:

My learned friend's case is really this – that Crippen would say to Le Neve, 'This is how I treated the woman who last shared my home, and

I invite you to come and share it with me now.' Does any one believe that the girl went back to live at Hilldrop Crescent towards the end of February, the month that this murder was committed – went to live in this house knowing that its last tenant had been murdered by the man she was going to live with?

Lord Alverstone was again the presiding judge. In his summing up he told the jury, 'The only matter upon which you have to concentrate your attention is, "Did Ethel Le Neve know when she fled with Crippen that Crippen was a murderer and had murdered his wife?"' Among the things that they had to consider were

what is the probability of this scoundrel having told her. So far as the evidence is concerned, it stands this way. When he was arrested he said, 'It is only fair to say she knows nothing about it. I never told her anything.' It is perfectly plain that that was a most serious statement so far as he was concerned. There is no secret about it. Crippen was most seriously cross-examined upon it, and he was asked to what it could refer except his wicked deed towards his wife.

The fact of this woman living with him and going with him to Dieppe, wicked and immoral as it is, is not evidence that he told her he committed the murder.

Upon that part of the case you are entitled to take into consideration what Mr Smith has said to you about her being gentle, sympathetic, and loving and affectionate towards Crippen. If he had told her, not only might it have been dangerous to himself, but do you not think that it might have changed her feelings towards him?

The jury took twenty minutes to find Ethel Le Neve not guilty. She was immediately liberated. Cecil Mercer said F. E.'s summing up was 'a lovely speech' but added, a little ungraciously, 'Any one could have got her off.'[7] Dew thought the outcome was correct and 'felt satisfied that justice had been done. Poor Miss Le Neve had suffered enough. Her association with Crippen had cost her many weeks of mental torture and doubt.'[8]

After the trial Lord Alverstone said to Smith, 'I think you ought to have put her in the box.' Smith enigmatically replied, 'No. I knew what she would say. You did not.'[9] Smith had been convinced throughout of Le Neve's innocence. 'Frail she was, and of submissive temperament, but not an accomplice in murder, or an ally in its concealment.'[10]

Smith never changed his view of Le Neve's innocence. In his account of her trial, written years later, he wrote,

> I am convinced that she was innocent in every sense of the word. I had the advantage of a close study of the case, including a great deal that was never in evidence.
>
> She was a girl whose character for truthfulness had never been questioned. She denied all knowledge of the crime, and I am convinced that she told the truth ... I was told that after the trial she left for America. But I never heard of her again.[11]

Smith's assessment of Crippen was that he had been guilty of 'a murder callous, calculated, cold-blooded, a murder which I say, in the whole annals of crime it would be hard to match for cold-blooded deliberation,' but 'he was at least a brave man and a true lover'.[12] Dew agreed, saying, 'Whatever may be said and thought about Crippen, one can only admire his attitude towards the girl who had shared his great adventure.'[13]

Le Neve visited Inspector Dew at Scotland Yard shortly after her trial to thank him for his 'kindness and consideration to her through her ordeal', adding that Crippen wished to add his thanks too. While Dew was pleased that they bore him no animosity, despite the fact that he had tracked them down and arrested them, he did not consider that he had done anything out of the ordinary in his dealings with them even though he had, like many other people, found Crippen an agreeable character. Dew admitted that 'detached from the crime, there was something almost likeable about the mild little fellow'.[14]

14

LET THE LAW TAKE ITS COURSE

Though in court you hear all sorts of lies told, in the end truth always prevails.

Richard Muir to Dr William Willcox, *The Detective Physician*

Immediately after being sentenced to death, Crippen's steely composure gave way. Arthur Newton saw him after he had been taken down from the dock, and found his client had 'completely collapsed, and sat there in a huddled heap, crying with his head between his hands, utterly broken and dejected'. 'We shall appeal,' Newton assured him, but Crippen's reply was, 'When is Ethel to be tried?'[1]

As with so many elements of the Crippen case, there are alternative and often quite opposite accounts of events in different sources. Oddie wrote that 'it was said in the Press that he broke down directly after he left the Court, I have good reason to know that the report was quite untrue'.[2] Joseph Meaney, who had attended Cora Crippen's funeral and Crippen's trial, did report that Crippen collapsed in the *Daily Express*:

> He collapsed at the foot of the staircase leading down to the cells. No one, apart from the warders who had to carry him along the passage to his cell, and the prison doctor who rushed to his aid, saw the pitiful drama behind the death sentence which closed the great Crippen trial.[3]

Crippen was transferred from Brixton to Pentonville Prison. Upon admission he was strip-searched. He held up his arms, then had his mouth, ears and beneath his private parts checked for concealed items. He was given a prison flannel shirt to put on before his feet were checked. Nothing was found between his toes or underneath his arches so he was given the remainder of his prison garb.

On 5 November Crippen appealed against his death sentence at the Court of Criminal Appeal before Mr Justice Darling, Mr Justice Channell and Mr Justice Pickford.

The grounds of his appeal rested upon the following points:

1. That one of the Jurymen, after I had been given in charge of the Jury absented himself from the rest of the Jury without either he or the rest of the Jury being given in charge of the proper Officer of the court.
2. That the identity of the remains found at 39 Hilldrop Crescent was not established.
3. That the Judge did not sufficiently place before the Jury the question of there being no navel upon the piece of skin measuring seven inches by six inches.
4. That the Judge misdirected the Jury in telling them that the onus of proof that the mark upon the piece of skin, measuring seven inches by six inches was not a scar, rested upon me.
5. I desire to be supplied free of charge with a shorthand note of the proceedings at the Central Criminal Court to be forwarded forthwith to my solicitor.

The member of the jury who absented himself during the trial was George Craig, who had fainted around midday on 19 October, the second day of Crippen's trial. He was taken from the court by an usher and two doctors while the case was adjourned. Craig had sufficiently recovered within fifteen minutes to be reunited with the eleven other jurors in their private room. During his absence Craig did not see anyone other than the doctors and court usher.

Ensuring the jury did not come into contact from any outside influences was taken very seriously. At the end of each day Crippen's jury were taken to the Manchester Hotel in Aldersgate Street. Their bedrooms were divided from the rest of the hotel by a corridor which could only be accessed by a private staircase. The door to the corridor was locked at night by the hotel manager. Several court staff stayed with the jury at the hotel to ensure their isolation.[4]

Crippen's appeal failed on every point. The judges were convinced the remains were Cora's as 'it is inconceivable that this woman, if she had left her husband as described by him, should, during all these months, have failed to communicate with any relative or friend: and further that she should have gone off in the depth of winter leaving her furs and clothing, as well as her jewels behind her'. Crippen's story about buying hyoscine for homoeopathic purposes was 'beyond belief'. In short, his trial had established his guilt 'beyond any doubt'. The appeal judges concluded,

> Crippen's motive for the murder was probably a mixed one – desire to establish closer relations with Le Neve and to possess himself of the jewels and money.
>
>   It was a cold blooded and deliberate crime carried out and concealed with horrible ingenuity. There can be no question of a reprieve.
>
>   Let the law take its course.

Upon hearing this Crippen 'turned round like an automaton and walked quickly out of the dock'.[5]

Undeterred, Newton drafted a petition for mercy in the hope that Crippen's death sentence would be commuted to one of life imprisonment. He made several hundred copies of the petition and sent them to cities and major towns throughout England to collect signatures from sympathetic members of the public. Newton quickly raised 150 signatures for the copy of the petition in his office alone. Many of those signing it were women.[6] The petitions raised over 15,000 signatures by the time they were submitted to the Home Secretary. This might have been more a reflection of a general opposition to the death penalty than a show of support for Crippen, who may not have been optimistic about his chances of a reprieve. On 8 November he wrote his will, witnessed by the chief warder and a warder at Pentonville. It left his entire estate to Ethel Le Neve.[7]

Madame Tussaud's waxworks had been prohibited from exhibiting an effigy of Dr Crippen, despite public demand, until his appeal had failed. Now they could unveil their creation. The waxen Dr Crippen bore a striking resemblance to the condemned murderer and stood in a dock, alongside the real Dr Crippen's armchair, purchased by Tussaud's at the recent auction.[8]

The high profile of the Crippen case was attracting the attention of cranks. Winston Churchill received several abusive letters. 'You are a dam waster,' wrote one. 'If Mr H. H. Crippen is Hung on Wednesday you and the Judge and jury will be in danger of your lives So take Heed.' It was signed 'The Black Hand Gang'. Another called him 'a Dam rotten liar … a fine liberal you are'. Churchill rejected a request from the British Phrenological Society for several of their members to take measurements of Crippen's head after his execution.

During his spell as Home Secretary, Churchill oversaw forty-three capital sentences. He granted reprieves in twenty-one of them, but not in Crippen's case. Churchill took the matter of deciding the fate of condemned prisoners very seriously and personally studied each case in great detail before making his burdensome decision. He would leave his verdict until the last possible moment should any new evidence come to light. Despite being a supporter of the death penalty, Churchill found such decisions very painful to make.[9] On 19 November Churchill announced that he had 'failed to discover any sufficient ground to justify him in advising His Majesty to interfere with the due course of law', (the prerogative of commuting death sentences belonged to the monarch but in practice the Home Secretary dealt with the matter). Crippen was informed of the decision at 9.15 that morning.

Churchill did make one concession in Crippen's favour. He had received a memo from his assistant under-secretary at the Home Office Ernley Blackwell, and Home Office advisor Sir Edward Troup, indicating that if Le Neve and Crippen wanted to kiss at their final meeting at Pentonville they should be kept apart to prevent a weapon or poison being passed, as they thought 'it is kinder to the parties themselves to keep such interviews as formal and unemotional as possible'. Churchill disagreed. He would not instruct the prison governor to keep Le Neve and Crippen apart as long as every precaution was taken to prevent Crippen obtaining any poison.

Ethel Le Neve's reaction to the news of Crippen's appeal failing was muted. The actor/manager Seymour Hicks was visiting a detective at Bow Street police station. Hicks was told that Le Neve was in the building to ask if she could borrow the pair of boy's trousers that she had worn on the *Montrose* because she had been offered money by a newspaper to pose as a boy for a photograph. The news of Crippen's failed appeal came through while Le Neve was still there. When she heard all she said was 'Oh!'

Coincidentally, Seymour Hicks was a cousin of Alfred Tobin and had previously met Dr Crippen. The pair enjoyed a 'long and pleasant chat together'. Hicks found Crippen to be of a gentle nature and whose most striking feature was his strong spectacles, which gave the impression that he had bulging eyes and, like many others, he admitted, 'I don't know why, I always had a sneaking pity for the wretched man Crippen.'[10]

Now that the normal courses of action had failed to save Crippen, desperate measures were being taken. His former employer Dr

Munyon offered a £10,000 reward for the reappearance of Cora Crippen or for anyone who could prove that she was still alive.[11] Francis Tobin, a Philadelphia lawyer, claimed to have proof that Cora Crippen was alive and in hiding in Chicago 'in order to carry out the most diabolical plan of revenge in the annals of crime'. However, Tobin failed to produce any evidence to support his story. In Cambridge an old soldier applied to the borough justices offering himself to be hanged in Crippen's place as a doctor should not be executed.[12]

While Crippen was languishing in Pentonville Prison awaiting his fate, the prison's governor, Major Owen Mytton-Davies, was paying close attention to his infamous charge:

> Crippen was another prisoner who remains impressed on my mind, chiefly, I must admit, owing to the notoriety surrounding his case, as there was nothing heroic about him. He was a sordid, mean, avaricious little man, whose one redeeming feature was his extraordinary devotion to Ethel Le Neve.
>
> My first glimpse of him in prison garb was in the central hall at Pentonville; in his drab convict clothes, stamped with a broad arrow and ill-fitting, he looked more than unprepossessing.
>
> I was very suspicious concerning Crippen, and even had the rims and ear-pieces of his spectacles examined for concealed poison.[13]

The prison's chief warder, Mr H. T. Boreham, had a more sympathetic attitude towards the prisoner. He recalled Crippen being 'a very pleasant little man'.[14] Another warder, J. Alan Shields, was similarly impressed by Crippen's demeanour. Upon his arrival at Pentonville, Crippen asked for the prison's regulations to be explained to him so that he could conform to them and be as little trouble as possible. Shields said that it was rare for a murderer to elicit any sympathy from the warders, but 'there was about Crippen something that made it possible to forget for the time being of the crime he was accused of'.

Shields noticed that Crippen was not sleeping at night. Crippen explained that he was seeing visions of the scaffold and of Cora passing through his cell. Crippen told Shields that this was not the first time he had figured in an execution: 'Years ago when I was living in Cleveland, Ohio, my wife and I both took part in private theatricals for the benefit of a local charity, and I played the part of a man falsely accused of murder and cut down from the gallows at the last moment on the arrival of the heroine, my wife, with proof of my innocence.'[15]

Crippen was visited in prison by a confidence trickster who masqueraded as Lady Mercia Somerset. Born Ada Alice Fricker, she had worked as an actress and was a client of Arthur Newton. Lady Mercia had no claim to a title and had served several prison terms. Somerset had initially become interested in the case as she thought there was a remote chance Crippen could be found not guilty, and if she could meet him first and get him to tell her his story 'it would be read with interest all over the world' and, no doubt, be profitable for her.[16]

Somerset wrote to Crippen and secured a visit. She promised to take him and Le Neve to live at her country house when they were released. Crippen and Somerset began a correspondence and were on friendly terms, although Le Neve did not appear to trust her. Le Neve later wrote in a series of reminiscences that after her acquittal 'a young man approached me and informed me that he had been sent by a person of title to take me away to a place of comfort and security'. This had to be Somerset because Le Neve described her as 'no titled person at all, but someone who has since served several sentences in prison for serious offences'. Le Neve made the disturbing allegation that Somerset 'planned to get me in the toils and use me to do things that a person with a chance in life would never dream of doing'.[17]

Neither did Major Mytton-Davies trust the bogus aristocrat. He read one of her letters which 'appears peculiar and it looks as if there were a hidden meaning in portions of it – viz the remarks regarding Miss Le Neve'. The last meeting between Somerset and Crippen took place at Pentonville on 27 October when 'he could talk of nothing else but the woman he adored'.[18] Somerset soon published a number of letters that Crippen had sent her, so she made some money for her efforts.[19]

Accepting that his days were numbered, Crippen published a statement that appeared in the *Daily Mail* and clearly showed the depth of his feelings towards Ethel Le Neve as well as emphasising her total innocence in the whole affair. Crippen took full responsibility for her plight, but not for the murder of Cora:

About my unhappy relations with Belle Elmore I will say nothing. We drifted apart in sympathy; she had her own friends and pleasures, and I was rather a lonely man and rather miserable. Then I obtained the affection and sympathy of Miss Le Neve. I confess that, according to the moral laws of Church and State, we were guilty, and I do not defend our position in that respect. But what I do say is that this love was not of a debased and degraded character. It was – if I may say so to people who will not perhaps understand or believe – a good love. She comforted me in my melancholy condition; her mind was beautiful to me; her loyalty and courage and self-sacrifice were of a high character. Whatever sin there was – and we broke the law – it was my sin, not hers...

In this farewell letter to the world, written as I face eternity, I say that Ethel Le Neve has loved me as few women love men, and that her innocence of any crime, save that of yielding to the dictates of the heart, is absolute. To her I pay this last tribute. It is of her that my last thoughts have been. My last prayer will be that God may protect her and keep her safe from harm, and allow her to join me in eternity.

Crippen wrote to Le Neve every day. One letter read,

How can I find the strength and heart to struggle through this last letter? God indeed must hear our cry to Him for Divine help in this last farewell.

How to control myself to write I hardly know, but pray God help us to be brave to help to face the end so near.

The thoughts rush to my mind quicker than I can put them down. Time is so short now, and there is so much that I would say.

There are less than two days left to us. Only one more letter after this can I write you, and only two more visits – one to-night before you read this letter, and one tomorrow.

When I wrote to you on Saturday I had not heard any news of the petition, and though I never at any time had hope, yet deep down in my heart was just a glimmer of trust that God might give us yet a chance to put me right before the world and let me have the passionate longing of my soul.

Your letter, written early Saturday, came to me last Saturday evening, and soon after the Governor brought me the dreadful news about ten o'clock.

He was so kind and considerate in telling me, in breaking the shock as gently as he could. He was most kind, and left me at last with 'God bless you! Good night,' so that I know you will ever remember him most kindly.

When he had gone I first kissed your face in the photo, my faithful, devoted companion in all this sorrow.

Oh, how glad I am I had the photo. It was some consolation, although in spite of all my greatest efforts it was impossible to keep down a great sob and my heart's agonised cry.

How am I to endure to take my last look at your dear face? What agony must I go through at the last when you disappear for ever from my eyes? God help us to be brave then.[20]

Another letter written by Crippen to Le Neve, after he knew his appeal had failed, showed him in a feistier mood. With all hope of a reprieve gone, Crippen protested his innocence with far more gusto than he had done at his trial:

In spite of my fate there is one working for me now in collecting fresh evidence, and it is still possible that after my death the real truth may be revealed. Face to Face with God, in Whose presence my soul shall soon stand for final judgement, I still maintain that I was wrongly convicted, and my belief that facts will yet be forthcoming to prove my innocence.

I solemnly state that I know nothing of the remains discovered at Hilldrop Crescent until I was told of their discovery by my solicitor, Mr Arthur Newton, on the next day after my arrival at Bow Street.

My conviction was obtained on purely circumstantial evidence, and I am positive that if I had at my disposal a sum equal to that spent by the Crown on the prosecution the important points of that evidence would have been rebutted so decidedly that a conviction would have been impossible.

Le Neve thought that he had written this letter in the hope that she would get it published, not only to make some money for her, but for 'justice in the future'.[21]

15

THE EXECUTION

> Hope has completely gone, and your hub's heart is broken. No more
> can he hold his wifie in his arms.
>
> Dr Crippen to Ethel Le Neve

Arthur Newton paid his final visit to Dr Crippen shortly after noon
on 21 November. They sat some 15 feet apart, separated by two
tables. 'Well I am sorry to say all our efforts have been in vain. I
have received an unfavourable reply to the petition,' said Newton.
Crippen replied, 'I have been informed there is no hope.' He had
known this for two days so Newton's visit seems a bit tardy. This
was the first time he had visited his client since 2 November. Several
newspapers reported that Newton had been in Nice 'on important
business' where he had been interviewed by the *Petit Parisien* on or
about 14 November. If Crippen was annoyed that his solicitor had
neglected him, he didn't show it and his manners were as perfect as
ever, thanking Newton for his efforts and saying he had been 'more
like a big brother' than just a solicitor.

Their conversation centred mainly on Ethel Le Neve. When the
time came for him to leave, Newton said, 'Goodbye Doctor, I am
sorry the Rules of the Prison won't allow me to shake hands with
you, but bear up as well as you can under the circumstances, and
I will do all I can for Miss Le Neve, so – Goodbye – Goodbye
– Goodbye.'

Newton waved as he said his departing words. Crippen replied,
'Goodbye.'

Le Neve visited Crippen eleven times at Pentonville from 31
October to 22 November. The first visit was in her own name, the
other ten as 'Mrs Hawley'. She was accompanied to the prison on
several occasions by journalist J. P. (John Percy) Eddy, who waited

for her outside the great, green, studded door. On one occasion 'she came away very subdued and clearly deeply anxious that he should, if possible, escape the gallows. There was no bitterness on her part that he had put her in a false position before the world; only a deep appreciation of the fact that her good friend was facing his extreme ordeal'.[1]

Ethel Le Neve paid her farewell visit less than twenty-four hours before Crippen's execution. Crippen's last words to her were 'Good-bye and God bless you'. Then, 'with a quick stride he made for the door, and, turning round, took a last, long farewell look upon my face and was gone'.[2]

On the night before his execution Crippen received a final telegram from Le Neve. Major Mytton-Davies watched as Crippen read it and then raised it to his lips, kissing it again and again. His last request to Mytton-Davies was for Le Neve's letters be buried with him.[3]

Crippen's executioner was John Ellis. As soon as the capital sentence was passed on Crippen, Ellis' troubles began. In addition to carrying out executions Ellis ran a barber's shop which was inundated with people coming in, not for haircuts, but to ask him about Crippen. People stopped in the street and pointed excitedly at him saying to their friends, 'That's him! That's the man who is going to hang Crippen!' To add to his woes, Ellis had to carry out an execution both the day before and after he hanged Crippen. Ellis said that the execution of Dr Crippen 'was about the only time in my life that I really almost regretted the office I held'.

Ellis arrived at Pentonville Prison on the afternoon of 22 November:

I learned that the condemned murderer had been deeply disappointed when he found that all hope of a reprieve must be dismissed from his mind. He seemed to have convinced himself that he would never be hanged, and when the truth came home to him he was on the verge of total nervous collapse.

Terrible though the shock was, he soon controlled his feelings once more and became his old cool, calculating self, a fact of which we were to have startling evidence that very night.

The peephole in his cell door provided me with means of observing him, and as I gazed in at the man who had set the whole world by the ears I marvelled at his calmness. He sat there writing, and would occasionally break off to chat pleasantly and in most affable fashion with the warders whose duty it was to watch him night and day until the scaffold claimed him.[4]

Like many people who came into contact with Crippen, Ellis was struck by his agreeable and helpful nature, which always came to the fore despite his awful predicament. He said that Crippen 'had a natural amiability and innate gentlemanliness that seized the affections of even his warders'. There must have been some inner turmoil under the calm façade, for Crippen attempted to commit suicide on the eve of his execution:

> Crippen undoubtedly committed a hideous crime which admits of no excuse but he had two sides of his nature, and it was the pleasant only that was uppermost during my contact with him.
>
> Yet that very night he showed that behind his suave graciousness lay power to make firm life and death decisions. Just before midnight one of the warders in that silent cell made a thrilling discovery.
>
> Crippen was in bed, and the men watching his progress through his last night on earth felt uneasy at Crippen's restless motions. The strain on warders in such a position is a most intense one, and these men would have been superhuman if they had not felt overweighted with the responsibility that was resting upon their shoulders.
>
> At last one of them went to Crippen's bedside to satisfy himself that the latter's movements were nothing more than the usual restless tossings of a condemned man on his last night, but to his amazement found he was just in time to prevent the scaffold being cheated of its victim![5]

Prison warder Mr Fellows had Crippen under close observation and recorded,

> Prisoner was crying for fully 10 minutes at 10.30 p.m. he undressed himself and went to the recess at 10.45, I heard something break while he was there and I asked him what was the matter, he said a button had burst off his pants, he then put his glasses on the cupboard and was getting into bed when I saw that his glasses were broken, I told him at once to give the other portion up to me & he then pulled the other part from under his pants, he had very little sleep during the night.

Ellis considered that 'this act was about the only one Crippen ever did that caused his custodians any trouble, for he was a most considerate prisoner, never making unnecessary trouble, and always doing exactly as he was told'.[6]

William Willis, Ellis' assistant, confirmed the story. Willis thought that Crippen had planned to puncture an artery and slowly bleed to death while he slept.[7] Willis was in the minority of people altogether less sympathetic towards the prisoner. In his reminiscences he wrote, 'Never was a man less deserving of sympathy than the monster who murdered Belle Elmore. He was a man unfit for the society of his fellow creatures.'[8]

Hawley Harvey Crippen barely touched his final breakfast, which consisted of a pot of tea, bread and butter and two eggs.[9] Being a Roman Catholic, Crippen was attended by Canon Thomas Carey. He changed from his prison uniform into the clothes he wore at his trial. Dr Crippen was hanged at nine o'clock on the dark, cold and foggy morning of 23 November. Ellis had determined that a drop of 7 feet and 9 inches would be sufficient to instantly dispatch Crippen, who stood 5 feet 4 inches tall and weighed 142 pounds clothed the day before the execution. The character of Crippen's neck was recorded as being 'normal'. Ellis described Crippen's last moments:

> As I stood on the scaffold I could see the procession come into view twelve yards distant. Behind the praying priest came the notorious Dr Crippen, no longer a murderer to fear but rather a man to be pitied. Yet his attitude was not that of one who asks for sympathy. If he had ever shown cowardice or collapse he displayed none now.
>
> I could see him smiling as he approached, and the smile never left his face up to the moment when I threw the white cap over it and blotted out God's light from his eyes for ever.
>
> In a trice he was on the trap-doors with his legs strapped together and a rope round his neck. One swift glance round to be assured that all was right and my hand shot to the lever.
>
> Thud! The fatal doors had fallen. The slack rope tightened, and in an instant was still. Dr Crippen was dead.[10]

Willis said that Crippen, polite to the end, 'employed his last breath to thank the Governor for his kindness and courtesy'.[11] All rumours of a last-minute confession made by Crippen were flatly denied. As with all executed criminals, a coroner's inquest was held to establish the cause of Crippen's death. Walter Schröder, who was the coroner at Cora Crippen's inquest, oversaw this formality. Hawley Harvey Crippen was then buried within the walls of Pentonville Prison in grave number sixteen.[12] A Home Office circular giving instructions for burying executed prisoners listed as its third point that 'lime will not be used'[13] The irony would surely have not been wasted on Crippen.

While reliable sources stated that Crippen made no confession to the murder of his wife, the possibility that a confession did exist led to dramatic scenes the day before his execution. On 22 November a young man entered the offices of the London *Evening Times*, a newspaper that had only been in existence for twenty days. He told the editor that Arthur Newton had a confession from Crippen and was prepared to sell it.

The *Evening Times*' crime reporter, Arthur Findon, hurried to Marlborough Street magistrates' court, where he found Newton. After much bartering, Newton settled on a price of £500 in cash for the confession, and an assurance that his name would not be mentioned. They agreed to meet at 8 p.m. at the Langham Hotel, where Newton would hand the confession over. Findon took Newton at his word and told his editor that it would be safe to announce in that evening's stop-press column that the next day's issue would contain the confession.

Findon, along with reporter James Little, met Newton at the Langham but the solicitor said he was reneging on the deal, fearing that he would be struck off the rolls by the Law Society if they ever found out what he had done. Findon threatened to print a story of how Newton tried to sell the confession. Newton backed down and said that an associate of his named Low would bring the confession to Findon's house at 2 a.m. on 23 November (the day of Crippen's execution). Low would show Findon the confession and then burn it. That way Newton could say that he had not given it to Findon.

Low duly arrived and read the confession to Findon and Little, who took notes. He then threw the papers on the fire but as soon as his back was turned Little plucked the half-burned confession from the grate. From this and their notes the two journalists pieced together Crippen's confession. By five o'clock in the morning on the day of publication the notes were being scrutinised by editorial staff, including Edgar Wallace, who had some affection for Crippen after learning that the fugitive had read his book *The Four Just Men* on the *Montrose*, which had resulted in a surge of sales of the title. The confession itself lacked the excitement they hoped for, but it was a definite statement that Crippen had deliberately poisoned Cora with hyoscine concealed in indigestion tablets. He then dismembered her with a surgeon's knife, which he later hid in the garden of an empty Hilldrop Crescent house.[14]

The *Evening Times* ran the story of Crippen's confession on 23 November, and the paper sold close to a million copies that evening.[15] The newspaper's problems started when another London evening paper ran a story the same day that they had interviewed officials at the prison and the Home Office who denied that there had been a confession. They had also interviewed Newton, who refused to comment. These denials were circulated by press agencies and appeared in the final editions of the evening papers.

At an *Evening Times* staff meeting the next day they discussed what to do to protect their reputation. According to Findon they decided to say nothing and save Newton's reputation. Furthermore, Findon did not reveal any of this until immediately after Newton's death in 1930. This remarkable altruism is surprising as Newton had pocketed £500 of the *Times*' money and humiliated them in front of their Fleet Street rivals. Findon said that he went to see Newton for an explanation and a statement. An unrepentant Newton told him, 'I can say nothing about the confession. I personally know of no confession, but beyond this I cannot discuss the matter except to say that it is not within the right of any man to throw doubt on the confession.' It was too little too late. By 26 November the *Evening Times*' sales had fallen from 1 million to 30,000, and it went out of business after just over a year.[16]

If Findon's story is to be believed, then that was not the only occasion that Newton profited from an alleged Crippen confession. In 1922 he sold his memoirs to *Thomson's Weekly News*. They included the claim that Crippen had signed a confession in Brixton Prison before his trial.

According to Newton, Crippen explained that he had been driven to murder by Cora's infidelity, nagging, drinking and jealousy. The murder was premeditated, for Crippen had bought a dissecting knife for the purpose of dismembering Cora. He had hidden the knife under his mattress, safe in the knowledge that Cora would not find it 'for she never even bothered to make my bed'. He burned the missing remains in the kitchen stove but could not finish the job as the fumes were overpowering and he did not want to arouse the suspicions of his neighbours. Newton added that the confession was either lost or destroyed by the time he gave up his practice.[17]

16

ETHEL

I've always wondered if Ethel Le Neve was in it with him or not.
Agatha Christie, *The Lernean Hydra*

The world-wide attention which the case has aroused has certainly made my future a very difficult problem.
Ethel Le Neve, *My Life Story*

Belief in Ethel Le Neve's innocence of any involvement in the murder of Cora Crippen was almost universal. Frank Dilnot, a journalist who attended the Bow Street committal hearings, was fairly typical in his assessment: 'Of course, Miss Le Neve knew nothing of the murder, and it is inconceivable that she should have had anything to do with Crippen if she had known him to be the murderer he was afterwards proved to be.'[1]

Captain Kendall shared Dilnot's view and 'no sort of doubt as to her innocence of crime remained in my mind. This was emphatically not the kind of girl who for weeks could spend all day alone in the Camden Town house knowing that below were the remains of the murdered Belle Elmore.'[2]

Very soon after Le Neve's acquittal she was 'captured at a price' by the *Daily Chronicle*.[3] That paper was affiliated with the popular Sunday tabloid *Lloyd's Weekly News*, which eventually published her story. Philip (later Sir Philip) Gibbs and J. P. Eddy, a future barrister and judge, were the two journalists assigned to interview Le Neve.

The Fleet Street duo spent several weeks with Le Neve at a furnished flat paid for by the newspaper and they both formed a favourable impression of her. Eddy described Le Neve as 'a brunette, with a slight figure, a finely-chiselled nose and expressive eyes'.[4] 'She was,' he thought, 'an understanding person who would be likely to give Crippen the affection and sympathy which he lacked. I had no shadow of doubt as to her innocence ... my faith in her innocence never faltered.'[5]

Gibbs gave a slightly different account. He wrote that Eddy 'cross-examined her artfully and persistently, with the firm belief that she knew all about the murder. Never once, however, did he trap her into any admission.' Gibbs described Le Neve as 'quite a pretty and attractive little creature' with 'astonishing and unusual qualities'. After Crippen's arrest 'she had no doubt now of his guilt'. But, as she also admitted, that made no difference to her love for him. 'He was mad when he did it,' she said, 'and he was mad for me.' Gibbs was struck by Crippen and Le Neve's affair, comparing them to 'mediaeval lovers in Italy of Boccaccio's time, when the murder for love's sake was lightly done'.[6]

On the morning of Crippen's execution Gibbs was with Le Neve, who dressed in black for the occasion 'and wished she might have died with him on the scaffold'. However, her ordeal had not appeared to affect her and 'many times she was so gay that it was impossible to believe that she had escaped the hangman's rope by no great distance'. She possessed 'a quick and childish sense of humour which had not been killed by the frightful thing that overshadowed her'.[7] Le Neve's own account of the day of execution was completely different. She said she had been at home in her flat; 'too ill to move out of bed, I lay there from dawn till the dread hour'.[8]

Gibbs was convinced of her innocence, but was 'glad to see the last of her' because he 'sickened at the squalor of the whole story of love and murder'.[9] When published in *Lloyd's Weekly News* over a four-week period, Le Neve's story proved somewhat disappointing. It offered no sensational revelations and served more as an advert for her innocence in the whole affair. The series was quickly reprinted in a booklet called *Ethel Le Neve Her Life Story* by a London publisher and soon afterwards as a facsimile by Daisy Bank publishing.

F. E. Smith never explained what he meant by his comment after Le Neve's trial, 'I knew what she would say'. Despite F. E.'s public support of Le Neve's innocence, could there have been some doubts lurking at the back of the sagacious barrister's mind? There was much more to her than met the eye and she would prove to be as enigmatic as Dr Crippen. One biographer of Bernard Spilsbury noted that 'Ethel Le Neve moves through the tragedy like a ghost. She is a completely baffling character, who glides from the scene without leaving trace or impression. Only this can be said: either there was nothing in her or there was a great deal.'[10]

In September 1911 a Post Office employee was making a routine examination of Post Office Savings Bank documents prior to their destruction. On one of them he noticed the name Belle Elmore and the address 39 Hilldrop Crescent. Remembering the names from the previous year's *cause célèbre*, he took a closer look.

The document related to a withdrawal of money from Cora Crippen's Post Office savings account. When cross-referenced with her account records it was discovered that between 5 April and 17 June 1910, eight withdrawals had been made totalling £196 11s 4d. All the withdrawals had been made from the Western Central District post office in London. The writing on the forged withdrawal papers was carefully examined and compared to Ethel Le Neve's. The Post Office concluded that Le Neve had forged Cora's writing and that the forgeries were 'very good'.

Details of the findings were handed to the Director of Public Prosecutions. He consulted with the Attorney General, who decided not to prosecute Le Neve because

> whatever the opinion an expert might form on the question of handwriting, it would be extremely harsh, after so great a lapse in time, to rearrest this woman, who had already stood her trial on a grave charge, and who had already been acquitted under a defence that what she had done was under the domination of a will stronger than her own, and under the domination of which she certainly was at the time of the occurrences upon which any fresh prosecution must be founded.

Eventually the embezzled money was refunded to the Post Office by the Treasury and given to the administrators of Cora Crippen's will.[11]

It is commonly believed that the journalist and prolific author Ursula Bloom was the first person to find Ethel Le Neve after she faded into obscurity at the end of 1910. One day in the early 1950s Bloom was discussing the Crippen case with Charles Eade, the editor of the *Sunday Dispatch*. Eade said that Ethel had 'disappeared into the limbo of lost things, and without a doubt she will never turn up again. Would you like to do the story? I propose to call it The Girl Who Loved Crippen.'[12] Bloom did want to do the story and would dine off it for the rest of her life.

The first instalment of *The Girl Who Loved Crippen* was published in the *Sunday Dispatch* on 4 April 1954. Two days after publication, a male relative of Le Neve turned up at the *Dispatch*'s office, ostensibly to complain about the article, but possibly hoping to profit from his connection to its subject. It may have been his grievance that led to subsequent instalments of the series including the disclaimer that 'this is a novel based on fact. The principal characters figured in the most famous crime of the century; some of the other characters are entirely fictitious.'

Bloom claimed not to have known Le Neve was alive and sent a letter of apology to her via the relative. Le Neve replied, saying that she had left England on the day of Crippen's execution, worked in Canada before returning to England in 1916 to nurse her dying sister. She stayed in England and married a co-worker with whom she had two children and one grandson, none of whom knew anything of her past and association with the Crippen case.[13]

Ursula and Ethel continued corresponding and eventually met. Le Neve told her she thought that Crippen was innocent and said that 'the nasty smell which haunted his house had been there during Belle Elmore's life. This was never taken up and there was never any inquiry into previous tenants.'[14]

After the series of *Sunday Dispatch* articles ended, Bloom added an appendix in which she described their meeting. In appearance Ethel 'could easily be anyone's next-door neighbour. Smally built, she is still pretty, with grey hair, and intelligent eyes out of which a strong personality looks. For 44 years she has remained unidentified, when there were hundreds who were curious about her.'[15]

The newspaper series had been completed before Bloom had met Le Neve[16] and was published in a book of the same title in 1955. It was virtually identical to the newspaper version. Bloom's meeting with Le Neve had not led to any new disclosures that would help sell the book, suggesting that Le Neve did not cooperate with the author.

Moving forward to 1961, and a new musical based on the Crippen story was about to open in London.[17] Ursula Bloom had stayed in contact with Le Neve and kept her promise never to divulge her whereabouts. Of the play 'she [Ethel] would not discuss it. She was not interested. She would not visit the theatre – for that would hurt her too much. All she seeks now is to retire into the background and be forgotten.'[18] Ursula Bloom kept in touch with Le Neve until the end. Shortly before Ethel died, Bloom allegedly accompanied her to Pentonville Prison at Le Neve's request.[19]

Bloom was famed for her association with Le Neve and occasionally recounted her story. In 1965, Bloom quoted from a notebook that she had filled in on the day she met Le Neve for the first time:

She said she still loved Crippen. Recalled that remains of Belle Elmore were unearthed and handed to the jury on a soup plate. Said they showed

an intensive hernia scar for removal of navel. But there was evidence that
Belle had retained her navel after her op. This was not pressed in court.

The pyjama sleeve unearthed was one of half a million sold in
neighbourhood by Jones of Holloway.

Hyoscine traces were found. But Le Neve said 'We seldom used
hyoscine, it was new, and he had never liked it.'

Then summed up: 'He did not die for any of those things. It was just
that he loved me.' Her face was very white.

I asked her if Crippen could have come back again, would she marry
him now? Her eyes almost pierced me. Then she nodded. 'Yes I would,'
she said.[20]

It is true that Ursula Bloom had tracked down Ethel Le Neve in the
1950s, but it is far from the truth to suggest that she was the first
person to do so since 1910.

In her youth, Bloom was an avid reader of the *News of the World*,
saying 'it was my relaxation from the classics, and nothing could have
enchanted me more'.[21] It was in the *News of the World* that she had
first read of the Crippen case in 1910. Maybe she had stopped reading
the paper, because in 1952 the front-page headline read, 'The Captain
Who Captured Crippen Tells His Story'.

Captain Kendall had read the serialised memoirs of Travers
Humphreys in the previous week's issue and wanted to give his
account about the Crippen case. At the end 'he revealed that Ethel Le
Neve is still alive – in a town in the South of England. She married, he
said, and is now a grandmother.'[22] Michael Gilbert had heard similar
rumours and wrote in his 1953 book on the Crippen case that

> whether she is alive or not today is uncertain. She worked as a
> dressmaker for a while, in England, and then departed for Australia,
> living under an assumed name. Her death has been reported at various
> times, but without much confirmation of identity. Lately it has been
> rumoured that she is still alive and living in England, a respected
> grandmother, happily married and immune from public inquisitiveness
> since nobody, save her husband, knows her secret. The truth of that
> report is not something which we have any intention of pursuing.[23]

Perhaps he had found some of this information in Kendall's article,
but it is worrying that Bloom did not appear to have read the most
recent book on Crippen, which was published just one year before
she wrote her articles.

There was much more Bloom had missed over the years. The *Daily Express* revealed in 1950 that Le Neve was still living in England and 'her husband is a good man who knows and keeps her secret, but her one fear is that her children will find out'.[24] More importantly Le Neve had sold her story at least four times to national newspapers after her appearance in *Lloyd's Weekly News* in 1910.

In 1920 *Thomson's Weekly News*, a popular Saturday tabloid based in Dundee, but having a London edition and a weekly circulation of 623,984, had a startling exclusive story to tell. 'My Life Story by Ethel Le Neve' was a huge series of lavishly illustrated articles running for twenty-three weeks.

Despite the sensational subject and billing as the 'Most Poignant Human Document Ever Written', the series was a little mundane and long-winded. It gave a reasonably straightforward account of the case: some of it is identical to the *Lloyd's* confessions. It is not clear how responsible Ethel was for the contents or if she told her story to a journalist who wrote it up for her. In it Le Neve refers to the 1910 series, saying she had presented 'the facts as I wanted them to be presented'.[25]

Le Neve spoke of her regret at having gone to live at Hilldrop Crescent, which she thought 'a terrible place, and I never felt at home in it'.[26] She seemed be very fond of Inspector Dew, whom she described as 'one of the smartest men that ever passed along the corridors of Scotland Yard'[27] and 'a very nice man and a real friend to a poor girl in distress'.[28]

The 1920–1 *Thomson's* series is of some interest because it offers Le Neve's account of her early life and what happened after her acquittal. However, as some of the story is provably false, the rest of it should be treated with caution. According to Le Neve, she left the Old Bailey with her sister and took a taxi to Fenchurch Street station. There they boarded a train for Southend where they stayed in a large hotel under false names. Against her sister's advice, Le Neve wanted to return to London to be near Crippen. She took a small flat in Chelsea, again under a false name.[29] Where she found the time to tell her story to the journalists Gibbs and Eddy, published in *Lloyd's Weekly News* in November 1910, wasn't explained.

Le Neve gave her opinion about how Cora Crippen died. It resembled Edward Marshall Hall's, but pre-dated it by eight years:

And now I think I may make the statement here that I do not think Dr Crippen murdered his wife in cold blood.

My own belief is that the murder may have been an accident. Cora Crippen, in a fit of pique, might easily have pretended to take poison in order to worry her husband, and unintentionally have taken a fatal dose.

But I do not think that this happened in the case of Cora Crippen. She had other and stronger means of frightening poor Dr Crippen. These, as he frequently told me, were so effective that there was never any need for her to employ more dramatic methods.

The only theory which appeals to me was that Dr Crippen killed his wife by accident, and afterwards was so terrified that he hid her body in the cellar … he was in the habit of taking small quantities [of hyoscine] from the office and administering them to his wife when he thought she was likely to break into one of her fits of passion.[30]

After Crippen's execution Le Neve's one desire was to leave England and start a new life in another country. Her choice of location was perhaps surprising:

Somehow or other I could not get it out of my head that if only I could get to Canada I would be able to throw off all the shackles of the past, all the fears that had beset me, and get what I never had got in England – a chance.[31]

So at the end of February 1911 she once again set sail for Canada. Passing Father Point and successfully disembarking at Quebec, Le Neve visited the prison she had been held in and was warmly greeted by the staff. Moving on to Montreal, she took various typing jobs, but living with the constant fear of recognition, she suffered a nervous breakdown and after nine months returned to England to stay with her sister in Tooting.[32]

After six months convalescing, Le Neve obtained an office job. One day when going to catch a train at Victoria station for Wandsworth she saw Inspector Dew walking towards her. Dew showed no signs of recognition and walked straight past her. Le Neve thought he must have known it was her, but Dew 'besides being a great detective, was one of the kindest, courtliest gentlemen I have ever met, and it is just the sort of thing he would have done to pretend that he had obliterated me from the tablets of his memory'.[33] Dew was working as a confidential enquiry agent at that time with an office near Victoria and had lived at Wandsworth until 1911 so the story may be true.

Another of Le Neve's stories was corroborated by Melinda May. May wrote,

I saw her myself on Easter Monday, 1913. And I saw her in an extraordinary manner.

I had been staying in Eastbourne and had entered a compartment in a train for London Bridge. A young woman was sitting opposite to me, and to my amazement I recognized her as Ethel Neave [May always disdainfully referred to Le Neve by her real name]. She saw me, too, and knew who I was, and she hung her head. I could not take my eyes off her all the time we were on the journey.[34]

Le Neve also recorded the confrontation and her description of May shows there was no love lost between the pair:

There was a middle-aged woman, hard featured and severe, with several valises and packages above her in the rack, and dressed in her unmistakable bizarre fashion of the touring music-hall woman. I was in a crowded compartment with the one woman who hated me most, who believed in my guilt, and who had given evidence against me at the Old Bailey.

To my surprise the woman did nothing. She looked at me several times over her newspaper then averted her gaze. As the train sped on I began to take refuge in the thought that she had failed to recognize me or if she knew me she preferred to treat me with contempt.

The woman rose from her seat, a big muscular woman, and towering above me she glared at me like a tigress. I shrank back into my corner, expecting a blow to fall. The other passengers looked at both of us in astonishment. There was going to be a scene.

'You think I don't know who you are, do you?' shrieked the woman. 'But I do!'[35]

With the outbreak of the First World War, Le Neve joined the VAD (Voluntary Aid Detachment) as a nurse. She was sent to a large old house in Kent that the owner had vacated to be used for the war effort. There Le Neve met an Australian soldier of Scottish descent who had been wounded at Gallipoli. He soon proposed and Le Neve confessed her true identity. To her surprise he had never heard of the Crippen case and his proposal stood.[36]

They married in the parish church in the village where they had met. A fellow soldier acted as best man while Le Neve's sister, brother-in-law and two VAD nurses were witnesses. After honeymooning in Eastbourne they sailed to Australia and lived at her husband's farm, where Ethel Le Neve's past was never mentioned.[37]

In 1922 Le Neve was telling her story again, this time to *The*

Mascot.[38] It was billed as the 'Greatest Series Ever Published' and told the tale of 'a wayward girl's struggle to live and love'.

Five years later Le Neve was interviewed by the *Sunday News*, which said she was in London on a brief holiday. She revealed that on visiting London, the first place she went to see was 39 Hilldrop Crescent. Other locations connected to the Crippen case had an inescapable lure for her. She went to a restaurant where she and Crippen often met, the Old Bailey and Holloway Prison.

Again she gave her opinion that Cora Crippen's death had been an accident:

> To this day I hold that the man who was so much to me then was innocent of the crime of murder. It is not for me to attempt to explain how Belle Elmore came to her death. I am convinced that her husband had no hand in the death, and I am inclined to accept his suggestion that she died accidentally and that the worst that can be alleged against him is that he buried the body unlawfully.

There were great discrepancies with the earlier *Thomson's* series. Le Neve said she was married and had met her husband 'far from the scene of the tragedy'. Her husband knew nothing of her past and 'had not the least idea that I was the tragic woman in the Crippen case'. She had married him under an assumed name and described him as 'the man who has made me so happy'.[39]

It wasn't long before Le Neve was telling her story again to *Thomson's Weekly News*. Now she was known as Mrs Brown and was 'the wife of one of the best men who ever drew breath, and the mother of two bonnie children – a girl and a boy'. Her husband 'knew all about my past' and she hoped her son would become 'a clean-living, open-hearted Englishman like his father'. The theme of this set of memoirs was 'How I Have Been Persecuted'.[40]

Her life in Canada was discussed, as was her return to England where she was recognised several times, forcing her to change jobs and addresses. Once she was tracked down by a representative of a film studio who were making a film about a girl who runs away dressed in boy's clothes. He had employed a private detective agency to find her. Le Neve declined the role and moved again, taking a job as a typist for a large firm of solicitors. When she was offered a permanent position, a copy of her birth certificate was required to join the company pension scheme. Le Neve had to confess her identity and her sympathetic employer found another job for her with a friend of his.[41]

Then came a repeat of the story of joining the VAD under the name of Ethel Grey and meeting an Australian soldier who knew nothing of Ethel Le Neve and Dr Crippen. This time he was described as being of Northumbrian stock rather than Scottish. The country church wedding was now abandoned as it would have required banns to be read out in her real name, so they married by special licence at 'an old fashioned church in the suburbs in which I had lived as a girl.' They set sail to Australia from Southampton to live on his farm.[42]

A son was born some eighteen months after arriving in Australia and a daughter, Kathleen, followed in 1921. The daughter was diagnosed with a nervous disorder and a doctor recommended treatment in Perth. Le Neve decided to return to England for treatment and so that her son could get a public school education.[43] Remaining in England, 'both our children are now growing up. The girl is strong and well, the boy almost finished with his education and just about to enter a profession.'[44]

Yet another interview with Ethel Le Neve appeared in 1931, this time in the *Sunday Post*. Again, it was at odds with her other declarations. This time she was 'Mrs B—', with a husband and two children, a son and a daughter, 'to whom, by mutual agreement, the past is a closed book.' On the day her first child was born, Le Neve destroyed all her old photographs in an attempt to eliminate her past. She was unable to socialise with her neighbours or join local clubs in case her real identity became known. Some people did realise who she was when newspapers ran stories about the famous Crippen case and published her photograph. This led to requests for money which Le Neve magnanimously excused by saying it was only done 'when they are hard up. It is not blackmail. Only they know that I will help them. I am too frightened to refuse. So I am always poor, and there are things I want in my home that I cannot have.'

Once again the family went to Australia, but this time they returned for medical treatment for her son, whose illness she attributed to her own fragile nervous system that had never recovered since her arrest. Le Neve's greatest fear was that one day her children would learn of her real identity, even after her death. Perhaps they would need to obtain a copy of her marriage certificate 'for the name on it is Ethel Le Neve'. The name on the certificate is Ethel Harvey.[45]

So what was the true story? Le Neve had told at least seven versions of her life story since 1910, all of which contradicted the others in some way. Ironically she had expressed annoyance that Inspector Dew had doubted her word that Crippen was not in when he first visited Hilldrop Crescent ('It annoyed me to think that this man should flatly contradict me, and practically accuse me of telling an untruth').[46] Can the conflicting memoirs be put down to unreliable tabloid sensationalism, or was Le Neve trying to create a smokescreen to protect her whereabouts? Perhaps it showed a streak of romantic imagination with her sailing off into the sunset to a new life in Australia.

Le Neve said 'it is my prayer that my children will also remain in ignorance of what I have been through'.[47] For decades they did. Then in 1985 crime historian Jonathan Goodman was finishing his book on Dr Crippen.[48] He knew that Ethel Le Neve had married a man named Stanley Smith and had died in South London in 1967. This would have been common knowledge by then, as in 1974 the *Evening News* ran a story about Le Neve that included a photograph of her marital home, 10 Parkway Road, Addiscombe. It further revealed that she had died seven years earlier at Dulwich Hospital, aged eighty-four, and had been a 'nice old dear … fond of a drink at the local. Always curious to learn more about world events. Always eager for a matey chat over a cup of tea. She was a tough old bird as well.'[49] In 1980 the theatrical journal *The Call Boy* noted that Ethel had two children and died on 9 August 1967.[50]

Armed with this information, Goodman searched for the death certificate of an Ethel Smith whose death was registered in South London in 1967. There was an Ethel Clara Smith of 62 Burford Road, Lewisham who died on 9 August 1967 at Dulwich Hospital from heart failure aged eighty-four. She had moved from Parkway Road after the death of her husband in 1960.

The death certificate bore the name and address of Ethel Smith's son Robert, so Goodman checked the telephone directory and found Robert Smith was still at the same West Country address and wrote to him, enclosing a stamped, addressed envelope for a reply. Robert Smith was a retired joiner aged seventy and his sister Nina Campbell, a retired secretary, was sixty-four. Robert opened Goodman's carefully worded letter:

Dear Mr Smith

I have learned your address from your mother's death certificate. I am at present completing a book which I trust will put an end to some of the many legends associated with the case of the death of Mrs Cora Crippen in 1910. I should be most grateful if you could assist me.[51]

Robert said to his wife, 'Some loony has written to me.' However, he replied the same day and invited Goodman to visit.[52] Goodman took with him a letter written by Le Neve and the handwriting matched that of a recipe for chocolate roll in her recipe book that Robert now owned.[53] Further proof came in the form of a photograph of their grandfather.

The mystery of Robert and Nina's parent's marriage certificate was now solved. It gave her name as Ethel Clara Harvey (Crippen's middle name).[54] She had married Stanley William Smith at Wandsworth Registry Office on 2 January 1915. His occupation was given as 'Household Furnishing Clerk', not Australian soldier. The validity of this certificate is proved by naming Ethel's sister Adine Brock as a witness and her father as Walter William Harvey, a coal merchant's commercial traveller. The Christian names and occupation matched Walter Neave. Stanley Smith had worked at Hampton's furnishing store when he met Ethel and their children were both born in London, not Australia.

Robert and Nina accepted their late mother had been Ethel Le Neve and were surprised that so many of her family members managed to keep her secret from them for so long. Ethel's father had lived with them for some time (apparently forgiven for selling her story to *Answers* in 1910). It is not certain whether their father knew her secret. Robert said, 'I would say that dad knew', while his sister said, 'I don't think she would have kept dad in the dark about it.'[55]

It seems likely that he did know, for in 1920 and 1928 her story was published in a mass-circulation newspaper containing up-to-date photographs of Ethel. If Stanley hadn't known, surely somebody would have seen them and commented on the likeness of his wife to Ethel Le Neve. Presumably she would have been paid reasonably well for her stories. Had she sold her memoirs purely for financial gain? In 1910 she would have needed the money from *Lloyd's* to start a new life. The first edition of the Notable British Trials volume on Dr Crippen had been published in 1920, which would have returned the case to the fore and made it a logical time to cash in.

Robert and Nina thought she had done the right thing by not telling them.[56] Nina later said in a documentary, 'I'm sure she must have known something about it [the murder].'[57] Robert said 'you could never discuss anything personal with her'. Even on her deathbed she refused to speak to them and kept her lips clenched tight.[58] Nina added, 'I can't honestly believe that she didn't know something. I would find that very very hard to believe.' Robert agreed, 'Yes, she did know something about it although she didn't take part. For that to happen and know nothing about it would be rather hard to accept.'[59]

Goodman had his suspicions about Le Neve. He claimed that a Professor William Wright noticed she had spent several weeks shortly before the murder in the library of the Royal College of Surgeons 'poring over toxicological tomes'. Goodman also noted a book called *A Wingless Angel* by J. E. Muddock, 'just the sort of purple pennyworth that Crippen's lady-love might have borrowed from a lending library'. The book, published in 1875, bore remarkable similarities to the Crippen story. It contains a character called Mrs Belmore, a murder by hyoscine, a murderer who disguises himself as a woman and a failed escape by boat.[60]

Ethel Le Neve always denied any knowledge of Cora Crippen's murder. She stood by Crippen until the end and would never say a negative word against him. From unwillingly being one of the most famous women in the world, she became a virtually anonymous 'cantankerous old lady, sitting there in a smock, and most of the time with her dentures out'.[61] With the passing of Ethel Smith in 1967, the last major player in the great Crippen drama had gone. It would be pure conjecture to guess at her true involvement and the extent of her knowledge. It is an old cliché, but in Le Neve's case an appropriate one. She took her secrets to the grave.[62]

17

PETER AND BELLE

Reading about the Crippen case sometimes makes one feel like setting up a Cora Crippen Defence Society.

Joan Lock, *Scotland Yard Casebook*

Mrs Crippen seemed a very charming woman, but as for him, I did not like the look of him at all.

Anonymous local tradesman, *Holborn and Finsbury Guardian*

A very pertinent observation was made by Michael Gilbert in his 1953 book about Dr Crippen:

By an odd romantic quirk the figure of Dr Crippen seems to become gentler and more sympathetic as the years pass. By contrast, the blowsy figure of Belle Elmore becomes blowsier with the passage of time and she appears as a slut who almost invited herself to a lethal dose of hyoscin. I fear that neither impression bears the bold stamp of truth.[1]

It certainly was not that simple. Broadly speaking, it appears that nearly everyone who knew Cora during her lifetime thought highly of her and held her in great affection. Since her death a great many writers and commentators have denigrated her name and reputation by accepting and embellishing later stereotypes. In the case of Dr Crippen, he was widely liked before his trial. The sympathy and regard for him continued unabated, even after his conviction for murder and execution. His abiding reputation led Tom Cullen to call his influential 1977 study of the case *Crippen: The Mild Murderer*.[2]

Perhaps it was his love for Le Neve and the romantic aspect of the story that evoked sympathy for Dr Crippen. Arthur Newton looked upon his client 'as the greatest lover I have ever met'.[3] One early writer on the case said, 'Sometimes great love goes hand in hand with a horrible and barbarous crime.'[4] The love story of Crippen and Le Neve was an integral part of the case for Inspector Dew, who said that the 'most extraordinary case in my career was that of the notorious Dr Crippen, in which cold, calculated murder and great love and devotion were mingled'.[5]

It is easy to find favourable post-1910 comments about Dr Crippen. One early account of the case neatly pointed out that Crippen 'would seem to have been a man of many minor virtues and of one monstrous crime'.[6]

'Quite apart from the sympathy everyone feels for a man who murders his wife, it was difficult not to admire Crippen for his courage and chivalry'[7] was the view of George Orwell, who made several references to Dr Crippen in his writings. Raymond Chandler, the author of hard-boiled American detective stories, commented in 1948 that 'you can't help liking this guy somehow. He was one murderer who died like a gentleman.'[8]

Ursula Bloom, whose sympathies were clearly on the side of Crippen and Le Neve, went further than most. 'The deeper one went into the life of Belle Elmore, the more disgusted one was with her, and the more sympathetic one became with poor little Dr Crippen who had been foolish enough to marry her.' Bloom may have been correct when she said, 'I never met anyone who did not like him ... everyone said that he was the kindest man alive.'[9]

There were some who were not so convinced of Crippen's virtues, such as assistant hangman William Willis and barrister Cecil Mercer. Barrister and author Helena Normanton considered that 'criminology has its own grim form of monarchy; and if criminals selected Murder Kings as they do Cat Burglar Kings and so on, Dr Crippen would easily rank among the first half-dozen candidates for the throne'. Normanton would compare Crippen to King Henry VIII, describing both of them as victims of 'a hunger for domesticity'. She thought that Crippen's 'elimination of his wife Cora Crippen is an imperishable classic'.[10]

Cora Crippen was very popular too during her lifetime. One newspaper reported, 'Nobody has an ill word to say concerning the dead woman, whom many affectionately remember, and who was often referred to in America as "Handsome Belle Elmore".'[11] She 'was at all times kindness and generosity itself; she was a large-hearted woman' according to Melinda May,[12] while Adelene Harrison remembered Cora as 'vivacious, full of the joy of life, and very kind hearted'.[13]

It is worth considering when this change of opinion about Cora took place. All of Cora's friends and family testified to her likeable character and popular standing among them. Why was it that after her death she became the complete opposite to most writers?

The series of Notable British Trials (NBT) volumes were, and remain, a hugely influential source of information for crime historians. Filson Young, who edited the 1920 Crippen volume, is partly responsible for Cora's posthumous reputation. Young was not particularly complimentary about Cora in his introduction, writing of her 'inordinate vanity ... It is distasteful to speak of Mrs Crippen's relations with other men, but it is obvious that the avenue to her affections was not very narrow or difficult to access.' Cora was noted for 'her vanity, her extravagance, her shrewishness' and her character was a 'loud, aggressive and physical kind that seems to exhaust the atmosphere round it, and is undoubtedly exhausting to live with'. Had Young been influenced by Crippen's lengthy statement to Dew that was reproduced in his book? He certainly repeated some of Crippen's unsupported claims about Cora as fact.

Filson Young's descriptions of Cora caused distress and outrage for some who had known her. When the 1950 reprint of the NBT was released it provoked Cora's sister Louise Mills to write to the publisher from her home in New York to refute Young's comments:

Unless you retract these lies, I shall be obliged to see my lawyer. She [Belle] was not the gay little peacock as you described her – she was a wonderful housekeeper, wife, cook and seamstress, making practically all of her clothes. I lived in Hilldrop Crescent with her for a while. She wanted me to live there permanently, but I did not stay because Crippen always bothered me as soon as his wife was out of sight – he also molested my other sisters when he came over and visited us in Brooklyn. He wasn't the little abused husband – he never, as you claim, cleaned the lodgers' boots, neither did he work in the kitchen – his wife always cooked our breakfast, and his dinner was always served regular.

They did not occupy separate rooms – I know because I occupied the room next to theirs. He was intimate with his typist, Le Neve, for a much longer period than he told. In 1906, five years before he did away with my sister, she told me she was afraid to stay alone with him, he often threatened her, she kept her jewellery in a safety deposit box because she did not trust him. He was a drug addict, and most of the drugs he bought as a doctor were consumed by himself.[14]

Obviously Louise Mills would have been supportive of her late sister and despised Crippen, but there are echoes of other people's views in her letter. Crippen's son Otto hinted that his father was a sexual predator when interviewed by the *Los Angeles Herald*, while the brother of his first wife believed he had threatened Charlotte. The image of a henpecked Dr Crippen cleaning the lodgers' boots is a common one in the literature on the case, but it may have been Cora who had to look after them. Maud Burroughs said 'Mrs Crippen got rid of them because they were too much work'.

Mills was not the only person who refuted later suggestions that Cora was a slatternly housewife. Neighbour Millicent Gillatt of 40 Hilldrop Crescent saw the charlady sweeping the carpet at No. 39, only for Cora to take the broom off her and do it herself.[15] German lodger Karl Reinisch remembered her as 'a good housewife, unlike many other English women. She cooked herself, quite excellently.'[16]

Adelene Harrison contradicted this, saying that Cora 'had a horror of servants or domestic help' that was only equalled by her love of fine clothes and jewellery.[17] She later gave a lengthy 'character study' to the newspaper *John Bull* in December 1910 when she described Cora's housekeeping skills:

> They lived practically in the kitchen, which was always in a state of dirt and disorder. On the dresser was a heterogeneous mass, consisting of dirty crockery, edibles, collars of the Doctor's, false curls of her own, hair-pins, brushes, letters, a gold jewelled purse and other articles. The kitchener and gas stove were brown with rust and cooking stains. The table was littered with packages, saucepans, dirty knives, plates, flat-irons, a washing basin and a coffee pot. Thrown carelessly across a chair was a lovely white chiffon gown, embroidered with silk flowers and mounted over white glace.
>
> But when she received her friends the whole scene changed. The table in one of the reception rooms was elegantly laid with a lace-bordered table cloth, dainty serviettes, gleaming silver and expensive flowers.[18]

Harrison made similar claims to Filson Young for the NBT but she did have some affection for Cora, whom she described as 'a brilliant chattering bird of gorgeous plumage. She seemed to overflow the room with her personality. Her bright, dark eyes were twinkling with the joy of life. Her vivacious rounded face, Slavonic in type, was radiant with smiles.'[19]

The publication of the first edition of the NBT of Crippen had provoked a response from one of Cora's friends. Lottie Albert had known the Crippens for twelve years and succeeded Cora as honorary treasurer of the Music Hall Ladies' Guild. After reading the NBT she wrote to the *Weekly Dispatch*, who had run a story about Crippen the previous week in their regular 'Real Crime and Mystery Stories' feature. 'Little do they who hurled these accusations at Belle Elmore know of the innermost character of that straight and true little woman. Hers was a temperament truly enigmatical. She was a creature of moods, passionately fond of children, possessing a heart of gold.' Lottie never suspected that Dr Crippen would 'turn out to be a fiend in human clothing, and that his pretty, vivacious, and lovable little wife would be done to death by those long, tapering, feminine-looking hands which were always their owner's pride'. Crippen had 'cold and calculating' eyes and at gatherings was an interesting conversationalist, speaking in a voice that never raised 'above the monotone which was habitually his style'. Lottie admitted that Cora had 'her little eccentricities. Who hasn't? But to accuse her of being extravagant and to state that she accepted presents from admirers is to blacken a character that was strictly honourable and upright.'[20]

When Philip Curtin told the story of Crippen in the *Weekly Dispatch* in February 1920, he was also critical of Young's recently published depiction of Cora Crippen:

Mr Filson Young has evidently taken great pains over his striking pen portrait of poor 'Belle Elmore.' But the present writer, who has in the past gone to some pains to find out what this woman was really like, ventures to think that his delineation errs on the hard side.

If Cora Crippen was as selfish, vain, frivolous, and, in little things, meanly natured as Mr Filson Young seems to believe she was, and has described her as being, then it is strange indeed that she made such warm, faithful friends.

The writer has met yet another friend of 'Belle Elmore,' the lady in question being a well-known clergyman's wife, and she, though apparently under no illusion as to certain incidents in her unfortunate friend's career, yet speaks with real affection and real admiration of the woman who met with so awful a fate on the night of January 31, 1910.

According to her account, 'Belle Elmore' was an eager, high-spirited, extraordinarily kind-hearted woman, always ready to do anyone a good turn; devoted to her friends, keenly interested in their affairs, and never speaking in any sense unkindly or even censoriously of the husband with whom she was undoubtedly not on good terms towards the end of their joint life.[21]

But the Notable British Trials study is normally the first volume an author will consult when writing about a famous crime, not a long-forgotten pair of articles in a long-defunct tabloid newspaper. Later authors may have been influenced by Young and their descriptions of Cora became increasingly vicious.

In the same year as the publication of the NBT, Ethel Le Neve had her memoirs serialised in *Thomson's Weekly News*. She repeated Crippen's claims of domestic misery, for which she only had his word:

'But after the company has gone she is quite a different person. Any excuse is good enough to pick a quarrel with me. There is not a night that she does not go to her room in a temper at me.' Everybody in the office was painfully aware that the Doctor was having a bad time, and Belle Elmore did not care a brass farthing how much she showed him up in his own office.[22]

In a later instalment Le Neve wrote that Cora 'at times was a very violent woman. When anything went wrong with her terrible scenes used to take place in the house at Hilldrop Crescent. She would abuse the doctor until the wonder was that he did not take the poison himself.'[23]

Yet despite his trials and tribulations Crippen's chivalrous reputation was enhanced by his concubine for 'at no time did he ever use a phrase or a word that would bring a blush to the cheek of a woman, and he never lost his respect for the sex'.[24]

The celebrated playwright and journalist George R. Sims wrote in 1922 that 'Belle Elmore, disappointed at her own personal failure, had taken to nagging the little doctor, frequently before company'.[25] For Edward Marshall Hall's biographer, Edward Marjoribanks, Cora Crippen 'was at once a peacock and a slut. To the outside world she appeared in all her finery; at home she kept no servant, and her husband seems to have performed what little housework was done.'[26]

There are a couple of sources, written by contemporaries who knew the Crippens, but not published until years later, that demonise Cora. One was by journalist W. Buchanan-Taylor, who wrote a gossipy, name-dropping memoir. He recorded that in 1910 he was asked by his editor to investigate Cora's disappearance as he was acquainted with many of the music hall personalities of the day. Buchanan-Taylor wrote that he met actress Marie Lloyd and her husband Alec Hurley:

> Marie made it quite plain that she didn't like either of the Crippens, and Belle Elmore was particularly in her disfavour. I asked Marie what she thought of 'Dr' Crippen.
>
> 'Blimey, I wouldn't trust him as far as I could throw him with my little finger. When he looks at you through them glaa-ses it makes you think you're going to have an operation,' declared Marie, as she fanned herself characteristically with a little lace-edged handkerchief.
>
> 'Cut that out, Marie,' said Alec, 'you know she's a bitch and you never know what's behind it. She'd make a man do anything.'
>
> 'There you are,' Marie interposed, 'when it's a man that's in trouble you men all stick up for him. All the same, if it came to choosing between 'em I'm not sure I'd pick her. What a cow!'
>
> Marie made many mistakes about men, but she was seldom wrong about women.[27]

Lloyd further confided that 'there was always suspicion among the women who knew them that Crippen, with his supposed knowledge of poisons, was liable to have "done her in"'.[28]

As for Crippen, Buchanan-Taylor thought he was 'one of the quietest, most unassuming chaps I ever knew intimately'. Crippen allegedly enjoyed his tenuous theatrical connections and became a member of the Vaudeville Club, where he played cards in the afternoon. The journalist probed the club's members for 'all the intimate details of Crippen's family life; the stories of Belle Elmore's misdeeds, her confirmed drinking habits, and her continuous abuse, verbal and physical, of Crippen. She was everything but a wife to him. Elmore was such a harlot that even her closest friends would not have regretted her disappearance or missed her companionship.'[29]

This last assertion is blatantly untrue and it must cast doubt on Buchanan-Taylor's other comments. He also claimed that it was 'well known among their most intimate friends that Crippen had on numerous occasions "quietened" Belle Elmore with the aid of sedative drugs. Her outbreaks were violent in the extreme and some of her friends have stated that it was a miracle that she had not killed him in one of her outrageous, drunken tantrums.'[30]

Another description of Cora was published in 1933 by one of Arthur Newton's clerks in a Sunday tabloid. He claimed to have met a theatrical client in a West End pub when his attention was drawn to

> a big, blousy woman, hotly flushed and obviously a shade the worse
> for her glasses of port. There were two or three men at her table and,
> I should judge, she was paying for the drinks.
>
> 'Calls herself Belle Elmore,' said our client, noting my curious gaze
> in the woman's direction. 'Thinks she can dance too. Holy Pete! We've
> got a lot of outside competition on the halls, but we haven't sunk to
> that.'
>
> She led Crippen the devil of a life. They were always quarrelling.
> She was a loud, vulgar woman of slovenly habits, very vain and
> extravagant, and she not only had no regard for his money or their
> home, she began also to treat him with a more and more open
> contempt.[31]

Despite both of these accounts being written by people who claimed to have known Cora in 1910, they more closely reflect post-1910 views and are in stark contrast to what her friends said about her. As the years passed the descriptions of Cora became evermore fearsome and no evidence was given to support them.

In 1934, writer Dorothy L. Sayers reviewed a novel based on the Crippen case called *Henbane* by Catherine Meadows. Sayers thought Crippen had been a nice man who had 'murdered only under overwhelming stress of circumstances' and thought it ironic that his name now had sinister connotations which was purely due to his method of disposing of Cora's body. The Cora character in the novel was 'noisy, over-vitalised, animal, seductive, and intolerable'.[32]

Cora still had loyal friends. Edith Field was one of them and she responded to Sayers' review by describing Cora as 'a delightful woman ... She was a sweet-natured woman, loved by all who came into contact with her. "Belle Elmore," Mrs Hawley Harvey Crippen, leaves behind her a fragrant memory'.[33] Sayers replied, not unreasonably, that 'Miss Meadows' interpretation of the personalities concerned agrees substantially with that offered in the majority of text-books dealing with the Crippen case'.[34]

A reviewer in the same newspaper held a similar view to Sayers when writing about Max Constantine-Quinn's 1935 case study of Dr Crippen, 'whom most intelligent people now believe to have been more sinned against than sinning (there are worse crimes than the murder of the body, and one of them is murder of the soul)'.[35]

By now the damage done to Cora's reputation was almost irreparable and descriptions of her were only too predictable. Horace Thorogood, who claimed to have attended every stage of Crippen's trial, seems to have forgotten everything that was said in the courts by the time he came to write about the case in 1935:

> The home life of this quiet, likeable little man was made wretched by an uncongenial wife who treated him with contempt. She was a worthless creature. She filled his house with people whom he despised and who despised him. Here, if ever, was an excusable crime. The woman had no known relatives and no children. There was no one to mourn her loss. She was out of the way, and not only was no one the worse for it but it made at last possible the happiness of the lovers.[36]

Harold Dearden wrote in 1948 of Cora that 'she had no room in her tawdry little mind for generosity to the man who had raised her from the gutter. She grew steadily lazier and more masterful and pleasure-loving, and their home life in consequence became a martyrdom for the Doctor.'[37] Captain Kendall, who had never met Cora, wrote in his memoirs that she was 'a flashy, faithless shrew, loud-voiced, vulgar, and florid'.[38]

It seemed that authors were trying to outdo each other when it came to writing nasty things about Cora. In 1954, Leonard Gribble added to the anti-Cora literature:

> This over-weight and overbearing female allowed her intimates to call her Belle, and never for a moment suspected the name could be comic in the circumstances. But then she had no sense of humour.
>
> His loud-mouthed wife, who openly sneered at his lack of the more obvious masculine attributes, was extravagant and utterly without taste. She cultivated friends who pandered to her conceit. She spent money recklessly on entertaining those friends, and on clothes and jewellery to deck her gross body.[39]

Ursula Bloom had a very unfavourable view of Cora Crippen, whom she described as 'a music hall lady with large bust and bottom ... she was hysterical and blowsy; she had affairs with other men; Crippen had rescued her from the streets of New York, where she worked as a prostitute, and she was for ever "kicking up a dust"'.[40]

The 1962 film *Dr Crippen*, starring Donald Pleasence and Coral Browne as Dr Crippen and Cora, perpetuated the myth of henpecked

Hawley and unfaithful Cora, as did Tom Cullen's 1977 book *Crippen: The Mild Murderer*, which was for years the standard text on the case along with the NBT volume.

In recent years opinions seem to favour Cora more and it has been realised that her outrageously tarnished image was far from the truth. Joan Lock jumped to Cora's defence in 1991. 'Reading about the Crippen case sometimes makes one feel like setting up a Cora Crippen Defence Society. For some strange reason, much of the sympathy in this case has gone to the murderer. Some writers appear to believe everything he said about Cora despite the fact that he was shown to have lied so effortlessly about everything else.'[41]

However, Dr Crippen's recent entry in the *Oxford Dictionary of National Biography* seems heavily influenced by the NBT and revives the archaic caricature: 'In reality Belle Elmore was a tipsy, plump and unfaithful shrew with inordinate vanity and a miserly streak.' It added for good measure, and with no supporting evidence, that in December 1906 Crippen found Cora in bed with a lodger.[42]

Just as the characters of the Crippens have provoked different reactions from people who knew them and later authors, their relationship is also open to interpretation. For every person who commented on their arguments there were more who would remark on how devoted the couple were. Lottie Albert said that during the twelve years she had known them, 'I never witnessed any signs of discord'. Something wasn't quite right though and there was 'an air of mystery about both of them. When it came to probing into their pasts one realised that it was forbidden ground.' Albert suspected that Cora was a wronged woman. About a month before Cora's death the pair were discussing men. Albert casually remarked that all the men she knew could be trusted. Cora gave her a look 'half sorrowful, half dubious and said, "Not all of them, Lottie, not all"', which made her friend wonder if she knew about Crippen and Le Neve.[43]

One of their German lodgers, Karl Reinisch, told a German newspaper years later that Crippen was

> extremely quiet, gentlemanly, not only in thought but also in behaviour, not only towards his wife but also to me and everyone else. He idolised his wife, and sensed her every wish which he hastened to fulfil.
>
> In contrast to the extremely placid nature of Dr Crippen, his wife was very high-spirited. Blonde, with a pretty face, of large, full, may I say of opulent figure, very ambitious, in spite of her former artistic

career, of which she often spoke to me a great deal in the presence of her husband.[44]

Adelene Harrison remembered 'they appeared always on the best of terms, she got a bit excited at times, but he was patient'. In a 1910 newspaper interview Harrison said, 'In fact, no one ever knew them to be otherwise than loveable and affectionate to each other. There was no indication that it was for "appearances sake" for he showed his love for her in every action in his life.'[45]

Actress Louise Smythson had been introduced the Crippens at the 1909 Music Hall Ladies' Guild dinner, where 'they seemed very happy, and pleasant to each other'. Melinda May said Cora 'always appeared to be devoted to Dr Crippen'. Clara Martinetti thought Cora seemed 'to get on very well with Dr Crippen', adding that the pair 'seemed always alike'. Her husband Paul 'had no idea he had any ill feelings towards her'. Dr Burroughs said 'they appeared to live very comfortably together. I never heard any quarrels', and his wife Maud agreed they 'appeared very happy together'. They considered Dr Crippen to be 'a model husband, he always seemed anxious to do his wife some little service and show her some attention,' although 'Mrs Crippen was at times somewhat hasty in her manner towards Dr Crippen, but not more so than one ordinarily meets in life. As far as I was able to judge she appeared to be fond of him.'

It was not only friends who thought the Crippens were a devoted couple. Their milkman, Thomas Brown, said 'they always seemed to be as happy as sandboys' when he saw them on his round. Cora, he added, 'was a well-built, handsome woman, and always was very chatty'.[46] Is it possible that the Crippens were able to portray such a united front if Cora was really making her husband's life so unbearably miserable and knowing that he was sleeping with his secretary? Even on the night of the murder, Clara Martinetti described them as being 'on affectionate terms while I was there'.

But there were people who said they quarrelled and Dew was told as much during his early enquiries, and isolated reports of a less than happy domestic life appeared in the 1910 newspapers. Their former servant Rhoda Ray remembered that 'Mr and Mrs Crippen were not altogether friendly to each other, and they spoke very little together'. Another German Lodger, Richard Ehrlich, was interviewed by the *Petit Parisien*:

The Crippens had then been married about six years, and the young man gathered from Mrs Crippen that her sole desire in life was to return to the stage. She admitted that she was bored to death at the routine of housekeeping, and bitterly regretted having abandoned the footlights. She explained that on her marriage the doctor made her promise never to return to the boards.

Ehrlich says that Mrs Crippen delighted to live in an atmosphere of adulation. The doctor was a calm, industrious type of business man. At the house in Hilldrop Crescent they received very few visitors. Mrs Crippen's friends were all theatrical folks, and the husband had no love for these.

'So you can imagine,' says Erlich, 'what were the sentiments of the wife towards her husband. She often lost her temper, and there were frequent bickerings and open quarrels. On the other hand, the doctor never lost his temper, though the wife's reproaches were frequently unjustified. He always answered in a gentle tone, and was never rude to her.'[47]

Cora had trodden the boards after her marriage to Crippen and her friend Lottie Albert stated that Cora had come to terms with her theatrical failings. So what was the truth? As with so many elements of the Crippen case, there are unanswerable contradictions.

Criminologist Nigel Morland offered the following assessment of the Crippens that seems reasonable:

A lot of people are still very sorry for Crippen, and, probably, an equal number are just as sorry for Cora Crippen. He was a nice little man, there is no doubt of it, and I do not think she was by any means a bad woman. Indeed, had Belle Elmore succeeded on the stage she might have gone off to a different life, perhaps a happier ending. Alternatively, had Crippen's chemical reactions been uninfluenced by Ethel Le Neve, he, too, might have gone on as he had always been.[48]

Morland also suggested that had Charlotte Crippen not died young, Dr Crippen 'would have been a decent and law-abiding citizen for the rest of his days'.[49]

With all the contradictions, Cecil Mercer's blunt assessment of the pair may be as close to the truth as it is possible to know:

I can honestly say that more rubbish has been written and published about the Crippen Case than ever has been written and published about any case in the world. Attempts have actually been made to palliate the crime. What is the truth? It was the sordid and barbarous murder by her husband of the Honorary Secretary (or Treasurer) of the Ladies' Music Hall Guild, to whom her many women-friends were deeply attached. Crippen had fallen for his typist: but, because a man falls for his typist he doesn't have to murder his wife. I have read that Mrs. Crippen led him a dog's life. Of that, there is not a tittle of evidence. She certainly had her interests, and he had his. What was their private relation, nobody ever knew.[50]

While Cora Crippen was a more brash and flamboyant character than her husband, she was, during her lifetime, generally perceived as a generous, friendly and vivacious woman who certainly did not deserve the posthumous reputation that she has been burdened with for nearly a century.

There is no denying that there were several positive aspects to Crippen's character. He was exceptionally courteous and thoughtful and his love for Ethel Le Neve cannot be doubted (though he also appeared to have been devoted to Cora before and since he met his mistress). Filson Young dryly observed that Crippen was 'always considerate – even in the weapon he used to kill his wife',[51] assuming that it had been the hyoscine that killed her, not a bullet, and that Crippen's real reason for using that drug was not because he hoped it would be difficult to detect.

In an interview with the *Daily Express*, Walter Dew said, 'Compared with Jack the Ripper, Crippen was an angel!'[52] But that was a very backhanded compliment. Even if he was likeable, Crippen was a faithless husband, seller of fraudulent medical cures, perjurer and murderer who lived quite happily with his mistress at 39 Hilldrop Crescent for months, knowing that the dismembered remains of his unfortunate wife lay buried in the cellar beneath their feet. His place in Madame Tussaud's Chamber of Horrors was hard earned and richly deserved.

18

THE INNOCENCE OF DR CRIPPEN: AN OLD MYTH RESURRECTED

...the Crippen case has been responsible for more weird and often nonsensical opinions than one would suspect.

Nigel Morland, *Hangman's Clutch*

After I am gone, thoughtful people will probably admit that the evidence was far too slender to send me to the scaffold.

Dr Crippen to Ethel Le Neve, *Thomson's Weekly News*

Ever since the discovery of human remains in the cellar of 39 Hilldrop Crescent, there have been some people who believed that Dr Crippen was innocent of murdering Cora Crippen. In recent years the case for Crippen's innocence has been revived with promises of new evidence. So what is the likelihood that Dr Crippen was wrongly hanged?

As early as August 1910, the *San Francisco Chronicle* asked, 'Is the Belle Elmore murder a fake for theatrical advertising purposes?' While dining with friends Inspector Dew allegedly hinted that the murder might have been a hoax. After all, he said, the remains at that date had not even been proved to be human and if Cora reappeared she could name her price for vaudeville and music hall appearances.[1] Since Dew never spoke publicly about the case until he gave evidence in court this story can easily be dismissed. It was reminiscent of the 'wild story' published in *The Times* the same day that Dew's wife Kate had a similar theory.[2]

Another American newspaper, the *New York Times*, also raised doubts over the remains that were merely 'a corrupt mass of mortality, indistinguishable by feature or by sex'. True, there was circumstantial evidence of Crippen's guilt, but 'conceivably the body is that of some other person or of an animal, placed there by someone else than Crippen'.[3] They failed to say who that other person might have been and how they could have concealed the remains. The previous day the same paper had made the peculiar suggestion that the remains could have been 'a person whom he had inadvertently killed in the course of his practice. It might be merely a body which Crippen, in the desire to perfect himself in his studies, had procured for the purpose of dissection'.[4]

In November 1910 a Reuters news agency story appeared in a number of newspapers, stating that a woman answering Cora Crippen's description was being watched by Canadian police. She fainted when overhearing a remark that Crippen would hang and swooned again in a shop after reading an account of his trial. Coincidentally, Ethel Le Neve encountered a Cora double while living in Montreal. The woman was 'Belle Elmore come to life again' but 'she spoke in French, with the accent of a Canadian Frenchwoman. The resemblance was striking, but the eyes were not the same.'[5]

A cutting of the Reuters report was sent to Winston Churchill, along with a letter published in *The Standard* on 12 November. It read,

> It is difficult to understand why he should have left so much incriminating material within easy reach of detectives (and for so many months), whilst being at the enormous trouble, as is assumed, of disposing of the rest elsewhere. As to the head, all the bones and a large proportion of the flesh, there is no evidence whatever. Let us hope they still form part of a living body to be yet forthcoming. It will then be clear that the so-called 'remains' were placed beneath the cellar floor, not for concealment, but to be found. I consider this by far the most reasonable inference from the evidence at our disposal, especially when it is stated that the stomach, though unwounded, was empty, notwithstanding the sumptuous repast that preceded the supposed murder.

Several letters survive in the Home Office files on the case that argue Crippen's innocence. One theorised that

> some rival or enemy of Crippen had wished, on the disappearance of Crippen's wife, and having Crippen's account, to form ground for a suspicion, it would have been material in finding 'human remains' as the groundwork of a plot ... The 'remains found' might with ease have been selected and removed from a newly buried body, exhumed for the purpose.

A correspondent signing himself 'X' asked, 'Has not Dr Crippen been the <u>victim</u> of a plot? The <u>unidentifiable</u> character of the remains found in the cellar points – if this feature of the remains affords any <u>points</u> – to a <u>plot</u>.'

Another story appeared in the *New York Times* in which lawyer Francis Tobin claimed to have evidence Cora was alive in America, but nothing came of this.[6] Back in England, the *News of the World* made mysterious hints in January 1911 that new evidence 'of a scientific character would soon be announced that would throw a new light on the Crippen case.[7] There was no follow-up to this tantalising rumour.

In 1926 a popular weekly tabloid, the *World's Pictorial News*, published a far-fetched story told by a former convict who had been recently released from Pentonville Prison. He remembered a Syrian vine that had mysteriously embedded its roots in Crippen's grave. When three years had passed 'the officials were amazed to see fruit growing upon the vine, and it was argued among the prisoners that this was a token of Crippen's innocence'. However, when the vine failed to bear fruit years later it was seen as a sign that Frederick Bywaters, who had been executed three years previously, was innocent.[8]

The next example of evidence of Crippen's innocence was almost as feeble. In 1943 Walter Dew received a letter from Colin Bennett of Devon suggesting that 'while Crippen did unquestionably cut up and bury his wife's body he did not kill her'. He made a vague suggestion that an assistant might have stolen poison from Crippen's office and committed the deed. Bennett claimed to have been in the crowd that gathered outside Madame Tussaud's waxworks when it burned down in 1925. When they heard Crippen's effigy had been saved 'a lusty cheer went up. The subconscious mind often knows more than the conscious mind.' After presenting his case, Bennett asked Dew, 'Are you still as sure as ever that in Crippen you hanged a murderer?' Dew was unimpressed and tersely replied 'my conscience is quite at rest as [to] the result of the case'.[9]

Moving on to the twenty-first century, and in 2004 Channel 4 broadcast *The Last Secret of Dr Crippen*. It promised that 'new evidence makes it clear that the most infamous murderer Hawley Harvey Crippen should never have hanged' and suggested that Crippen was hastily condemned under pressure from the Director of Public Prosecutions and the media.

The programme claimed it was significant that Lord Chief Justice Alverstone had been the judge at Crippen's trial, having been hand picked by the Director of Public Prosecutions, who was worried about the outcome. This was 'against regular practice' and he 'virtually directed the jury to convict' Crippen. Alverstone was still an assize circuit judge and presided over many cases. Cecil Mercer did recall that Alverstone was not initially scheduled to appear, but he insisted, allegedly saying, 'This man deserves to hang, and I'm not going to see him get off on a point of law.' However, Mercer added that 'I never remember a case more beautifully tried.'[10]

Claims that the outcome of the trial was ever in doubt were scoffed at by those involved. Such stories had been around for years. Mercer called them 'utter rubbish', peddled 'by men who knew no more of that case than did the butlers of Mayfair'.[11]

They then moved on to Cora's alleged lover Bruce Miller. Believing the lone word of Dr Crippen, who had only said they were fond of each other, it was stated that Cora was definitely having an affair with Miller and was also sleeping with her German lodgers. The programme makers thought it suspicious that Miller and Cora's sister Theresa Hunn had been paid expenses to travel from America to give evidence at the Old Bailey. And why were Pinkerton's detective agency, not the American police, used to track Bruce Miller down? Scotland Yard collaborating with Pinkerton's was nothing new and the answer is in the Crippen files held at the National Archives, which clearly state,

> The Director of Public Prosecutions considered it important that Bruce Miller should be found, and communications were made to the American Police asking them to make enquiries.
>
> No very satisfactory result came of this, and so the Director decided to instruct Messrs Pinkerton's to make enquiries, and requested us [the Metropolitan Police] to communicate with them in respect of Bruce Miller, and also to see the deceased woman's friends to ascertain what they knew of an operation performed upon her which would leave a scar on the lower part of her abdomen, and also make enquiries at hospitals etc to ascertain if any operation had been performed on her.

Bruce Miller was obviously a vital witness for the trial as Dr Crippen had said Cora had run off to be with him. The American police could only find one Bruce Miller in Chicago, who knew nothing about Crippen, so Pinkerton's were engaged and they succeeded in finding Miller. Knowing the potential importance of the scar on the remains, the Director of Public Prosecutions wanted to investigate the matter fully.

Miller was not, as the programme said, 'paid richly' for denying that he had been Cora's lover and that she had run away to live with him. They said Miller had been paid 'a staggering $450 to give his evidence'. If Miller had been making $10,000 a year and expecting a $25,000 commission on a deal, as he told Pinkerton's, then $450 was hardly a great inducement to cross the Atlantic and have his private life laid bare at the Old Bailey. He did not have to come to England to give evidence. In doing so he lost earnings and accepted less money than the Director of Public Prosecutions' original offer of $25 a day for a minimum of thirty days, plus $5 a day while in England.

Theresa Hunn and Cora's stepfather, Frederick Mersinger, were also tracked down by Pinkerton's. They agreed to testify at the Old Bailey that Cora had an operation scar. All they asked for was that 'their travelling expenses and subsistence are paid, and receive compensation for their loss of time'. Mersinger would have had to sell his horses as there would be no one to look after them and purchase new ones upon his return. He asked for some compensation for this but was not called as a witness. Theresa Hunn received just $100 for her troubles.

Nor was there anything mysterious about Miller returning home after the first day of the trial. The documentary had it that 'Miller was skilfully whisked out of the court and returned to America on the first day of the trial'. Day one of the trial was taken up by prosecution witnesses. Miller had given his evidence, Tobin was asked if he had any objection to Miller going and he had none. There was no reason for him to stay any longer.

Inspector Dew's evidence at the trial was called into question, especially the pyjama top he had found among remains. The programme declared, 'It's questionable whether the pyjamas were indeed found in the cellar, and whether Dew had discovered them the way he told the court.' Why was it questionable? No evidence was presented to support this assertion. Sergeant Mitchell had been with Dew when the remains and pyjamas were discovered. Does this make him part of a conspiracy?

The inference was obvious. It suggested the police had planted evidence to help convict Crippen. But Dew hadn't even bothered establishing the fact that the pyjama top was manufactured after the Crippens had moved into Hilldrop Crescent. Richard Muir and Travers Humphreys had to chivvy Sergeant Mitchell into finding out the pyjamas were first delivered to Jones Brothers' shop on 7 December 1908. Mitchell only found this out one day before the Old Bailey trial started. Cecil Mercer and Samuel Oddie both thought Crippen had used the pyjama top to transport slippery remains,[12] which is a far more prosaic explanation as to how they ended up in the cellar. If Dew had planted the pyjama top it would have been in July 1910 and it would still have looked fresh, unlike the putrid state it was found in.

The 'new evidence' offered by the documentary was a letter in the Home Office's Crippen records held at the National Archives, which have been open to the public for decades. The reason nobody had mentioned it before is because it was a hoax and has no bearing on the case. Allegedly from Cora Crippen, it read,

Chicago, Ill.
Oct 22 – 1910.

Dr Hawley Harvey Crippen.

Brixton Prison
London
England

Doctor:-
As I saw your conviction
coupled with the death
penalty, I come from
seclusion long enough
to try and save your
worthless life at least; as
I don't want to be responsible
for your demise, if I can
save you in this way,
but I will never come
forward personally, as
I am happy now.
I informed the judge;
now save yourself.

Belle Elmore Crippen

The Chicago letter was sent to the Home Office by the governor of Pentonville Prison (it had been wrongly addressed to Brixton Prison). A Home Office official wrote on the file cover that 'this is certainly a hoax but to be on the safe side it should be compared with the late Cora Crippen's writing of which no doubt the Police have specimens'. Indeed they did, and after examining the letter they soon replied, 'The handwriting is <u>not</u> that of Mrs Crippen, alias Belle Elmore.'

Julian Duffus, described in the programme as a historian, believed the letter was authentic. In a later interview for a student film maker he stated 'this letter at the time was suppressed'. He added that he had compared the writing of the Chicago letter with samples of Cora's handwriting 'and of course it [the Chicago letter] was legitimate'.[13] There is a sample of Cora's very distinctive handwriting in the National Archives in the form of a letter she wrote to a former German lodger in 1906.[14] It is in a different hand to that which wrote the Chicago letter (see picture section). 'I can only assume charitably that people imagined it to be a hoax,' added Duffus.[15] But the letter had been carefully examined at the time by the Home Office and Scotland Yard and quickly discovered to be a hoax.

Another letter, supposedly from Cora, was mentioned in the programme. A tiny extract was shown of a document in the Prison Commission papers held at the National Archives. It was a note from the governor of Brixton Prison to the Home Office about a letter he had received and forwarded to them on 19 September 'purporting to come from Mrs Crippen'. He wrote again on 22 October, the day Crippen was sentenced to death, reminding them of it as he had received no acknowledgement. The programme alleged that the letter was sent to the Home Office, who informed the governor of Brixton Prison that it had been forwarded to Winston Churchill who put it into his pocket and forgot about it. Thus Dr Crippen's defence team was deprived of two important pieces of evidence that Cora was alive. What the document actually said was that the 'letter was sent on to the Secretary of State as soon as it was received'.

Clearly this is not evidence that Churchill ignored the letter. It does not appear to have survived, which makes it impossible to know whether it needed to be taken seriously, or was just another hoax. It is extremely unlikely that Churchill would have forgotten or ignored any genuine evidence pointing to Crippen's innocence. Furthermore, there is documentary proof that when a prison governor sent a supposed letter from Cora to the Home Office they examined it before forwarding it to Scotland Yard to double-check it.

It is a mystery why the programme makers should have presented the Chicago letter as evidence of Cora being alive when it is described as a hoax in the file that contained it. There are several other hoax Cora letters in the Home Office records, no doubt written in response to Munyon's offer of a reward for proving Dr Crippen had not killed his wife. An obvious way of doing this was to prove Cora was still alive.

The programme pointed out that Cora had tried to empty her bank account before her disappearance. This was true. She had written to the Charing Cross Bank on 15 December 1909 requesting that an account containing £600 be closed. However, the terms of the account meant that one year's notice of closure had to be given, meaning she could not have obtained the money until 15 December 1910. Cora had access to the more readily available and considerable funds in her Post Office savings account but does not seem to have used it. As Le Neve demonstrated, this money could be quickly withdrawn.

John Trestrail, an American forensic toxicologist, is a leading advocate of Crippen's innocence. He was bemused that hyoscine had been used as a poison as it had never been used before for murder and Crippen would have had access to more effective poisons. However, there was no denying Crippen had bought large quantity of hyoscine before Cora disappeared that he could not account for and the remains in the cellar contained it.

Other 'evidence' was given of Crippen's innocence: the scar on the remains was not really a scar, but this was used by Crippen's defence team in 1910 and not believed either at the Old Bailey or the Court of Appeal.

The 2004 documentary offered no genuine evidence whatsoever of Dr Crippen's innocence and was about as convincing as the story of the Syrian vine from the *World's Pictorial News*. It attracted little attention in comparison to what was to follow.

19

THE DNA DILEMMA

Public opinion as to the guilt of Dr Crippen was not by any means
unanimous.

Ethel Le Neve, *Thomson's Weekly News*

One swallow does not make a summer, nor yet, presumably, does one
Hinde's curler make an absent lady.

Harold Dearden, *Death Under the Microscope*

In 2007, newspapers worldwide ran a story about Dr Crippen having
been proved innocent by new DNA evidence. The following year
John Trestrail made a more elaborate case for Crippen's innocence
in the Channel 5 documentary *Revealed: Was Crippen Innocent?*
Announcing that 'no one has seriously questioned Crippen's guilt ...
until now', it left viewers wondering if the 2004 documentary had
been serious, and indeed there had been several questions about his
guilt since 1910.

'Previously confidential documents' were consulted, but they were
just the files on the Crippen case held at the National Archives that
had been open to the public since 1985. They had at one time been
confidential and subject to a closure period, but so had every other
official file concerning murder. Trestrail had 'been given access to
the original Crippen case files ... confidential until recently'. Calling
the twenty-three-year-old declassification recent was a stretch of the
imagination. Furthermore, anybody who visits the National Archives
can get access to the files, but these grandiose claims can probably be
dismissed as hyperbolic television publicity.

Incidentally, between 2005 and 2007, four new books on the
Crippen case had been published.[1] In each instance the authors
had carefully been through all of these so-called confidential files

at the National Archives and many more sources besides and their conclusions were identical. Crippen was guilty. There is nothing in the files to suggest he was innocent, therefore it is necessary to examine the modern arguments for Crippen's innocence.

The programme cited a Metropolitan Police telegram dated 12 July 1910 from Inspector Thomas Davis:

> Re A. S. message this morning asking for Special Enquiry to trace a carman who collected boxes from No. 39 Hilldrop Crescent, Camden Town and telegram sent to you at 2.45 to-day, Sergt. Yard has since accompanied the carman, John Mc'Crindle, to Hilldrop Crescent, and he is now sure that it is No. 39 he went to. He says that about five months ago, he thinks, he collected five boxes from that address and delivered them in the forenoon at the ground floor at No 10, Nottingham Terrace, Marylebone Road. to a woman age 35 to 40, 5ft 7 or 8, dark, appearance of a prostitute,. She complained to the carman, as to the length of time he took to collect the boxes. The exact date cannot be given until Mc Crindle's employer returns on Thursday next.

This was just one of several documents concerning McCrindle, but it was the only one quoted, albeit incompletely. It had been written in response to a telegram sent earlier that day by Melville Macnaghten, that was not mentioned, requesting 'Careful and Special enquiry to be made by experienced C. I. D. officers at Passenger & Goods Stations, Railway & other carriers, Carmen, Greengrocers, etc, to ascertain if they have collected boxes or other luggage from 39 Hilldrop Crescent on or since the 31st of January last'. Macnaghten's missive appears to show how diligently the police were searching for Cora Crippen before her remains were discovered.

The telegram sent by Davis on 12 July was presented in isolation as proof that Cora Crippen had cleared her possessions from Hilldrop Crescent shortly before her disappearance and it was suggested that the police ignored an important piece of evidence. Barrister Andrew Rose commented 'the police in effect suppressed that piece of evidence because it didn't support their interpretation of the facts'.

Far from being suppressed, McCrindle's story was fully investigated when McCrindle's employer Mr Frost returned, and it proved to be a false lead. In the same file, dated 20 July, was the sequel that demolished McCrindle's tale and the suggestion that the police had suppressed evidence:

According to the carman McCrindle, he moved 6 trunks from 39 Hilldrop Crescent on the 15th of January last.

McCrindle describes the woman he met at Hilldrop Crescent, as being about 34 or 35 years of age complexion fresh, thin build, appearance of a prostitute.

She requested him to take the 6 trunks to Paddington station, where she said she would be met by another woman who would take charge of them, but if she was not there, he was to take them to 10 Nottingham Terrace, Marylebone Road.

McCrindle says he visited the Railway Station, for about twenty minutes, and as no one turned up to take possession of the trunks, he then took them to 10 Nottingham Terrace, where he found the same woman, that he saw at Hilldrop Crescent. She was waiting and took the trunks into the house, which at the time was unoccupied, paid the account and signed her names in the attached counterfoil from the carman's book.

I have also made enquiry at No. 5 Nottingham Terrace, Marylebone Road, and was informed by Miss Hamilton that in January last she had the letting of No. 10 Nottingham Terrace, and that she was quite sure no one could have taken trunks into the house as described by the carman, because the keys were never out of her possession for more than a few minutes at a time, and she generally when anyone was viewing the house, waited on the steps for the keys to be returned.

I beg to suggest that if there is any truth in McCrindle's statement it can have no bearing on the murder, as the murdered woman was seen alive at least a fortnight after he moved the trunks.

None of this was mentioned, and the woman at Hilldrop Crescent was described as thin, which would rule out Cora. Furthermore, Cora's friend Maud Burroughs described Cora as being 'not very tall' and estimated her height at 5 foot 4 or 5 inches, shorter than the woman described. Despite these discrepancies John Trestrail described the woman allegedly seen by McCrindle as being of Cora's stature. The 2004 documentary had also stated as fact that Cora had hired a removal company to remove the crates. If she had, why were all her clothes and jewellery left behind? Dew said there were enough women's clothes at 39 Hilldrop Crescent to fill a large van and 'enough ostrich feathers to stock a milliner's shop'.[2] A possible explanation for McCrindle's story was that the police had circulated a notice to all cab ranks, shelters and other places used by cabmen that offered a £1 reward to any cab driver who came forward that had removed luggage from 39 Hilldrop Crescent.

Trestrail was still puzzled by the dismemberment of the corpse as 'it is so unusual that a poisoner should dismember the victim, because a poisoner attempts to get away with murder without leaving any trace. In my database of 1,100 poisoning cases, this is the only one which involves dismemberment.'[3] While it was improbable, it was not impossible, and if it is looked upon as a murderer dismembering his victim to dispose of the body then there are many examples. Trestrail thought a poisoner would have tried to obtain a 'natural causes' death certificate. However, Crippen is remembered for his many mistakes, and if Cora had died and not been dismembered there probably would still have been a coroner's inquest to establish why a woman in the prime of life and known to enjoy good health had suddenly died. That could lead to a post-mortem which might have revealed hyoscine.

Besides, there were other poisoners who dismembered their victims. Crime historian Robin Odell noted the cases of mass murderer Dr Marcel Petiot who injected his victims with poison before dismembering and incinerating them in the 1940s and that of Dr Herman Schmitz who poisoned his lover with cyanide before mutilating her body in 1920s Vienna.[4]

Why wouldn't Dr Crippen dismember the corpse? He had the skill to do it and had to get rid of the body somehow, especially if Samuel Oddie's hypothesis was correct and there were gunshot wounds. Cora's corpse would have been too substantial to get rid of in one piece, so it had to be dismembered. The only real mystery is why he left some behind and this can only be speculated about. Cecil Mercer thought Crippen lost his nerve. Perhaps, having removed all the bones, he believed that the lime would have destroyed the remaining soft tissue. Trestrail's assertion that Crippen had 'disposed of 99% of her body' was a disingenuous exaggeration.

Trestrail raised the interesting issue of Dr Crippen's dog, who would surely have noticed the smell of a cadaver. This theory suggests that the remains were not in the house during Crippen's residence there and thus planted by the police after Crippen had fled. Clara Martinetti remembered that, at the last supper on 31 January, Cora 'had a funny little Bull terrier and she tried to show us how funny he was, but complained he was not clean being only a puppy, but she said she liked him and made a fuss of him'. Le Neve said that in early February 1910 Crippen owned a bull terrier 'of which he was very fond'.[5] She also claimed to have fed the dog one day.[6] Of course a dog would be infinitely more sensitive to smells, but other than these fleeting mentions, there do not appear to be any other references to the dog.

Cora had two cats, a white Persian and an ordinary black cat. Crippen told Melinda May that the Persian had disappeared a few days before Cora had 'gone to America'. May later suggested that Crippen had done away with the felines as well.[7] Millicent Gillatt remembered that she had once kept fowls in the garden and also kept birds.[8] Seven canaries were given to William Long, which accounts for the birds. Another neighbour spoke of a covered fresh-water aquarium in the back garden that Cora tended to.[9] If Crippen did have a dog that he was so fond of, what became of it? Like Dr Watson's bull pup, mentioned in the first Sherlock Holmes story, it was never heard of again.

There is some contention over whether there was a smell in the house. The remains were buried under soil and bricks. At the request of Dr Pepper, Dew had measured the distance between the top of the remains to the surface of the floor as 8 inches, so they were substantially covered. Dew and Mitchell didn't notice any smell when they visited the house. It was only when the remains were uncovered that the stench became obvious. Dr Pepper suggested the lime had acted as a disinfectant that absorbed any gasses given off by the decomposing body.

Emily Jackson visited 39 Hilldrop Crescent in February 1910 and 'noticed a very strange smell all over the house, particularly downstairs, and I spoke to Ethel about it, she said "Yes" the place is very damp, and in a filthy condition'. Jackson described the smell as 'a damp frowsy one, and might have resulted from the damp and dirt. It was a stuffy sort of smell.' There had been a leaking pipe and the dining room wallpaper was damp. Adelene Harrison thought the basement smelled 'earthy and unpleasant' but she attributed this to a lack of ventilation.[10] Le Neve told Ursula Bloom that there had been a nasty smell in the house when Cora lived there, and the police never investigated the previous tenants.[11]

By now Trestrail did not believe the remains could be those of Cora Crippen and wanted a DNA test carried out. Besides Cora's remains buried at St Pancras Cemetery, there were two other options for obtaining a DNA sample. The first was the hair discovered with the remains in the cellar, which is now on display at Scotland Yard's Crime Museum (popularly known as the Black Museum). According to one newspaper, Scotland Yard agreed to test two strands of the hair for £17,500.[12] However, the DNA testing was to be done in America at Michigan State University and 'owing to concerns about transport via commercial carriers and chain of custody, a hair was not offered for testing'.[13]

The alternative was one of the microscope slides of tissue from the remains that are held at the archives of the Royal London Hospital. But what were the chances that the tissue had not been contaminated in the time between its discovery and being encapsulated in the slide used for the twenty-first-century DNA test? The 2004 programme had expressed concerns that the police had 'contaminated the murder scene and cast doubt over the validity of the forensics'. This appears to have been a reference to the fact that on 13 July Inspector Dew had told PC Charles Pitts to buy a bottle of disinfectant fluid, which he diluted with water and poured on the soil around the remains. Pitts reported that 'some might have gone on to the remains'.

Unlike today, keeping the remains pristine was not the primary concern of the police at the time, who did not know of the existence of DNA. Their priority was to find Dr Crippen as quickly as possible. As Melville Macnaghten colourfully put it, 'we had to catch our hare before we need bother our heads about the subsequent culinary operations'.[14]

Dr David Foran, who conducted the DNA tests, was sure the sample from the slide would not be contaminated by being touched by a pathologist creating the slide in 1910. But who else had come into contact with the remains and how had they been handled since the moment of discovery? Fortunately the case files are detailed enough to answer this question.

13 July 1910

Dew digs up the cellar floor 'with a spade and other things'. Once he and Mitchell had uncovered part of the remains, they sent for help from the nearest police station and called for Dr Marshall and Macnaghten. PCs Daniel Gooch and Frederick Martin arrive and complete the excavations, which were done between 4 p.m. and 11 p.m. PC Martin deposed that 'in scraping the clay off the top of the remains we also scraped off some of the bits of flesh'. Macnaghten recalled that two police constables used pickaxes to excavate the cellar.

Dr Marshall arrives, stays and hour and returns at 9.15 p.m., by which time most of the remains were visible. He 'touched the remains slightly then'. PC Pitts sloshes disinfectant around the cellar. Macnaghten and Froest were also present in the house that day along with coroner's officer PC Robert Thompson.

14 July 1910

Drs Marshall and Pepper inspect the house with Dew and 'other members of the Police'. The doctors 'spent some considerable time in making what examination was possible'. PC Thompson asks local undertaker Albert Leverton to bring two large shells (coarse coffin-like boxes used to transport corpses) to 39 Hilldrop Crescent. Leverton returns with one shell and one large coffin. There is no indication whether they were new or had been used for conveying corpses before. The remains were placed in the large coffin by PCs Gooch and Martin. Leverton was 'unable to see if the remains were put in coffin by hands being used or a spade'. Gooch explained, 'I used my hands for the purpose of removing them. Police Constable Martin was with me, and helped to remove them. He used his hands.'

Pepper asked that the uppermost portions of the remains be placed at the bottom of the coffin 'so that on taking the remains out of the coffin one could reconstruct the heap if thought necessary'.

The coffin was taken outside and the remains were again examined by Pepper and another man (no doubt Marshall). Dew asked Leverton to screw down the coffin and take it to the mortuary in Holloway Road. Leverton loaded the coffin onto his undertaker's van and 'I also took some remains on a tray'. These were the hair, a curler, coarse string, paper, cloth and a piece of buttock and thigh.

Mortuary keeper Arthur Robinson received the coffin and placed it on two trestles. The coffin was unscrewed and the remains taken to the post-mortem room for Pepper and Marshall to examine. Afterwards Robinson put them back in the coffin.

15 July 1910

The remains were removed from the coffin and a post-mortem examination was carried out at the mortuary by Dr Pepper and Dr Marshall. Sergeant Mitchell and Arthur Robinson were also present along with Inspector Dew, who would never forget the many hours he spent with Dr Pepper and Dr Marshall 'examining again and again every portion of those terrible remains'.[16] Pepper finds the skin with the scar on it 'which attracted my attention, and I afterwards examined it with particularity. I spent several hours examining it.' Some internal organs, hair and clothing were placed in five glass jars. The jars were sealed with stoppers, tied with white tape and kept on a mortuary slab until 22 July.

18 July 1910

The coroner and his jury view the remains. Several newspapers say this took place at the coroner's court, where the remains were behind glass. Afterwards, or possibly on the next day, Arthur Robinson, on his own initiative, sprinkles carbolic powder on the remains 'to prevent smell arising'.

18–22 July 1910

Three other post-mortems are carried out at the mortuary by five different doctors. The jars remained in the same room during these visits. It is not known if the post-mortems were carried out on the bodies of men or women, how many slabs there were at the mortuary, or what method was used to clean the slabs between post-mortems. Dr Pepper thought that 'it would have been better for the jars not to remain in a room where post-mortems were carried on,' but 'it would certainly not be possible for the remains, secured as these were, to become impregnated from germs from their being kept in a room where post-mortems were carried on'.

22 July 1910

PC Thompson takes the five jars to St Mary's Hospital and gives them to Dr Willcox.

25 July 1910

Dr Marshall makes a further examination of the remains left at the mortuary, lasting between two and three hours. He finds another curler with hair on it which he places in a jar along with some of the liver and intestines and takes it to St Mary's Hospital.

8 August 1910

Drs Pepper and Marshall examine the piece of skin with a scar on it at the mortuary. Pepper hands the skin to Dr Willcox who preserves it 'by a special process to prevent putrification' (the Kaiserling process using formalin, water, potassium nitrate and potassium acetate). By September it 'had the exact appearance that it had on delivery and is preserved in a solution of glycerine'. Between 8

August and 15 September Willcox examined the skin four or five times.

Arthur Newton is granted permission by the Home Office to view the remains along with an analyst and a pathologist working on behalf of the defence.[17]

14 August 1910

Dr Marshall makes yet another examination of the remains at the mortuary. He finds another curler, which he puts in a jar, adding the lungs, some more intestines 'and one or two other matters'. Marshall gives the jar to Dr Willcox at St Mary's Hospital.

9 September 1910

The piece of skin bearing the scar was shown by Dr Pepper to Dr Marshall, Dr Willcox, Dr Wall and Dr Turnbull, who 'made a complete examination of the remains'. After their examination, which lasted for three hours, Dr Pepper cut off a piece of the scar, leaving a piece of skin on either side. This he handed to Dr Willcox. Dr Spilsbury then examined the skin for the first time, firstly with his naked eye, before preparing a section for a slide and looking at it under a microscope. This was the tissue that was sealed on the microscope slide.

So numerous men had repeatedly and extensively handled the remains over a period of nearly two months. They had been excavated with dirty shovels, placed by hand into a coffin, which may have been used before, and examined on mortuary slabs which were being used for other post-mortems. There is no evidence that the police officers, doctors or mortuary attendant wore gloves or masks when handling them. Spilsbury later wrote that Dr Pepper 'occasionally stroked his moustache during an operation'.[18]

An illustration of the care taken over medical evidence in 1910 is demonstrated by Cecil Mercer's recollection of Crippen's trial, where 'the slab of flesh upon which the scar appeared, was exhibited in court. It was lying in a large meat dish – the kind of dish in which sirloins used to be served – soused in spirits of wine or some preservative. It was presented to counsel, and I inspected it.'[19] The flesh had arrived in court in a glass jar. Dr Willcox sent out for the dish and forceps. Dr Pepper removed the flesh from the jar and put it in the dish. Oddie remembered it was 'preserved in formalin, was handed about in Court on a dish and was carefully inspected by the Jury. Finally it was taken into an adjoining empty Court where a series of microscopical slides prepared by Spilsbury from the supposed scar were set out and peered at through microscopes by the Jurymen.'[20] Presumably these were the same slides that ended up in the hospital's archives.

Today such repeated handling of a piece of evidence would make the result of any DNA test inadmissible as evidence. However, there could be no question about Dr Foran's exacting standards when examining the slide. He used 'full personal protective equipment, and supplies were autoclaved, filter-sterilized, and UV-irradiated'. The cover slip of the slide was sealed tight and stuck fast so it was necessary to chip open the glass cover with a sterile scalpel to expose the tissue. Foran managed to extract enough tissue to create a mitochondrial DNA (mtDNA) reading.[21]

Living descendants of Cora Crippen had to be located to compare their DNA with the mtDNA from the slide. Cora had no children, thus no direct lineal descendants. As mtDNA passes down through the female line, it was necessary to find an unbroken chain of female descendants from one of Cora's sisters or half-sisters.

Genealogical research was undertaken by Beth Wills at the behest of John Trestrail. Wills confessed, 'I am a hobby genealogist that has taken a few courses in Family History Research.' Initially she only presented 'a synopsis of my research journey' rather than a full pedigree of Cora's family and descendants with the exact sources she obtained the information from. 'I feel that if anyone needs more information, or doubts the results of my research that they are certainly fee [*sic*] to do any research that they want on their own dime,' she said.[22]

When Foran and Wills published their research in 2010 the scanty genealogical information sat incongruously alongside the detailed scientific explanations. Names of Cora's relatives were restricted to one letter, images of genealogical documents had names blacked out and descriptions of sources consulted were as vague as 'Baptismal/christening records' and 'Genealogical websites'.[23] Wills was confident she had correctly traced Cora's great niece, from whom a DNA sample was taken. When compared to the mtDNA sample from the slide, Dr Foran announced the samples did not match.

The genealogical findings were brought into question when it was independently discovered that on Cora's marriage certificate her mother's maiden name was given as Mary Wolff, while on her half half-sister Bertha's (from whom it seems descendants were traced) it was Mary Smith.[24] This seemed to explain why the slide's mtDNA excluded the living descendants as being related, as they did not appear to have descended from the same female line.

Wills had calculated Cora's birth date from her marriage licence and census returns. A look through the Crippen case files at the National Archives would have revealed that a birth certificate existed. Cora's sister, Theresa Hunn, gave a statement in which she said, 'She [Cora] was born on the 3 September, 1873. I produce her Birth Certificate.' Cora's birth certificate was later discovered by a poster on an internet message board and it gave Mary Schmidt as her mother, indicating that she had the same mother as Bertha.[25]

If the remains were not Cora's, why were human remains in the cellar of 39 Hilldrop Crescent? No explanation was offered other than Crippen may have worked as an illegal abortionist for extra income and an unknown woman died during a botched operation. Trestrail said that hyoscine was used in obstetrics and although 'we don't know that Crippen carried out abortions, but he dabbled in all sorts, so it is quite plausible'. He added that an abortion would have to be carried out on a patient with an empty stomach, so the remains couldn't be Cora's because she had dined on the night she disappeared.[26] Dr Pepper's report on his examination of the remains had concluded the stomach was 'empty and intact'.

There was never any evidence of Crippen carrying out abortions at Hilldrop Crescent and this theory was created to fit a particular hypothesis. Surely if Crippen had used hyoscine during an abortion, he would not have administered such a large and lethal dose. This was all forgotten when a new type of test was carried out at the laboratory to determine the sex of the tissue sample the slide contained. It was declared to be male.

Trestrail abandoned his abortion hypothesis and wondered how male remains could have ended up in the cellar. 'I'm running scenarios through my mind of planted evidence'. A different and arguably better scenario would be that the tissue sample had become contaminated with male DNA. After being discovered, the remains were in the presence of at least seventeen men, at least half of whom had handled the remains before the slide was made. They were Inspector Dew; Sergeant Mitchell; Assistant Commissioner Melville Macnaghten; Superintendent Frank Froest; PC Gooch; PC Martin; PC Pitts; PC Thompson; Albert Leverton, the undertaker; Arthur Robinson, the mortuary keeper; Dr Marshall; Dr Pepper; Dr Wall; Dr Turnbull; Dr Spilsbury; Arthur Newton; and Dr Willcox.

On the day that the slide was made, the remains were examined for three hours by Drs Willcox, Pepper, Spilsbury, Marshall, Wall and Turnbull. Other contamination could obviously have come from Dr Crippen, any male cadavers who shared the mortuary slabs and unsterilised instruments used to cut the tissue when preparing the slide.

Instead of this, the programme declared it was Dew and Mitchell who had planted the pyjama top and possibly the remains because they 'had the opportunity to plant evidence in the cellar'. The viewer was not enlightened on how this could have been achieved. For it to be true, Dew and Mitchell would have needed to be impossibly lucky:

They would have had to been sure that Cora Crippen would never turn up alive anywhere in the world.

They would have had to have known that the pyjama top they had thrown into the remains could not have existed before the Crippens moved into 39 Hilldrop Crescent.

They must have magically made the pyjama top appear that it had been buried for months rather than a couple of hours.

And if they had planted the remains, they would have had to dig the grave and dispose of the soil unobserved.

they would have had to obtain a corpse for themselves. But rather than use a female corpse as a substitute for the missing woman, they decided a male cadaver would do just as well. They would then need the anatomical and surgical knowledge to dismember it, eliminating any evidence of sex and make sure their remains had an old surgical scar in the same place as Cora Crippen, which neither of them knew about at that time.

They would have had to make sure that when the remains were under the scrutiny of a post-mortem examination they would have the appearance of being buried shortly after death and buried for several months.

They would have had to dispose of the unwanted body parts without being discovered.

They would have had to obtain a large quantity of hyoscine from a chemist (larger than Crippen's chemist usually stocked), signed the poisons register then distributed it through the remains as if it had been taken orally, without knowing Crippen had recently bought a large quantity of hyoscine.

Then they would have had to obtain a sack of lime and covered the remains, mixing it with water, without knowing Crippen had bought a quantity of lime.

This would all have to have been done on either 12 July (Flora Long and Valentine Lecocq were still in the house on 11 July), or within a few hours on 13 July. That day Dew had spent the morning making various enquiries and digging up more of Crippen's garden. PC Gooch arrived at about 4 p.m., although Sergeant Mitchell estimated the time of the discovery at about 5 p.m.

Dew had rushed to fortify himself with brandy after uncovering the Hilldrop Crescent remains.[27] Surely the discovery would not have come as a shock if he had just planted them. The suggestion is particularly unpleasant as it implies that Dew and Mitchell lied under oath at the magistrates', coroner's and Central Criminal Court and watched while Crippen was sentenced to death, knowing that they had planted the evidence that resulted in his execution.

Even the planted evidence myth is an old one. The *New York Times* suggested it in 1910 when they asked 'whether this was a clever police "plant" formulated in deference to the criticism of the police after Crippen's disappearance'.[28] It had been ninety-eight years since this fantasy was first proposed, and in all those years not a shred of evidence has been found to support it. Neither was an explanation forthcoming about how the remains could be male. It seems highly unlikely that the long, dyed hair (the longest strand being 8 inches long) found with the curlers (which were the same brand that Cora used) would have proved male in origin if it had been tested.

An attempt was made by the programme to show Cora was still alive in New York in 1920, living with her sister and using the name Belle Rose. Belle Rose appeared on the 1920 New York census living with Bertha Mersinger. The census page was not shown, but had it been it would have been obvious that Belle Rose was not Belle Elmore. The census enumerator's head of household number (forty-eight) had been mistaken with Cora's possible age. Belle Rose's occupation was designer, not singer, which would have fitted Cora and Belle was described as Bertha's cousin, not her sister. John Trestrail was not deterred. He told the *Guardian*, 'Are Belle Rose and Cora Crippen one and the same? We can't prove any of that – that is another investigation.'[29]

The documentary was broadcast in America on the PBS channel under the title *Secrets of the Dead: Executed in Error*. It contained additional footage including an examination of the Chicago letter, but this time the 1910 file cover denouncing it as a hoax was shown, as was a photocopy of a postcard written by Cora, which they admitted was written in a different handwriting. Still the letter was given credence and the impossible-to-prove suggestion was made that Cora had dictated it, or even that Bruce Miller was the author.[30]

The 2008 documentary repeatedly compared the Crippen case to the Jack the Ripper murders of 1888, as if this was Scotland Yard's chance to redeem itself, especially Inspector Dew, who had failed to catch Jack the Ripper as a detective constable in Whitechapel. Dew was quite open about the police's failure to catch Jack the Ripper. He was reconciled to the dreadful events of the autumn of terror, admitting that 'failure it certainly was, but I have never regarded it other than an honourable failure'.[31] His name barely appeared in the press coverage at the time and his reputation had not suffered. Indeed, he was promoted to the rank of detective sergeant in December 1889.

A dubious claim was made that Dew's 1938 autobiography, *I Caught Crippen*, had been a bestseller and Dew had exploited his involvement in Crippen case to make it so. Far from being a bestseller, the book was remaindered and never reprinted.[32] If Dew had planted evidence it would have been in his interest to stay quiet about the case rather than continually laud it in public as his greatest achievement.

More aspersions were placed on Dew in a 2011 interview with Julian Duffus. He said that when Dew retired from Scotland Yard 'he gave up his pension and took on other work. Why?'[33] There is nothing in Dew's pension papers to support this unsubstantiated claim[34] and printed Metropolitan Police orders refer to Dew as 'Pensioned' after his retirement.[35] The matter of Dew's pension was raised in Parliament by Horatio Bottomley on 20 February 1911. He asked whether Dew had retired with a pension. Winston Churchill made it quite clear in his reply that Dew had retired voluntarily 'on full pension'.[36] He worked as a confidential enquiry agent for many years, but that was a common career choice for officers who were entitled to retire at a relatively young age with a decent pension after a lengthy service.

The historical claims made by the 2004 and 2008 documentaries are disproved by the same documents that were used to present them and the modern scientific findings are overwhelmingly contradicted by the historical evidence. Headline-grabbing DNA results do not explain why nobody seriously believed in Crippen's innocence in 1910:

After Cora's disappearance nobody ever saw or heard from her again, despite there being a large reward for finding her.

Cora disappeared without taking her beloved jewellery and furs with her.

Human remains found in Crippen's cellar were wrapped in his pyjamas which could not have existed before 1908, well after the Crippens had moved in.

Hair and curlers identified by friends as resembling Cora's were among the remains.

The remains were laced with hyoscine. Crippen had bought a large quantity of hyoscine shortly before Cora's disappearance, none of which could be accounted for.

The remains were covered in lime. Crippen had bought a quantity of lime.

Dr Crippen was found guilty of Cora's murder by a coroner's jury.

Dr Crippen was found guilty of Cora's murder at the magistrates' court.

Dr Crippen was found guilty of Cora's murder by an Old Bailey jury.

Dr Crippen was found guilty of Cora's murder by the Court of Criminal Appeal.

No contemporary police officer or legal figure involved in the case believed that Crippen had not killed his wife.

Crippen's solicitor Arthur Newton thought his client was guilty.

Even Ethel Le Neve believed Crippen had killed Cora, albeit accidentally.

In the 2004 documentary, Lord Chief Justice Alverstone was portrayed as part of an establishment conspiracy to convict Crippen and was accused of directing the jury to find Crippen guilty. However, in the 2008 documentary he was praised for supposedly pointing out to the jury in his summing up that they had to decide whether the remains were male or female. John Trestrail was shown reading from the trial transcript: 'Gentlemen, I think I may pass to the question of whether it was a man or a woman. Of course if it was a man, the defendant is entitled to walk out of that dock.'

This was presented as 'final evidence of a miscarriage of justice'. Far from being 'bombshell' evidence, Alverstone's summing up had been published in the Notable British Trial volume of Crippen in 1920, which was republished in 1933 and 1950.

Disconcertingly, the extract Trestrail was pointing to did not say what he had just read. Alverstone's real words, which were shown on the screen, were, 'Gentlemen, I think I may pass for the purpose of your consideration from the question of whether it was a man or a woman. Of course if it was a man, again the defendant is entitled to walk out of that dock.' This could be interpreted as meaning the opposite to Trestrail's misquote; that Alverstone was directing the jury away from the non-issue of whether the remains were male or female, rather than addressing them to the possibility.

In the previous paragraph on the same page that Trestrail was reading from, Alverstone said, 'Gentlemen, that they are the remains of a woman now is really not seriously disputed', and he points out that a woman's clothes were found with the remains and the defence did not dispute that the hairs found were also a woman's. The sentence following Trestrail's misquotation was 'Now, being a woman, was that Cora Crippen or not?' Alverstone had no doubts that the remains were a woman's. In his autobiography, published in 1914, Alverstone wrote, 'The identity of the remains with those of Mrs Crippen was further proved by the presence of a scar,' while the evidence 'though purely circumstantial, left no doubt in the mind of any impartial man of the prisoner's guilt.'[37]

It is worth remembering Alverstone's 'test applied in these Courts, and it ought to be applied. How did the man behave when the charge was brought against him?' Dr Crippen:

Lied to the police about Cora running off to live with Bruce Miller.

Made no attempt to trace Cora as Inspector Dew had asked.

Pawned Cora's jewellery.

Bought a suit of boy's clothes to disguise his mistress as a boy.

Left his job without notice.

Left his house without notice.

Assumed a false name.

Shaved off his moustache and took off his glasses to change his appearance.

Fled the country.

As Richard Muir summed up at Dr Crippen's trial, 'Where is Belle Elmore? Is your answer to be that she is dead? Then, whose remains were those in the cellar? Is your answer to be Belle Elmore's? If not Belle Elmore's, what conceivable explanation is there? None in the world.'

20

THE AFTERMATH OF THE CRIPPEN CASE

39 Hilldrop Crescent

In December 1910, several residents wrote to Islington Borough Council asking them to rename Hilldrop Crescent as its new-found notoriety was affecting property prices and deterring tenants from moving in. Henry Trutch at No. 41 suggested Camden Gardens or Camden Crescent, but the council found no evidence of falling house prices and Hilldrop Crescent has retained its name to this day.[1]

The next occupier of 39 Hilldrop Crescent was the Glaswegian comedian Adam Arthur, who performed under the name of Sandy McNab. By his own questionable account, he guessed that the owner of the property would be keen to be rid of it as it now had a gruesome reputation. Even an official taxation record noted that 'this house was occupied by Crippen and is notorious in consequence'.[2]

McNab's letter to the house's owner had been returned undelivered, so he wrote to Inspector Dew, who passed it on to the property's agent, who subsequently agreed to the sale. McNab was well satisfied with acquiring the property he claimed was worth more than £1,000 for £500. He may also have taken into account the publicity value of the story of his purchase, which saw his photograph splashed across the front page of a weekly tabloid with a circulation of over 430,000.

McNab described his new property:

> When I went through it as I did from top to bottom, I felt fully convinced that the authorities had left not the slightest trace of the terrible crime behind them. Every wall had been stripped of its wallpaper and here and there the plaster and lath had been removed. Floor boarding had been taken up, and ceilings had been pierced during the search for clues.
>
> On my first visit I made my way all over the premises, and at last I

came to the fatal cellar. I will not attempt to hide the fact that as my foot stepped upon the concrete floor, hardly yet dried, I felt a queer sensation at the pit of my stomach and a choking sensation in my throat. In my mind's eye I could see again the culprit working with feverish haste to bury the last trace of the crime from the eyes of man. Then I imagined the officers of the law examining the dark, damp, dungeon-like cellar, while the culprit stood calmly upon the steps behind them. The detectives were probably wise to leave the cellar at that time without making farther examinations, and I felt I could do no better than follow their example.[3]

He became known as 'The Man Who Made Crippen's Cat Laugh', and allegedly opened a museum of Crippen relics, but public disapproval led him to convert the house into theatrical lodgings.[4] McNab soon became the subject of headlines himself. In 1912 he was attacked in Hilldrop Crescent by three men who robbed him of a valuable diamond-studded gold medal that had been presented to him by the South African Amalgamated Theatres Limited after a recent tour.[5]

The following year his son William Arthur was fined £500 for breach of promise. He had proposed to his pregnant girlfriend, Lily Target, before joining his father's South African tour. On his return William informed Lily he wanted to marry another woman, and the best thing she could do was blow her brains out. When he gave her a gun she fainted and upon coming round he took her to the railway station. When the train approached, William told Lily, 'I would like to push you under there.'[6]

The new residents of 39 Hilldrop Crescent were a vile family. In 1914, Sandy McNab was found guilty at the Kent Assizes of sexually abusing a thirteen-year-old girl. The trial judge was Mr Justice Darling, who had rejected Dr Crippen's appeal.

When sentencing McNab to two years' hard labour, Darling said, 'I am satisfied from what has been brought to my notice since your conviction, that you are a man who makes a practice of this sort of thing.' He then turned to the jury and apologised for not having the power to pass a more severe sentence.[7]

After McNab's departure, No. 39 was occupied by numerous other tenants. The house survived when a high-explosive bomb landed in the back garden of 40 Hilldrop Crescent on the night of 8 September 1940, damaging the rear of Nos 37–40.[8] Writer Eric Ambler visited the Crescent after the war and found No. 39 'a little shabby, perhaps a little run down, but still proudly intact'.[9] On a return visit Ambler was uninspired by the location, writing, 'After ten minutes of Hilldrop Crescent in the wet, almost any explanation of the crime would seem credible. The visiting student is advised to take a raincoat and to keep his taxi waiting.'[10]

It remained unoccupied and was eventually demolished around 1951. A block of ten flats was built on the site in 1954, named Margaret Bondfield House after the first woman to become a member of the British Cabinet.[11] In 1969 the council considered erecting a blue plaque to commemorate Dr Crippen's association with the property, but public opposition halted the scheme.[12]

As recently as 2010 there were rumours that the house was haunted. One resident complained of a spooky atmosphere at night and possessions going missing without explanation.[13]

Chief Inspector Walter Dew[14]

The Crippen case had made Chief Inspector Walter Dew an international celebrity. He retired from the Metropolitan Police on 5 December 1910, with an exemplary certificate and some 130 commendations and rewards. He was forty-seven years old and had served a total of twenty-eight years and 176 days. Dew was considering resigning before the Crippen investigation, but he stayed on to see the job through to the end. He cited 'special private reasons' for his decision, and quite rightly thought it a 'fitting moment to retire'.

One national newspaper printed the following tribute to the departing detective:

> On the Continent, as in this country, his astuteness and tact have won him fame. His quiet, unassuming disposition secured him considerable popularity among his colleagues, and the intimation of his ensuing resignation has been received with universal regret.

Always sensitive to criticism, Dew sued nine newspapers for libellous comments they had made about his conduct during his final investigation. The *Daily Chronicle* paid out £400 in damages for having said that Dew told their correspondent that Crippen had confessed in Canada. Dew argued that this made it appear that he was failing in his duty and ignoring instructions not to speak about the case except as a witness at the trial.

Now working as a confidential enquiries agent, Dew was concerned that the scurrilous stories suggesting he was guilty of misconduct could damage his chances of gaining employment. Every libel action was judged in Dew's favour. Even F. E. Smith, representing *John Bull*, could not secure a victory against Dew.

Dew's son Walter, said by his father to have been the only other member of his family to have set foot inside a police station, joined the Metropolitan Police. He eventually rose to the rank of inspector in Special Branch and retired in 1933. His other son, Stanley, died in the First World War in France in 1915. In 1916 Dew was featured in a series of newspaper profiles on 'The Twelve Greatest Detectives of the World'. He told the paper that being a detective 'is the finest profession in the world, and if I could start life all over again I would rather be a detective than anything else'. Dew's name was still inextricably linked with that of Dr Crippen. The paper commented, 'Ask the average person who Walter Dew is, and he will answer, "The man who arrested Crippen." Some will cut down the answer to "Crippen Dew". Such is fame.'

Dew continued working as a private detective until the late 1920s. In 1926 he won a £100 prize in a *Daily Express* writing competition. The title of his piece was 'My Race With Crippen'.[15] It was to be his first foray into writing.

In 1927 Dew's wife Kate died from cancer, and the widowed detective left London and retired to Worthing on the south coast. He moved into a bungalow called 'The Wee Hoose' that he had bought from a family named Hawley. Dew married widow Florence Idle in 1928.

He spent the remainder of his retirement gardening and writing. National newspapers would sometimes ask Dew for his opinion on sensational cases that were being investigated. In 1934 *Thomson's Weekly News* ran a series of lengthy articles entitled 'The Whole Truth About the Crippen Case'. This was followed the next year by 'My Hunt for Jack the Ripper' and in 1936 by 'From Pitch and Toss to Murder', a series of articles about the variety of other cases Dew had worked on. These memoirs were published in a single-volume autobiography in 1938 called *I Caught Crippen*, which is today a valuable collector's item.

Dew still remembered Crippen kindly. He recalled the arrest to his local newspaper, the *Worthing Gazette*: 'Old Crippen took it quite well. He always was a bit of a philosopher, though he could not have helped being astounded to see me on board the boat ... He was quite a likeable chap in his way.'

Walter Dew occasionally fired off angry letters to newspapers that printed articles criticising the Crippen investigation. He eventually died at the Wee Hoose on 16 December 1947, aged eighty-four, and was buried at Worthing Cemetery. In 2005 the Wee Hoose was renamed 'Dew Cottage' in his honour.

Sergeant Arthur Mitchell

Mitchell rose to the rank of Detective Inspector and became the head of CID for the Tottenham division. He later returned to Scotland Yard before retiring from the Metropolitan Police in 1925. A career as a private detective ended abruptly with Mitchell's early death in 1929 aged fifty-one from double bronchopneumonia and cardiac collapse. He was buried at Tottenham Cemetery.[16]

Superintendent Frank Froest

After thirty-three years of service, Froest retired from Scotland Yard in 1912 at the age of fifty-four. King George V sent him the following message: 'Good-bye Mr Froest, and God-speed. The detective and police organization in which you have served so long is, in my opinion, the best in the world.'

Froest would later write several crime novels. He moved to Weston-super-Mare, Somerset, where he became a Justice of the Peace and an alderman. Frank Froest died on 7 January 1930 aged seventy-three at Weston-super-Mare hospital. He had been ill for a year and went totally blind shortly before he died. He was buried in the churchyard of Uphill Old Church.[17]

Sir Melville Macnaghten

Magnaghten remained at Scotland Yard as Assistant Commissioner until his retirement in 1913, after two years of declining health. His memoir, *Days of My Years*, was published in 1914 and he died in 1921.

Captain Henry Kendall

Captain Kendall's celebrity status resulted in his being inundated with crank letters about Crippen. These included a marriage proposal from a woman in Philadelphia, and a plea from a Canadian woman to locate her husband who had run off with another woman. He was offered £4,000 for a twenty-week theatrical engagement in America, and was pestered by a man who tried to tempt him with £100 for a cast of his face that could be exhibited in a waxworks.[18]

In 1914 Kendall was the captain of the *Empress of Ireland* when it collided with another vessel in the St Lawrence River, leading to the deaths of 1,012 people.

Kendall retired in 1939 and his autobiography, *Adventures on the High Seas*, was published the same year. Henry Kendall died in 1965, aged ninety-one, in a London nursing home. In 1974 the telegrams he sent during Crippen's voyage on the *Montrose* were sold at auction for £1,600.[19]

The *Montrose* was sold to the Admiralty in 1914. They intended to fill her holds with concrete and scupper her off the Dover coast as a block ship to deter German U-boats. The last man to ever leave the ship was named William Crippen.[20] The *Montrose* broke free from her moorings, drifted and foundered on the Goodwin Sands where she remained, until breaking up in June 1963.[21]

Lord Alverstone

During Dr Crippen's trial a joke was doing the rounds that was attributed to Alverstone. 'Oh, the Crippen case. Tried for the murder of his wife – and she was in court all the time.' 'Nonsense.' 'She was, indeed. But she was too cut up to say anything.'[22] Alverstone, a regular member of the church choir of St Mary Abbotts, Kensington, and known to sing comic songs,[23] retired in 1913 on account of ill health, and was made a viscount. His autobiography, *Recollections of Bar and Bench*, was published in 1914. He died the following year and was buried at Norwood Cemetery.[24]

Richard Muir

Muir was appointed Recorder of Colchester in 1911 and knighted in 1918. In January 1924 he had a bout of influenza which developed into double pneumonia, from which he died at his London home aged sixty-seven. He was buried at Norwood Cemetery.[25]

Travers Humphreys

Humphreys worked on a number of other high-profile cases, including those of the poisoner Frederick Seddon, the Brides in the Bath murders and the prosecution of Roger Casement for treason. Knighted in 1925, he became a judge, and after the Second World War sat on the Court of Criminal Appeal. Humphreys penned two volumes of memoirs, published in 1946 and 1953, and died in 1956.[26]

Samuel Ingleby Oddie

Oddie was appointed coroner for Westminster in 1912, a position he held for twenty-seven years, retiring when he turned seventy. He lived at Croxley Green, Hertfordshire, and served on the Rickmansworth Urban District Council for thirty-two years, including a spell as chairman in 1918–21. Oddie wrote his memoir, *Inquest*, in 1941 and died in May 1945 aged seventy-six.[27]

Cecil Mercer

Not long after the Crippen case Mercer gave up practising law and became a writer, employing the pen name Dornford Yates. He served in Egypt and Greece during the First World War, where he contracted severe rheumatism, which blighted him for the rest of his life. Moving to the warmer climes of southern France, he was forced to move again in 1940 when the Germans invaded. Settling in southern Rhodesia, Mercer continued writing popular thrillers and two volumes of autobiography. He died in 1960 aged seventy-four, having sold over two million books.[28]

Arthur Newton

Newton was found guilty of professional misconduct by the Law Society, and struck off as a solicitor for twelve months after publishing false information in the newspaper *John Bull* in the form of a letter, allegedly written by Crippen.[29] In 1913 he was permanently struck off and sentenced at the Old Bailey to three years in prison. This time he had fraudulently obtained £13,500 from an Austrian for some Canadian land.[30] Upon his release, Newton worked as a private enquiry agent and died in 1930 aged seventy.

Alfred Tobin

Tobin was elected Member of Parliament for Preston in 1910 and held the seat until 1915. He was awarded a knighthood in 1919, the same year that his friend F. E. Smith arranged his appointment as judge of Westminster County Court. Tobin held that position until his retirement in 1935. He died in Switzerland in 1939 aged eighty-three.[31] Crippen's other defender Huntly Jenkins died in 1923 aged fifty after a stroke. The previous year he had unsuccessfully defended

Frederick Bywaters. His colleague Henry Delacombe Roome died in 1930 aged forty-eight after being involved in a car crash.

F. E. Smith

Smith's career flourished after Le Neve's acquittal. In 1914 he became solicitor general and then attorney general. He was knighted the same year. Three years later Smith was created Baron Birkenhead, and made a life peer in 1918, sitting regularly as Speaker at the House of Lords. In October 1924 he accepted the office of Secretary of State for India. Lord Birkenhead died in 1930 aged fifty-eight.[32]

Dr Augustus Pepper

The Crippen case was Pepper's last as Home Office Pathologist. He remained a popular teacher at St Mary's Hospital until his retirement in 1919. Pepper spent much of his retirement gardening at his home in Sidcup, Kent. He died there on 18 December 1935, aged eighty-six, having been 'largely responsible for the raising of medico-legal work to its present high level'.[33]

Dr William Willcox

Willcox continued working as a lecturer on chemical pathology and forensic medicine at St Mary's Hospital until the 1930s. During the First World War he was given the rank of colonel and acted as a consultant to the British Army in Mesopotamia. In 1919 Willcox was made medical advisor to the Home Office. Known as 'the King's Poisoner' among journalists, on account of his unrivalled knowledge of poisons, Willcox died aged seventy-one in 1941 and was cremated at Golders Green.[34]

Dr Bernard Spilsbury

Spilsbury succeeded Pepper as Home Office Pathologist, holding that position until 1934. He gave evidence at many famous murder trials, including those of Frederick Seddon, Herbert Rowse Armstrong and the Brides in the Bath murders.

Knighted in 1923, Spilsbury worked as a lecturer in morbid anatomy at St Bart's until 1947, and in pathology at St Mary's until 1919. He conducted an estimated 25,000 post-mortems during his career.

Spilsbury suffered a stroke in 1940, and arthritis made working increasingly difficult. Further depressed by the death of two sons, Spilsbury died in 1947, the day after Walter Dew, aged seventy, after gassing himself in his laboratory at University College, London.[35] He never finished his book, which was to be the standard work on medical jurisprudence.

NOTES

PRO – Public Record Office documents held at the National Archives.

1. The Case of the Missing Actress

1. Unless otherwise stated the information contained in this book was obtained from PRO CRIM1/117, PRO DPP1/13, PRO HO144/1718/195492, PRO HO144/1719/195492, PRO MEPO3/198, PRO P/COM8/30, and Young, *The Trial of Hawley Harvey Crippen*.
2. Dilnot, *Great Detectives*, p. 47.
3. *The Sunday News*, 12 January 1930.
4. *The Saturday Post*, 29 January 1916.
5. Dew, *I Caught Crippen*, pp. 7–8.
6. *Daily Express*, 2 January 1950.
7. *Ibid.*, 23 November 1926.
8. *The Era*, 23 July 1910.
9. Rose, *Red Plush and Greasepaint*, p. 29.
10. *Weekly Dispatch*, 15 February 1920.
11. *Ibid.*
12. *Evening News*, 14 July 1910. This was possibly Michael Bernstein, who checked passenger lists on behalf of the Guild, although Guild secretary Melinda May thought that a solicitor's wife named Mrs Osborn had employed a private detective.
13. Buchanan-Taylor, *Shake the Bottle*, p. 93.
14. *The Era*, 26 February 1910.
15. Smythson had visited Scotland Yard on 31 March to ask how to find out where Cora's death would be registered and she was directed to the American embassy. She also gave a statement conveying the Guild's suspicions, but there was insufficient reason for the police to investigate (Wood, *Survivors' Tales*, p. 271); *Daily Mail*, 18 July 1910.
16. *Sotheby's Sale Catalogue*, 24 February 1976. This letter was sold at auction in 1976.
17. Wood, *op. cit.*, p. 272.
18. Dew, *op. cit.*, p. 11.

2. The American Dentist

1. *The Music Hall and Theatre Review*, 7 April 1910.
2. *The Stage*, 7 April 1910.
3. Dew, *op. cit.*, p. 11.
4. *Answers*, 27 August 1910.
5. Dew, *op. cit.*, 12.
6. *Ibid.*, p. 15.
7. *Ibid.*, pp. 13-4.
8. *Ibid.*, p. 14.
9. *Ibid.*, p. 19.
10. *Ibid.*
11. *Ibid.*, p. 20.
12. *Ibid.*, pp. 20-1.

3. The Cellar

1. Dew, *op. cit.*, p. 23.
2. *Ibid.*, p. 22.
3. *Ibid.*, p. 25.
4. *Daily Mail*, 19 July 1910.
5. *Daily Chronicle*, 18 July 1910.
6. *Answers*, 27 August 1910.
7. *Ibid.*
8. *Ibid.*, 3 September 1910.
9. Dew, *op. cit.*, p. 26.
10. *Ibid.*, p. 27.
11. *Daily Express*, 23 November 1926.
12. Dew, *op. cit.*, p. 27.
13. *Ibid.*, pp. 27-8.
14. *Ibid.*, p. 28.
15. Macnaghten, *Days of My Years*, p. 195.
16. Adam, *CID: Behind the Scenes at Scotland Yard*, p. 20.
17. Macnaghten, *op. cit.*, p. 195.
18. *The Times*, 14 July 1910.
19. *Islington Daily Gazette*, 15 July 1910.
20. Gooch later became a chief inspector and head of the Flying Squad. He died in a car crash in 1936.
21. *Pall Mall Gazette*, 15 July 1910.
22. *Ibid.*, 14 July 1910.
23. *The People*, 17 July 1910.
24. Dew, *op. cit.*, p. 11.
25. *Liverpool Daily Post*, 6 August 1910. The lodger was probably Richard Erlich, whose interview in the *Petit Parisien* appeared in many English newspapers at that time.
26. *New York Times*, 15 July 1910.
27. *Los Angeles Herald*, 15 July 1910.
28. *The Times*, 19 July 1910.
29. Dew, *op. cit.*, p. 30.

4. The Fugitives

1. Yates, *As Berry and I Were Saying*, p. 250.
2. Dew, *op. cit.*, pp. 31–2.
3. *Cleveland Plain Dealer*, 16 July 1910.
4. *San Francisco Chronicle*, 17 July 1910.
5. Wood, *op. cit.*, p. 264.
6. *Ibid.*, pp. 266–7.
7. *The Times*, 19 July 1910.
8. *Ibid.*, 21 July 1910.
9. Dew, *op. cit.*, p. 25.
10. *Ibid.*, pp. 33–4.
11. *The Times*, 20 July 1910.
12. *Ibid.*, 22 July 1910.
13. A photocopy of the page from the visitors' book is kept at Camden Local Studies and Archives.
14. *Daily Mail*, 20 July 1910.
15. *The Times*, 22 July 1910.
16. *Islington Daily Gazette*, 21 July 1910.
17. Gibbs, *Adventures in Journalism*, p. 73.
18. Dew, *op. cit.*, 79.
19. The controversy over Crippen's title was later discussed in the letters column of *The Times* on 2 November 1938 and 5 November 1938.
20. *The British Medical Journal*, 29 October 1910.
21. *Western Mail*, 26 September 1898.
22. *Ibid.*
23. *The American Homeopathic Journal of Obstetrics and Gynaecology*, 1885, p. 242.
24. *Ibid.*, p. 102.

5. The Inquisitive Sea Captain

1. Kendall, *Adventures on the High Seas*, p. 160.
2. In his memoirs, Kendall wrote that he could see Crippen's teeth were not false and Scotland Yard had been mistaken in their description (Kendall, *op. cit.*, p. 162).
3. *Ibid.*, p. 150.
4. Dew, *op. cit.*, p. 37.
5. Macnaghten, *op. cit.*, p. 197.
6. Dew, *op. cit.*, p. 39.
7. Macnaghten, *op. cit.*, p. 199–200.
8. *Durban Daily News*, 12 November 1938.
9. *Liverpool Courier*, 25 July 1910.
10. *Montreal Daily Star*, 30 July 1910.
11. Dew, *op. cit.*, p. 40.
12. Kendall, *op. cit.*, p. 169.
13. *The Umpire*, 27 July 1910.
14. Kendall, *op. cit.*, p. 171.
15. *The Times*, 29 July 1910.
16. *Montreal Daily Star*, 30 July 1910.
17. Dew, *op. cit.*, p. 49.
18. *Montreal Daily Star*, 30 July 1910.
19. Dew, *op. cit.*, p. 41.

6. The Arrest

1. *Daily Mail*, 12 August 1910.
2. When interviewed decades later Kendall claimed Dew did not immediately recognise Crippen saying, 'My God, captain, that isn't Crippen!' Kendall said he replied, 'That's Crippen all right – and if you won't arrest him I will' (*News of the World*, 3 February 1952).
3. Dew, *op. cit.*, p. 43.
4. *Ibid.*, p. 44.
5. Macnaghten, *op. cit.*, p. 189.
6. Kendall, *op. cit.*, p. 187.
7. *Reynolds's Weekly Newspaper*, 7 August 1910.
8. *The Times*, 1 August.1910.
9. *Ibid.*, 2 August 1910.
10. Dew, *op. cit.*, pp. 50–1.
11. *Islington Daily Gazette*, 4 August 1910.
12. *Daily Chronicle*, 8 August 1910.
13. *The Times*, 9 August 1910.
14. *San Francisco Chronicle*, 9 August 1910.
15. *The Times*, 5 August 1910.
16. *Montreal Daily Star*, 15 August 1910.

7. The Return Voyage

1. *Liverpool Daily Post*, 22 August 1910.
2. Grant, *To The Four Corners*, p. 45.
3. *The Times*, 29 August 1910.
4. Dew, *op. cit.*, p. 50.
5. PRO BT26/422. Mitchell's name was wrongly recorded as Charles.
6. *Cleveland Plain Dealer*, 22 August 1910.
7. Dew, *op. cit.*, pp. 53–6.
8. *Ibid.*, p. 56.
9. *Lloyd's Weekly News*, 13 November 1910.
10. Dew, *op. cit.*, pp. 56–7.
11. Yates, *op. cit.*, p. 243.
12. Dew, *op. cit.*, p. 7.
13. *Ibid.*, p. 57.
14. Yates, *op. cit.*, pp. 255–6.
15. Grant, *op. cit.*, p. 46.
16. *Ibid.*, p. 45.
17. *Answers*, 17 September 1910.
18. *Daily Mail*, 29 August 1910.
19. *Liverpool Courier*, 29 August 1910.
20. *Reynolds's Weekly Newspaper*, 28 August 1910.
21. Dew, *op. cit.*, p. 60.
22. Adam, *op. cit.*, p. 158.
23. Macnaghten, *op. cit.*, p. 193.

8. The Crooked Solicitor

1. Humphreys, *A Book of Trials*, p. 162.
2. Humphreys, *Criminal Days*, p. 112.

3. *Sunday Express*, 31 December 1923. Crippen said he remembered Newton from a 1898 case when they were on opposing sides.

4. Cullen, *Crippen: The Mild Murderer*, p. 146.

5. Yates, *op. cit.*, pp. 159–60.

6. *The People*, 23 April 1933.

7. *Sunday Express*, 6 January 1924.

8. Dew, *op. cit.*, p. 60.

9. Dilnot, *Adventures of a Newspaper Man*, pp. 130–1.

10. *Thomson's Weekly News*, 6 November 1920. The cell Crippen occupied at Bow Street had other notorious residents. Forger John Hurley hanged himself in it just hours before he was due to stand trial in 1923 (*Daily Express*, 26 September 1923). It was later occupied by William Joyce, otherwise known as 'Lord Haw Haw', who was executed for treason in 1946 (*Daily Mail*, 18 June 1945).

11. Macnaghten, *op. cit.*, p. 189.

12. *The Times*, 1 August 1910.

13. Morland, *Hangman's Clutch*, p. 146.

14. *The New Statesman*, 16 November 1940.

15. Dew, *op. cit.*, p. 7.

16. *Daily Mail*, 2 August 1910.

17. Dilnot, *Great Detectives*, pp. 44–5.

18. Yates, *op. cit.*, pp. 254–5.

19. *The Times*, 7 September 1910.

20. *Ibid.*, 15 September 1910.

21. *Ibid.*, 17 September 1910.

22. *The Globe*, 21 September 1910.

23. *Ibid.*, 19 September 1910.

9. Pre-Trial Proceedings

1. *Oxford Dictionary of National Biography*. Newton had briefed Marshall Hall in his first ever case in 1894 (Marjoribanks, *The Life of Sir Edward Marshall Hall*, p. 87).

2. Bowker, *A Lifetime With the Law*, pp. 23–4.

3. Marjoribanks, *op. cit.*, pp. 281–2.

4. *Ibid.*, p. 283. Travers Humphreys denied this was the case. He wrote that Marshall Hall 'declined to accept it for reasons which seemed good to him and which had nothing to do with the suggested defence of manslaughter' (*Book of Trials*, pp. 62–3).

5. Crippen said he 'wrote an account (12 foolscap pages finely written) of my experiences of seven weeks, and my solicitor has this, *yet unpublished.*' (Ellis, *Black Fame*, p. 312). Apparently the first instalment was published in the *Sunday Budget*, a London newspaper owned by American press baron William Randolph Hearst and staffed by American journalists. A court injunction quickly ended the series (Buchanan-Taylor, *op. cit.*, p. 97).

6. *The People*, 23 April 1933.

7. *The Times*, 27 September 1910.

8. Croall, *Fourteen Minutes: The Last Voyage of the Empress of Ireland*, p. 25.

9. *Sotheby's Auction Catalogue*, 24 February 1976. This letter was auctioned along with other Crippen ephemera including letters written by Cora and a signed photograph of her. They once belonged to Dr John Burroughs, who had died in 1940 (*Evening News*, 30 January 1976).

10. Meaney, *Scribble Street*, p. 59.

10. Rex v. Crippen Part One: Prosecutors and Defenders

1. *Dictionary of National Biography*.
2. *Pall Mall Magazine*, August 1913. Cecil Mercer described Alverstone as 'a splendid chief and a splendid Judge. So far as I ever saw, he had only one fault. And that was that he was impatient. But he couldn't fairly be blamed, for he had a lightning brain.' (Yates, *op. cit.*, p. 96)
3. Alverstone, *Recollections of Bar and Bench*, p. 274.
4. *The Saturday Post*, 17 February 1917.
5. Browne and Tullett, *Bernard Spilsbury: His Life and Cases*, p. 48.
6. Oddie, *Inquest*, p. 74.
7. Yates, *op. cit.*, p. 179.
8. Lieck, *Bow Street World*, pp. 59–60.
9. Felstead, *op. cit.*, p. 116.
10. Humphreys, *Criminal Days*, p. 113.
11. *Ibid.*, p. 106.
12. Oddie, *op. cit.*, p. 13.
13. Yates, *op. cit.*, p. 246.
14. *Ibid.*, p. 255.
15. *Ibid.*, p. 254.
16. *Ibid.*, pp. 242–5. Mercer concluded the hair found with the remains had been torn out when Crippen dragged Cora downstairs.
17. Oddie, *op. cit.*, p. 80. Unfortunately for Oddie's theory the post-mortem revealed the heart 'was in a good state of preservation and showed no sign of disease'.
18. *Ibid.*, p. 81.
19. Yates, *op. cit.*, p. 262.
20. Humphreys, *A Book of Trials*, p. 59.
21. *Ibid.*
22. Humphreys, *Criminal Days*, p. 82.
23. Humphreys, *A Book of Trials*, p. 55.
24. *Ibid.*
25. Bowker, *op. cit.*, p. 24.
26. *Daily Mirror*, 5 February 1914.
27. *Ibid.*
28. *The Times*, 4 December 1939.

11. Rex v. Crippen Part Two: The Trial

1. *The American Law School Review*, 1920, p. 557.
2. *Empire News*, 27 August 1922.
3. Felstead, *op. cit.*, p. 88.
4. *Empire News*, 27 August 1922.
5. Constantine-Quinn, *Doctor Crippen*, p. 45.
6. *Chicago Sunday Tribune*, 23 October 1910.
7. *Pall Mall Gazette*, 19 October 1910.
8. *The Lancet*, 28 December 1935.
9. Yates, *op. cit.*, p. 259.
10. Dew, *op. cit.*, p. 65.
11. Browne and Tullett, *op. cit.*, p. 51. Much is made of Spilsbury's appearance at Crippen's trial by some authors. However, Pepper and Willcox were hugely experienced and respected, and their evidence would have been just as influential, if not more so.

12. *Ibid.*, pp. 38–9.
13. *British Medical Journal*, 19 July 1941.
14. De Villiers, *My Memories*, pp. 74–5.
15. *Daily Mirror*, 2 March 1914.
16. *The People*, 23 April 1933.
17. *Pall Mall Gazette*, 21 October 1910.
18. Humphreys, *Criminal Days*, p. 109.
19. Dew, *op. cit.*, p. 69.
20. *Ibid.*, p. 73.
21. Bixley, *Guilty and the Innocent*, pp. 49–50.
22. Yates, *op. cit.*, p. 246.

12. Rex v. Crippen Part Three: The Verdict

1. *Sunday Express*, 27 February 1927.
2. De Villiers, *op. cit.*, pp. 75–6.
3. Yates, *op. cit.*, p. 258. Mercer stated that Crippen had obtained two sacks of lime (*Ibid.*, p. 243).
4. *Ibid.*
5. Alverstone, *op. cit.*, p. 276.
6. Bowker, *op. cit.*, p. 24.
7. Meaney, *op. cit.*, p. 57.
8. *Daily Mail*, 20 July 1910.
9. Oddie, *op. cit.*, p. 81.
10. Macnaghten, *op. cit.*, p. 201.
11. *Thomson's Weekly News*, 9 October 1920.
12. *World's Pictorial News*, 4 October 1925.

13. Rex v. Le Neve

1. Yates, *op. cit.*, p. 261.
2. Felstead, *op. cit.*, p. 117.
3. *Dictionary of National Biography*.
4. Oddie, *op. cit.*, p. 43.
5. Humphreys, *Book of Trials*, p. 63.
6. Birkenhead, *Famous Trials of History*, p. 295.
7. Yates, *op. cit.*, p. 261.
8. Dew, *op. cit.*, p. 80.
9. Birkenhead, *Frederick Edwin Earl of Birkenhead*, p. 129.
10. Birkenhead, *Famous Trials of History*, p. 300.
11. *Ibid.*
12. *Ibid.*, p. 297.
13. Dew, *op. cit.*, p. 47.
14. *Ibid.*, p. 8.

14. Let the Law Take its Course

1. *Sunday Express*, 6 January 1924.
2. Oddie, *op. cit.*, p. 79.
3. *Daily Express*, 23 September 1930.
4. *The Sketch*, 20 October 1910.

5. *The Globe*, 5 November 1910.
6. *Islington Daily Gazette*, 11 November 1910.
7. The will was proved on 8 February 1911 and valued at £268 6s 9d. Theresa Hunn's solicitor handled Cora's will that was proved on 11 March 1911 and valued at £175.
8. *Sunday Times*, 13 November 1910.
9. Churchill, *Young Statesman: Winston S Churchill 1901–1914*, p. 418. Churchill does not appear to have written anything about his involvement in the Crippen case, nor have his biographers. This seems a little odd as he was so closely involved with it, as was his best friend, F. E. Smith. It may be an indication that, despite its notoriety, the Crippen case was of little historical significance compared to other events in Churchill's epic life. In a report to the King, written on 22 November 1910, Churchill wrote 'no fewer than eight capital cases wh [*sic*] have descended from the summer assizes have been a great burden in the last few days...' (Churchill, *Volume II Companion*, p. 1027).
10. *Sunday Express*, 23 June 1935.
11. *Daily Mail*, 7 November 1910.
12. *The Umpire*, 13 November 1910.
13. *Sunday Express*, 27 February 1921. A more sympathetic account of Mytton Davies' feelings towards Crippen can be found in Cullen, *Crippen: The Mild Murderer*. Cullen spoke to Mytton Davies' son Cynric, who recalled his father 'found Crippen to be a very mild, inoffensive little man who never gave anyone any trouble. He believed that Crippen was covering up for the real culprit, and was going to his death on that person's behalf.' (p. 178).
14. *The Leader*, 17 June 1930.
15. *Thomson's Weekly News*, 1 March 1919.
16. *Ibid.*, 19 May 1923. Mercia Somerset is sometimes confused with Isabella Somerset, the noted member of the temperance movement and estranged wife of Lord Henry Somerset. Crippen referred to her as 'Lady Henry Somerset' in a letter to Ethel Le Neve (Ellis, *Black Fame*, p. 309), but Isabella Somerset died in 1921 and could not have been Lady Mercia, who revealed her true identity and sold her memoirs in 1923.
17. *Ibid.*, 11 August 1928.
18. *Ibid.*, 26 May 1923.
19. *Penny Illustrated Paper*, 26 November 1910. Nine of Crippen's letters to Somerset were auctioned at Christie's in 1990 (*South London Press*, 14 September 1990).
20. Other letters are transcribed in Ellis, *Black Fame*, pp. 308–20.
21. *Thomson's Weekly News*, 22 January 1921.

15. The Execution

1. Eddy, *Scarlet and Ermine*, p. 57.
2. *Thomson's Weekly News*, 15 January 1921.
3. *Sunday Express*, 27 February 1921. His wish appears to have been granted. Filson Young said in the *Trial of Hawley Harvey Crippen* that Mytton-Davies agreed to the request. The book was published around February 1920 and contains an acknowledgement to 'the Governor of Pentonville Prison'. Mytton-Davies held that post until November 1919. Le Neve also said her letters were buried with Crippen (*Thomson's Weekly News*, 22 January 1921).
4. *Thomson's Weekly News*, 19 July 1924.

5. *Ibid.*
6. *Ibid.*
7. *Sunday Dispatch*, 26 February 1956.
8. *Empire News*, 24 April 1927.
9. *Reynolds's Weekly Newspaper*, 27 November 1910.
10. *Thomson's Weekly News*, 19 July 1924.
11. *Empire News*, 10 March 1924.
12. PRO HO324/1. Crippen would later be joined in the burial ground by other executed felons including Frederick Seddon, Roger Casement and Louis Voison. Casement's corpse was exhumed in 1965 and returned to Eire. It was rumoured that Crippen's remains had been sent by mistake as the initials on the worn headstones, 'RC' and 'HC', looked similar (*New Law Journal*, 30 May 1997).
13. Smith, *Supper With the Crippens*, p. 2.
14. Lane, *Edgar Wallace the Biography of a Phenomenon*, p. 237.
15. Despite its huge print run that day, no copies appear to have survived.
16. *The Leader*, 14 October 1930.
17. *Thomson's Weekly News*, 16 September 1922. Newton again made the claim the Crippen had confessed to murdering Cora in the *Sunday Express*, 6 January 1924.

16. Ethel

1. Dilnot, *Adventures of a Newspaper Man*, p. 129.
2. Kendall, *op. cit.*, p. 185.
3. Gibbs, *op. cit.*, p. 75.
4. Eddy, *op. cit.*, p. 49.
5. *Ibid.*, pp. 57–8.
6. Gibbs, *op. cit.*, pp. 75–6.
7. *Ibid.*, pp. 76–7.
8. *Thomson's Weekly News*, 22 January 1921.
9. Gibbs, *op. cit.*, p. 77. J. P. Eddy wrote that whenever he subsequently met with Gibbs and spoke about Le Neve 'it was to express our surprise and regret that we had lost all contact with her' (*The Times*, 17 March 1962).
10. Browne and Tullett, *op. cit.*, p. 41.
11. PRO T1/11335. In February 1910, Emily Jackson was told by Le Neve that 'she had been up to the house helping the Dr search for a bankbook which was worth £200 and that they eventually found it'. It is unclear what they did with the money.
12. Bloom, *The Mightier Sword*, p. 88.
13. *Ibid.*, p. 93. The *Daily Mail* (23 November 1910) reported that Ethel had sailed to New York on the day of Crippen's execution under the name of Miss Allen.
14. *Ibid.*, p. 95.
15. *Sunday Dispatch*, 20 June 1954.
16. Bloom, p. 92.
17. *Belle, or the Ballad of Dr Crippen* by Wolf Markowitz and Monty Norman was not a success and soon closed.
18. *Sunday Dispatch*, 29 January 1961.
19. *Guardian*, 12 July 1972.
20. *Sunday Citizen*, 28 March 1965.
21. Bloom, *op. cit.*, p. 14.
22. *News of the World*, 3 February 1952.

23. Gilbert, *Doctor Crippen*, p. 118.
24. *Daily Express*, 9 September 1950.
25. *Thomson's Weekly News*, 8 January 1921.
26. *Ibid.*, 9 October 1920.
27. *Ibid.*, 13 November 1920.
28. *Ibid.*, 16 October 1920.
29. *Ibid.*, 1 January 1921.
30. *Ibid.*, 8 January 1921.
31. *Ibid.*, 22 January 1921.
32. *Ibid.*, 29 January 1921.
33. *Ibid.*, 5 February 1921.
34. Wood, *op. cit.*, p. 282.
35. *Thomson's Weekly News*, 11 August 1928.
36. *Ibid.*, 12 February 1921.
37. *Ibid.*, 19 February 1921.
38. I have been unable to locate any issues of this periodical. There is an advert for the Le Neve series in the *Hull Daily Mail*, 3 April 1922.
39. *Sunday News*, 13 March 1927.
40. *Thomson's Weekly News*, 11 August 1928.
41. *Ibid.*, 1 September 1928.
42. *Ibid.*, 8 September 1928. Another interview with a woman claiming to be Le Neve had her living in poverty in Australia, having fled there from India. (*Daily Express*, 28 June 1932). Sir Hugh Rhys Rankin claimed to have taken tea with Le Neve in the red-light district of Perth in 1930. She had been 'a pretty hard woman' who had been through several divorces in Canada before emigrating to Australia. This woman told Rankin that Crippen had killed Cora because she had syphilis (*Sunday Times*, 11 October 1981).
43. *Ibid.*, 22 September 1928.
44. *Ibid.*, (Dundee edition), 22 September 1928.
45. *Sunday Post* 8 March 1931.
46. Le Neve, *Ethel Le Neve Her Life Story*, p. 29.
47. *Sunday News*, 13 March 1927.
48. Goodman, *The Crippen File*.
49. *Evening News*, 14 December 1974. The *Sunday Times* also reported in 1974 that Ethel had married, was a grandmother and had died in 1967 (*Sunday Times*, 7 July 1974).
50. *The Call Boy*, Summer 1980.
51. *Living with the Legend*, a radio broadcast presented by Roger Wilkes.
52. *You Magazine*, 14 July 1985.
53. *Sunday Telegraph*, 16 March 1997.
54. After his trial Crippen wrote to Le Neve that 'it would please me so much if you would take my first name or my second Christian name, which you prefer – probably you prefer Hawley' (Ellis, *Black Fame*, p. 309).
55. *Living with the Legend*.
56. *You Magazine*, 14 July 1985.
57. *Secrets of the Black Museum*, Discovery Channel, 1999.
58. *You Magazine*, 14 July 1985.
59. *Living with the Legend*.
60. *New Law Journal*, 30 May 1997. J. E. Muddock discussed the coincidences in *The Sketch*, 26 October 1910.
61. *Daily Telegraph*, 26 January 2002.
62. It is sometimes stated that Le Neve requested a locket containing Crippen's photograph to be buried with her. Goodman tells the story in *The Crippen*

File (p. 95), but admitted it was unconfirmed. Two years later Goodman stated 'it is not true' (*The Black Museum*, p. 156), but later writers have repeated it as fact. In 1928 Le Neve said that she had destroyed her photograph of Crippen years before, and that a photograph of her had been buried with Crippen (*Thomson's Weekly News*, 22 September 1928). Le Neve left no will containing such instructions.

17. Peter and Belle

1. Gilbert, *op. cit.*, p. 125.
2. Cullen's book was provisionally titled *No Meat for the Hangman* (*Guardian*, 24 February 1976). The phrase was taken from *The Edwardians* by J. B. Priestly; 'He must have had something that was not so much meat for the hangman.'
3. *Thomson's Weekly News*, 16 September 1922.
4. Constantine-Quinn, *op. cit.*, p. 13.
5. *Daily Express*, 23 November 1926.
6. Parrish and Crossland, *The Fifty Most Amazing Crimes*, p. 119.
7. *The New Statesman*, 16 November 1940.
8. Gardiner and Walker, *Raymond Chandler Speaking*, p. 197.
9. Bloom, *op. cit.*, p. 90.
10. *Pall Mall Magazine*, May 1928.
11. *Lloyd's Weekly News*, 17 July 1910.
12. Wood, *op. cit.*, p. 264.
13. *Daily Express*, 15 July 1910.
14. *New Law Journal*, 30 May 1997.
15. *Pall Mall Gazette*, 14 July 1910.
16. PRO MEPO2/10996.
17. *The People*, 17 July 1910.
18. *John Bull*, 10 December 1910.
19. *Ibid.*
20. *Weekly Dispatch*, 15 February 1920.
21. *Ibid.*, 8 February 1920.
22. *Thomson's Weekly News*, 25 September 1920.
23. *Ibid.*, 8 January 1921.
24. *Ibid.*, 25 September 1920.
25. *Sunday Illustrated*, 3 September 1922.
26. Marjoribanks, *op. cit.*, p. 277.
27. Buchanan-Taylor, *op. cit.*, pp. 93–4.
28. *Ibid.*, p. 94.
29. *Ibid.*, pp. 96–7.
30. *Ibid.*, pp. 98–9.
31. *The People*, 23 April 1933.
32. *Sunday Times*, 7 October 1934.
33. *Ibid.*, 14 October 1934.
34. *Ibid.*, 21 October 1934.
35. *Ibid.*, 23 June 1935.
36. Thorogood, *East of Aldgate*, pp. 97–8.
37. Dearden, *Death Under the Microscope*, p. 66.
38. Kendall, *op. cit.*, p. 151.
39. Gribble, *Adventures in Murder*, pp. 114–5.
40. Bloom, *op. cit.*, p. 88.
41. Lock, *Scotland Yard Casebook*, pp. 191–2.

42. The origin of this accusation is unclear and it is probably fallacious. Cullen tells the story without giving an authority and gives the date as November 1906 (Cullen, p. 79).
43. *Weekly Dispatch*, 15 February 1920.
44. PRO MEPO2/10996.
45. *The People*, 17 July 1910.
46. *The Morning Advertiser*, 15 July 1910.
47. *Pall Mall Gazette*, 6 August 1910.
48. Morland, *op. cit.*, pp. 178–9.
49. *Ibid.*, p. 149.
50. Yates, *op. cit.*, p. 240.
51. Browne and Tullet, *op. cit.*, p. 43.
52. *Daily Express*, 3 May 1934.

18. The Innocence of Dr Crippen: An Old Myth Resurrected

1. *San Francisco Chronicle*, 9 August 1910.
2. *The Times*, 9 August 1910.
3. *New York Times*, 2 August 1910.
4. *Ibid.*, 1 August 1910.
5. *Thomson's Weekly News*, 29 January 1921.
6. *New York Times*, 7 November 1910.
7. *News of the World*, 9 April 1911.
8. *World's Pictorial News*, 19 April 1926.
9. Letter from Colin Bennett to Walter Dew, 18 October 1943, reproduced in the *Western Daily Press*, 10 August 2007. The letter was sold at auction in 2007 and purchased by the Crime Through Time Museum in Gloucester. Dr Crippen's waxen effigy suffered further indignity when it was decapitated, after England was hit by an earthquake in 1931 (*Daily Mirror*, 8 June 1931).
10. Yates, *op. cit.*, p. 257.
11. *Ibid.*, p. 258.
12. *Ibid.*, p. 243; Oddie, *op. cit.*, p. 82.
13. http://vimeo.com/32201595.
14. PRO MEPO2/10996. Another example of Cora's writing appears in *Lloyd's Weekly News*, 17 July 1910.
15. http://vimeo.com/32201595.

19. The DNA Dilemma

1. Connell, *Walter Dew, the Man Who Caught Crippen*; Smith, *Supper With the Crippens*; Larson, *Thunderstruck*, and Watson, *Dr Crippen*. Surprisingly there were no centenary publications in 2010.
2. Dew, *op. cit.*, p. 21.
3. *Guardian*, 17 October 2007.
4. Odell, *Written and Red*, p. 81.
5. Le Neve, *op. cit.*, p. 19.
6. *Thomson's Weekly News*, 2 October 1920.
7. Wood, *op. cit.*, p. 270–1. Le Neve said the cats were still there in early February (*Thomson's Weekly News*, 2 October 1920).
8. *Pall Mall Gazette*, 14 July 1910.
9. *Evening News*, 15 July 1910.
10. *John Bull*, 10 December 1910.

11. Bloom, *op. cit.*, p. 95. The Post Office Directory lists a Mrs Fitzgerald as the previous occupant of 39 Hilldrop Crescent, preceded by Adriana Hagart, a woman in her nineties who boarded with mechanic, Mark Ryder, his wife and four children.
12. *Daily Mail*, 20 October 2007.
13. *Journal of Forensic Sciences*, January 2011 (online edition).
14. Macnaghten, *op. cit.*, p. 196.
15. *Ibid.*, p. 194.
16. Dew, *op. cit.*, p. 34.
17. *Daily Mail*, 9 September 1910.
18. *The Lancet*, 28 December 1935.
19. Yates, *op. cit.*, p. 259.
20. Oddie, *op. cit.*, p. 78.
21. *Journal of Forensic Sciences*, January 2011 (online edition).
22. Posted on www.jtrforums.com
23. The article was first published online by the *Journal of Forensic Sciences* on 23 August 2010. It was later published as part of the January 2011 online issue of the journal.
24. http://forum.casebook.org/; http://www.jtrforums.com/.
25. *Ibid.*
26. *Daily Mail*, 20 October 2007.
27. Dew, *op. cit.*, p. 28.
28. *New York Times*, 22 November 1910.
29. *Guardian*, 17 October 2007.
30. The postcard appeared as an illustration in Goodman's *Crippen File* (p.8). This may have been the source for the copy shown in the documentary. PBS did not examine the original postcard which is undated, although the documentary stated it was written in 1908. It was also alleged that the postcard was the document used to make the handwriting comparison with the Chicago letter, but the Home Office file does not say what sample of Cora's writing the police used. The postcard was held by book dealer Camille Wolff who loaned it to Goodman before selling it to crime historian Stewart Evans. He sold it in 2012 and it is now part of the Neil Storey Crime Collection.
31. Dew, *op. cit.*, p. 87.
32. The price of the book was 12s 6d. My copy has a 'reduced to 10s 6d' sticker on the cover and crime historian Richard Whittington-Egan bought his in 1938 for 1s 6d from Boots in Liverpool.
33. http://vimeo.com/32201595.
34. PRO MEPO21/39.
35. PRO MEPO7/72.
36. Parliamentary Debates, fifth series, vol. XXI, 20 February 1911, p. 1533. Bottomley owned the newspaper *John Bull* who Dew successfully sued for libel in 1911 for implying he had been compelled to resign in 1910. That newspaper had also published a bogus confession from Dr Crippen on 26 November 1910. In 1922 Bottomley was sentenced to seven years penal servitude for fraud.
37. Alverstone, *op. cit.*, p. 276.

20. The Aftermath of the Crippen Case

1. *Islington News & Hornsey Gazette*, 23 December 1910.
2. PRO IR58/43163.

3. *Thomson's Weekly News*, 19 November 1910. An Inland Revenue survey states that the property was only let to McNab and valued it at £580 (PRO IR58/43163).
4. *Islington Daily Gazette*, 14 May 1963.
5. *The Saturday Post*, 24 August 1912.
6. *Daily Mirror*, 26 November 1913.
7. *Kent Messenger*, 27 June 1914.
8. Islington Local History Centre, Second World War Bomb Damage Register.
9. Ambler, *Ability to Kill*, p. 95. Ambler suggested the house had been renumbered describing it as 'the immortal 39 (now 30)'. The caption beneath the photograph of the house in the Notable British Trials volume also says '30'. This may have been a typographical error copied by Ambler. A comparison of the 1910 Finance Act map (PRO IR121/14/37) and the 1952 Ordnance Survey map of Hilldrop Crescent show the street was not renumbered. The eight surviving houses in the Crescent have retained their 1910 numbers.
10. *Ibid.*, p. 98.
11. Islington Local History Centre, Islington Borough Council Housing Committee Minutes, volume 13. The minutes of the October 1951 meeting record that the plot of land containing 37–40 Hilldrop Crescent had been cleared.
12. *The Times*, 17 November 1969.
13. *Sun*, 10 August 2010.
14. Unless otherwise stated the details about Walter Dew are taken from Connell, *Walter Dew: The Man Who Caught Crippen*.
15. *Daily Express*, 23 November 1926.
16. *Tottenham and Edmonton Weekly Herald*, 29 March 1929.
17. *The Times*, 8 January 1930.
18. Kendall, *op. cit.*, pp. 188–9.
19. *The Times*, 31 July 1974. Kendall had given the documents to his friend Sir Norman Vernon, whose son found them in his attic (*Sunday Times*, 7 July 1974).
20. *Daily Mirror*, 13 July 1937.
21. *Sunday Telegraph*, 9 March 1997.
22. Yates, *op. cit.*, p. 260.
23. *The Musical Journal*, February 1908.
24. *Dictionary of National Biography*.
25. *The Times*, 15 January 1924.
26. *Dictionary of National Biography*.
27. *Watford Observer*, 11 May 1945.
28. *The Times*, 7 March 1960.
29. *Guardian*, 21 June 1911. The letter appeared in *John Bull* on 26 November 1910.
30. *Ibid.*, 24 July 1913.
31. *The Times*, 4 December 1939.
32. *Dictionary of National Biography*.
33. *The Times*, 19 December 1935; *British Medical Journal*, 28 December 1935; *The Journal*, 28 December 1935.
34. *British Medical Journal*, 19 July 1941; *The Lancet*, 19 July 1941; *Dictionary of National Biography*; Willcox, *Detective Physician*, p. 324.
35. *Dictionary of National Biography*; *British Medical Journal*, 27 December 1947.

BIBLIOGRAPHY

Primary Sources

PRO BT26/422.
PRO CRIM1/117.
PRO DPP1/13.
PRO HO144/1718/195492.
PRO HO144/1719/195492.
PRO HO324/1.
PRO IR58/43163.
PRO IR121/14/37.
PRO MEPO2/10996.
PRO MEPO3/198.
PRO MEPO21/39.
PRO PCOM8/30.
PRO T1/11335.

Islington Local History Centre.
Borough of Islington bomb damage reports.
Borough of Islington Housing Committee minute book no. 13.

Books

Adam, H. L., *The Story of Crime* (London: T. Werner Laurie, 1908).
Adam, H. L., *CID: Behind the Scenes at Scotland Yard* (London: Sampson Low, 1931).
Alverstone, Viscount, *Recollections of Bar and Bench* (London: Edward Arnold, 1914).
Ambler, E., *The Ability to Kill* (London: Bodley Head, 1963).
Andrews, V., *Sherlock Holmes and the Hilldrop Crescent Mystery*, (Cambridge: Breese Books, 2011).
Arthur, H., *All the Sinners* (London: John Long, 1931).
Bierstadt, E. H., *Murder by Inspiration* (London: Chapman & Hall, 1935).
Birkenhead, Earl of, *Famous Trials of History* (London: Hutchinson & Co., 1926).
Birkenhead, Earl of, *Frederick Edwin Earl of Birkenhead* (London: Thornton Butterworth, 1933).

Bishop, C., *From Information Received* (London: Hutchinson & Co., 1932).

Bixley, W., *The Guilty and the Innocent* (London: Souvenir Press, 1957).

Bloom, U., *The Girl Who Loved Crippen* (London: Hutchinson & Co., 1955).

Bloom, U., *The Mightier Sword* (London: Robert Hale, 1966).

Blumenfeld, R. D., *R. D. B.'s Procession* (London: Ivor Nicholson & Watson, 1935).

Bowen-Rowlands, E., *In the Light of the Law* (London: Grant Richards, 1931).

Bowker, A. E., *A Lifetime with the Law* (London: W. H. Allen, 1961).

Bowker, A. E., *Behind the Bar* (London: Staples Press Ltd, 1947).

Broad, L., *Advocates of the Golden Age* (London: John Long, 1958).

Browne, D. G., Tullett, E. V., *Bernard Spilsbury: His Life and Cases* (London: George G. Harrap, 1951).

Browne, D. G., *Sir Travers Humpreys: A Biography* (London: George G. Harrap, 1960).

Buchanan-Taylor, W., *Shake the Bottle* (London: Heath Cranton, 1942).

Churchill, R. S., *Young Statesman: Winston S. Churchill 1901–1914* (London: Heinemann, 1967).

Churchill, R. S., *Winston S. Churchill, Volume II Companion Part 2 1907–1911* (London: Heinemann, 1969).

Connell, N., *Walter Dew the Man Who Caught Crippen* (Stroud: Sutton, 2006).

Constantine-Quinn, M., *Doctor Crippen* (London: Duckworth, 1935).

Croall, J., *Fourteen Minutes: The Last Voyage of the Empress of Ireland* (London: Michael Joseph, 1978).

Cullen, T., *Crippen: The Mild Murderer* (London: The Bodley Head, 1977).

De Villiers, J., *My Memories* (London: Grant Richards, 1931).

Dearden, H., *The Mind of the Murderer* (London: Geoffrey Bles, 1930).

Dearden, H., *Death Under the Microscope* (London: Hutchinson & Co., 1948).

Dew, W., *I Caught Crippen* (London & Glasgow: Blackie & Son Ltd, 1938).

Dewes, S., *Doctors of Murder* (London: John Long, 1962).

Dilnot, F., *Adventures of a Newspaper Man* (London: Smith, Elder & Co., 1913).

Dilnot, G., *Great Detectives and Their Methods* (London: Geoffrey Bles, 1927).

Eddy, J. P., *Scarlet and Ermine* (London: William Kimber, 1960).

Ellis, J., *Diary of a Hangman* (London: True Crime Library, 1996).

Ellis, J. C., *Black Fame: Stories of Crime and Criminals* (London: Hutchinson & Co., 1926).

Ellis, J. C., *Blackmailers & Co.* (London: Selwyn & Blount, 1929).

Emsley, J., *Molecules of Murder: Criminal Molecules and Classic Cases* (Cambridge: RSC Publishing, 2008).

Felstead, S., *Sir Richard Muir: A Memoir of a Public Prosecutor* (London: John Lane, 1927).

Fordham, E. W., *Notable Cross-Examinations* (London: Constable & Company, 1931).

Gardiner, D., Walker, K. S. (eds), *Raymond Chandler Speaking* (London: Hamish Hamilton Ltd, 1962).

Gibbs, P., *Adventures in Journalism* (London: William Heinemann Ltd, 1923).

Gilbert, M., *Doctor Crippen* (London: Odhams Press Ltd, 1953).

Goodman, J., *Bloody Versicles: The Rhymes of Crime* (Newton Abbot: David & Charles, 1971).

Goodman, J., *The Crippen File* (London: Allison & Busby, 1985).

Goodman, J., Waddell, B., *The Black Museum: Scotland Yard's Chamber of Crime* (London: Harrap, 1987).

Graham, E., *Lord Darling and His Famous Trials* (London: Hutchinson & Co., 1929).

Grant, B., *To the Four Corners* (London: Hutchinson & Co., 1933).

Greenwall, H. J., *The Strange Life of Willy Clarkson* (London: John Long, 1936).

Gribble, L., *Adventures in Murder* (London: John Long, 1954).

Haestier, R., *Dead Men Tell Tales* (London: John Long, 1934).

Harris, M., *ITN Book of Firsts* (London: Michael O'Mara, 1994).

Hicks, S., *Not Guilty, M'Lord* (London: Cassell & Company, 1939).

Humphreys, T., *Criminal Days* (London: Hodder & Stoughton, 1946).

Humphreys, T., *A Book of Trials* (London: William Heinemann Ltd, 1953).

Huson, R. (ed.), *Sixty Famous Trials* (London: Daily Express, 1938).

Jackson, S., *The Life and Cases of Mr Justice Humphreys* (London: Odhams Press, 1952).

Kendall, Captain H. G., *Adventures on the High Seas* (London: Hurst & Blackett, 1939).

Lane, M., *Edgar Wallace the Biography of a Phenomenon* (London: William Heinemann Ltd, 1938).

Larson, E., *Thunderstruck* (London: Doubleday, 2006).

Le Neve, E., *Ethel Le Neve Her Life Story* (Manchester: Daisy Bank, 1910).

Le Queux, W., *Things I Know About Kings, Celebrities, and Crooks* (London: E. Nash & Grayson, 1923).

Le Queux, W., *Dr Crippen: Lover and Poisoner* (London: George Newnes, 1966).

Lieck, A., *Bow Street World* (London: Robert Hale, 1938).

Lock, J., *Scotland Yard Casebook* (London: Robert Hale, 1993).

Machen, A., *The Cosy Room and Other Stories* (London: Rich & Cowan, 1936).

Macnaghten, M., *Days of My Years* (London: Edward Arnold, 1914).

Marjoribanks, E., *The Life of Sir Edward Marshall Hall* (London: Victor Gollancz Ltd, 1929).

Meaney, J., *Scribble Street* (London: Sands & Co., 1945).

Morland, N., *Hangman's Clutch* (London: Werner Laurie, 1954).

Moss, A., Skinner, K., *The Scotland Yard Files* (Surrey: The National Archives, 2006).

Oddie, S., *Inquest* (London: Hutchinson & Co., 1941).

Odell, R., *Written and Red 2, The True Crime Lectures* (Salisbury: Timezone Publishing, 2011).

Oxford Dictionary of National Biography.

Parrish, J. M., Crossland, J. R. (eds), *The Fifty Most Amazing Crimes of the Last 100 Years* (London: Odhams Press, 1936).

Parry, L,. *Some Famous Medical Trials* (London: J. & A. Churchill, 1927).

Pearson, E., *Murder at Smutty Nose and Other Murders* (London: William Heinemann Ltd, 1927).

Prothero, M., *The History of the Criminal Investigation Department at Scotland Yard From Earliest Times Until To-Day* (London: Herbert Jenkins Ltd, 1931).

Randall, L., *The Famous Cases of Sir Bernard Spilsbury* (London: Nicholson & Watson, 1936).

Roberts, B., *Sir Travers Humphreys: His Career and Cases* (London: John Lane, 1936).

Rose, A., *Lethal Witness: Sir Bernard Spilsbury Honorary Pathologist* (Stroud: Sutton, 2007).

Rose, C., *Red Plush and Greasepaint* (London: Museum Press, 1964).

Rowland, J., *Poisoner in the Dock* (London: Arco Publications, 1960).

Saward, J., *The Man Who Caught Crippen* (Morienval: Morienval Press, 2010).

Shore, W. T. (ed.), *Crime and its Detection* (London: The Gresham Publishing Company Ltd, 1931).

Smith, D. J., *Supper With the Crippens* (London: Orion, 2005).

Speer, W. H., *The Secret History of Great Crimes* (London: A. H. Stockwell,, 1929).

Thompson, C. J. S., *Poison Mysteries in History, Romance and Crime* (London: Scientific Press, 1923).

Thorogood, H., *East of Aldgate* (London: George Allen & Unwin Ltd, 1935).

Townsend, W. & L., *Black Cap: Murder Will Out* (London: Albert E. Marriott Ltd, 1930).

Wall, W. J., *The DNA Detectives* (London: Robert Hale, 2005).

Watson, K., *Dr Crippen* (Surrey: The National Archives, 2007).

Willcox, P., *Detective Physician: The Life and Work of Sir William Willcox* (London: Heinemann Medical, 1970).

Wood, W. (ed.), *Survivors' Tales of Famous Crimes* (London: Cassell and Company, 1916).

Yates, D., *The House That Berry Built* (London & Melbourne: Ward, Lock & Co., 1945).

Yates, D., *As Berry and I Were Saying* (London & Melbourne: Ward, Lock & Co., 1952).

Young, F. (ed.), *Trial of Hawley Harvey Crippen* (Edinburgh & London: William Hodge & Company Ltd, 1933).

Periodicals

The American Homeopathic Journal of Obstetrics and Gynaecology (1885).

Cook, C., 'A Famous Murder Trial in Old Bailey', *The American Law School Review* (1920).

'Doctor Crippen', *Murder in Mind*, 13 (1994).

Early, J. E., 'Technology, Modernity, and 'the Little Man': Crippen's Capture by Wireless', *Victorian Studies*, 39(3) (Spring 1996).

Eastaway, E., 'What Mother Never Told Us', *You Magazine* (14 July 1985).

Foran, D., Kiley, B., Jackson, C., Trestrail, J., Wills, B., 'The Conviction of Dr Crippen: New Forensic Findings in a Century-Old Murder', *Journal of Forensic Sciences* (online), 56 (1) (January, 2011).

Goad, A., 'A Life on the Road', *The Call Boy* (Summer 1980).

Goodman, J., 'Much Ado About Crippen', *New Law Journal* (30 May 1997).

Lovesey, P., 'Dr Crippen & the Real Inspector Dew', *The Armchair Detective* (Summer 1984).

Menges, J., 'Another World Another Judge. Do New Scientific Tests Clear Crippen?', *Ripper Notes*, 28 (2008).

'The Mild-Mannered Murderer', *Murder Casebook*, 9 (1990).

Normanton, H., 'The Trial of Dr Crippen. The Criminal Who Was Betrayed by His Own Conscience', *Pall Mall Magazine* (May 1928).

Real Life Crimes... and How They Were Solved, 21 (1993).

Documentaries

Forensic Casebook, ITV (2008).

Revealed: Was Crippen Innocent?, Channel 5 (2008).

Secrets of the Dead: Executed in Error, PBS (2008).

Tales From the Black Museum, Discovery Channel (1999).

The Last Secret of Dr Crippen, Channel 4 (2004).

Websites

http://drcrippen.co.uk/
http://forum.casebook.org/
http://jtrforums.com/
http://vimeo.com

Recordings

'Doctor Crippen', *Great British Trials* (Mr Punch Audio Ltd, 1999).
Living With the Legend, first broadcast on BBC Radio 4, 9 November 1991.

Newspapers Consulted

Answers.
British Medical Journal.
The Bystander.
Chicago Sunday Tribune.
Cleveland Plain Dealer.
Daily Chronicle.
Daily Express.
Daily Mail.
Daily Mirror.
Daily Telegraph.
Durban Daily News.
Empire News.
The Era.
Evening News (London).
The Globe.
The Graphic.
Guardian.
Holborn and Finsbury Guardian.
Hull Daily Mail.
Illustrated Police News.
Islington Daily Gazette.
Islington News & Hornsey Gazette.
John Bull.
Kent Messenger.
The Lancet.
The Leader.
Liverpool Courier.
Liverpool Daily Post.
Lloyd's Weekly News.
Los Angeles Herald.
Montreal Daily Star.
Morning Advertiser.
Mrs Bull.

The Music Hall and Theatre Review.
The Musical Journal.
The New Statesman.
New York Times.
News of the World.
Pall Mall Gazette.
Penny Illustrated Paper.
The People.
Reynolds's Weekly Newspaper.
San Francisco Chronicle.
The Saturday Post.
The Sketch.
South London Press.
The Stage.
Sun.
Sunday Citizen.
Sunday Dispatch.
Sunday Express.
Sunday Illustrated.
The Sunday News.
Sunday Telegraph.
Sunday Times.
Thomson's Weekly News.
The Times.
Tottenham and Edmonton Weekly Herald.
The Umpire.
Watford Observer.
Weekly Dispatch.
Western Daily Press.
Western Mail.
World's Pictorial News.

INDEX